Charles F. Lummis

Charles F. Lummis as he appeared following his trek across the continent in 1885.

Charles F. Lummis

The Man and His West

By Turbesé Lummis Fiske
and Keith Lummis

607313

University of Oklahoma Press : Norman

Library of Congress Cataloging in Publication Data

Fiske, Turbesé Lummis.
   Charles F. Lummis: the man and his West.

   Bibliography: p.
   1. Lummis, Charles Fletcher, 1859–1928
Biography.
I. Lummis, Keith, 1904–   joint author.   II. Title.
PS3523.U49Z65 917.94'03'40924 [B] 74–15910
ISBN 0–8061–1228–X

MY FATHER was a many-sided person. Only slightly less complex was his daughter Turbesé. As an old friend put it, "There were many Turbesés."

One Turbesé was occupied on and off for forty years preparing a biography of her father. Her sources were her memory, his letters and handwritten memos, his forty-volume diary, official museum and library reports, his widely distributed journal, his reminiscences, scrapbooks containing hundreds of articles written by or about him, his published writings, stories she had heard firsthand, and letters from friends. When she died in 1967 at the age of seventy-four the manuscript was impressive but hardly ready for publication.

The search for an inspired poet-historian to finish the reconstruction of the life of this remarkable personality was unavailing, and it became evident that, if the biography was to be completed, it would be up to me.

With considerable help of my patient wife I have rewritten my sister's manuscript, reducing it by one half and adding new material that seemed essential to the story. I have also attempted to identify the source of all quotes—a matter with which Turbesé had not concerned herself.

The difficulty of searching for specific quotes in the vast quantity of source material was compounded by the fact that in the process of making a meager living with his pen, my father told the same story many times, each time varying the wording slightly. He usually managed to sell a story to a newspaper and then to a magazine before it appeared as a chapter in a book. It could also be found in his diary, his journal, and his autobiographical reminiscences, "As I Remember." Suffice it to say that it has not always been possible to determine the exact source of a specific quote. Perhaps it could be done, but we lack another forty years.

KEITH LUMMIS

San Francisco, California
May 9, 1975

Contents

Illustrations

FROM THE HOUSE BOOK

Charles F. Lummis

There are certain men who are as vital as our Frontiers

Oct 12/1924

Douglas Fairbanks

Douglas Fairbanks
October 12, 1924
From the House Book

1

Early Days

THE THOUSANDS who roar through the Pasadena Freeway in the modern city of Los Angeles pass within yards of a stone castle that arose when the crowded highway was still a wide arroyo, when the sky was clear, the air faintly perfumed with orange blossoms, and the city still remembered as El Pueblo de Nuestra Señora la Reina de Los Angeles.

The castle was crowded with works of art and treasures of the past gathered by the builder, an adventurer, poet, and scholar known to his friends as Don Carlos. The great "noises" held at this gathering place for the literary and artistic were eagerly attended by scholars, wits, and musicians of the time. They consumed the frijol and the claret, heard choice operatic voices, sang the songs of early California, and enjoyed the droll fabrications of old cowhands.

The gallant little figure of Don Carlos was something of an anachronism even then. He lived in the past that was dear to him and preserved it for the future. Many who now pass through those halls decorated with Navajo blankets and Pueblo pottery sense the impact of his life and work.

To say *the Southwest* is practically to say his name. That is the region he christened and loved. Those who "See America First" are obeying his injunction. Whether they see it in the Indian pueblos of New Mexico, in the cave dwellings of the first Americans, or in the swimming rainbows of the Grand Canyon, they are following trails he helped break many years ago.

This controversial personality, reckless, pugnacious, and romantic, who seems to have made more friends and more enemies than anyone in the West, is first mentioned in a diary entry, in the style typical of the day, on March 13, 1859.

When last I was writing here, February was tracing upon the Earth her latest lessons—now March is ringing out wild jubilant choruses. And in the wildness of the opening symphony my baby came to me. My Baby! My eyes are dim with tears when I say over the sweet words. As I sit in my room this charming spring morning and think of the mysterious little life entrusted to my watchcare—and of the young spirit that will take its impress from my own life and character, I tremble in my weakness and pray to God for strength.[1]

The precise, graceful hand is that of Harriet Lummis, the young wife of the Reverend Henry Lummis. He was at that time principal of the Lynn [Massachusetts] High School, a sage and personable teacher students never forgot. Old family papers indicate that the first of his clan, Edward Lummis, arrived in Massachusetts from Essex, England in 1635. Henry's father, William, four generations later, had been a preacher and circuit rider whose obituary in 1843 credited him with more than five thousand conversions during his ministry. The principal Methodist functionary of the area, one Bishop James, recalled that "Father Lummis could knock more sinners than any of us."

Family tradition has it that the wife of William Lummis brought the blood of John Paul Jones into the family strain—an interesting speculation since there is no record that the "seagoing Casanova," whose own paternity was questioned, ever himself took a wife.[2] In view of her age and his reputation, it

[1] The diary of Harriet Fowler Lummis is in the possession of Keith Lummis.
[2] S. E. Morrison, *John Paul Jones*, 4.

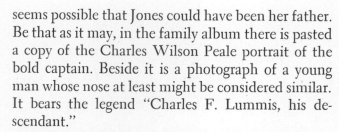

Harriet Fowler Lummis, 1858.

The Reverend Henry Lummis, 1855.

seems possible that Jones could have been her father. Be that as it may, in the family album there is pasted a copy of the Charles Wilson Peale portrait of the bold captain. Beside it is a photograph of a young man whose nose at least might be considered similar. It bears the legend "Charles F. Lummis, his descendant."

Harriet Fowler Lummis' diary reveals her absorption with closet prayer, spiritual yearnings and skating caps, "zephyr" sleeves, God and the *Atlantic Monthly*, wifely duties and the history of Methodism—until the coming of her "Charlie Bird" on March 1, 1859. From then on her life was completely devoted to "this spotless soul who daily almost, gains some new grace, some cunning, winning way . . . ." She petitioned the Heavenly One to give her child "a meek and quiet spirit and grace to guide his infant feet aright."

The baby was so frail that he had to be carried on a

pillow, and the mother suffered ever more frequent spells of coughing.

Less than two years after Charlie came, Harriet's health was further weakened by the birth of Louise Elma. The twenty-two-year-old mother began to have "moments of great sadness, fear that the months are hurrying me to life's close." Though she believed firmly that we should long for a heavenly existence, she confessed to feeling "a clinging in my heart to this earth life—especially to my darling baby Charl."

It was a few weeks after Charlie's second birthday that the last entry was made in her diary, a prayer "that the Good Sheperd carry him tenderly in his bosom."

When sixty-nine and knowing his own time was running out, Charles Fletcher Lummis wrote of her goodbye.

"The first thing I remember seeing in this world was the old parlor, a forbidden room and always dark

4

But today my grandma Fowler led me in. It was an afternoon in May 1861. I was a trifle over two years old. No picture is clearer to me."[3]

During the turbulent years that followed, every important event was commemorated with verse. In these lines Charles expressed the loneliness he always felt because of the early loss of his mother.

> Thin fingers, like as petals, cling . . .
>   Cold to a baby's cheeks.
> Big eyes so deep I cannot see
>   Til stars come up in them for me;
> The shadow of a breath that speaks
> "God keep my little boy!" and then
> Slow lids—and Nothing
>   And they bore me out again.[4]

Shy, sickly, little Charlie and his baby sister, Lulie, were taken to the home of their maternal grandparents, Judge Oscar Fitzallen Fowler and Louise Waterman Fowler. As he recalled it later in his reminiscences:

Bristol was a dear little typical New Hampshire village with perhaps 400 people and five or six stores around the enormous bare commons. Through the town ran the quick clear river, pausing at the dam of the tannery before plunging down some 300 feet in marvelous cascades to the Merrimac below.

Granpa was the village harness and saddle maker. He was also the village probate judge and the most famous trout fisherman in half the state. His saddlery and harness shop was built on piles over the New-found river. Below his shop was an unused room on the piling about four feet above the river. I could hang my bamboo pole out the window and fish in four to six feet of the clear water where I could see minnows, chubs, shiners and perch as in an aquarium and sometimes an eel.

He remembered with pride that his grandfather, standing only five feet six inches and carrying 230

The Fowler home in Bristol, New Hampshire, where Charlie lived after his mother's death until he was eight years old. Pictured are his grandparents and his sister, Louise.

pounds of muscle, was locally famous for his strength. When nearing sixty he raced and outran the eighteen year olds across the commons, and at the end placed one hand on a five-foot rail fence and vaulted cleanly over it. He was also known as the champion fisherman of several counties and often carried his little grandson on his shoulders when pursuing the elusive trout, talking softly all the time of the arts and tricks of the craft.

When Charlie was about eight, his grandfather decided that it was time for his education to begin. He took Charlie to his father, who was then principal of the New Hampshire Seminary and Female College at Sanbornton Bridge, New Hampshire. There was a primary class for the village children.

This was taught by Jennie B. Brewster, an extremely able young woman. Soon after Granpa brought me down from Bristol to live with Father, the latter put me in this primary class. That is, he led me to the door and presented me to Miss Brewster and she seated me at a desk. I knew how to read very well, the

[3] Charles F. Lummis, "As I Remember." When Lummis discovered, as an old man, that he had only a year to live, he began dictating his reminiscences under the general title "As I Remember." These memoirs are grouped under headings such as "Youth," "New Mexico," "Californy," and the like. None of these writings has ever been published. Portions of the reminiscences are now in the possession of the University of Arizona Library, the Southwest Museum in Los Angeles, and Keith Lummis. Hereinafter cited as Lummis, "As I Remember."

[4] Charles F. Lummis, *A Bronco Pegasus*, 5.

multiplication tables and some spelling and made quite an impression on the teacher when she called me up to read some childish page.

But classrooms had no vital appeal to me and when Teacher stepped out into the hall for a moment I "ducked." When she came back she was first conscious of a subdued titter in the room, then noted my empty seat and looked around to find what had become of me. The eyes of the class were guides enough and she looked under a long wide table in the corner where I was crouched close to the wall. She bade me come out—no answer. Repeat—still no answer. She used a birch switch as well as she could from the distance without success and, red in the face, stepped out down the hall. Shortly I heard a Step—one that I knew. It stopped at the door and its owner said in a quiet but reaching voice, "Charlie!"

And Charlie came out and assumed his seat but that is the last day he ever sat there. I told Father I couldn't learn that way and asked him to teach me himself. And that marvellous man, one of the most scholarly and beloved men I have ever known, did exactly that for the next ten years.

When I was about eight Father resigned as principal of the Seminary, accepting a professorship at Lasell College in Auburndale, Massachusetts . . . and there I discovered that the school teacher from whom I had escaped was now my stepmother and no escape! We were greatly unsuited for the relationship by temperament but our mutual love for my father went a long way. And while she caused me a great deal of unhappiness in my young years, it was not all her fault. She was a noble woman as well as a brainy one and a model wife to my father.[5]

It is also possible she furnished some of the discipline Charlie needed. In any case, Charlie had his way with his father who taught his son his own specialties—Latin, Greek, and Hebrew. Charlie read from the Vulgate Bible every morning at family prayers. By the time he was ready for college, he had read nearly everything in Latin and Greek that was on the Harvard elective list.

The grandparents, too, suffering from the loss of their gentle daughter, were inclined to let her son do as he wished. It set a pattern that the "school marm"

[5] Lummis, "As I Remember."

Charles Fletcher Lummis, 1868.

stepmother was not able to break. He was punished at least once, however, for the unique crime of putting a mass of polliwogs through the sausage machine.

The boy read extensively, and, in addition to his father, grandfather, and a brash young uncle, he had two special idols. Many of the long days of his youth were spent absorbed in the adventure tales of Captain Mayne Reid and many hours in dreaming of the incredible career of his presumed ancestor, the fearless Scotsman, John Paul Jones.

Charlie actually left little information about his childhood, a strange thing for a man who made such a complete record of his later life, even to keeping coded portions in his diaries which minutely described acts customarily unmentioned, as though he were preserving and treasuring every moment of his fleeting existence. It was not then the fashion, however, to attribute to the travail of childhood every idiosyncrasy and quality of adult personality. To his childhood he credited his knowledge of the classics and his love of trout fishing, nothing more. His life began when he left the cloisters and entered college.

I had no violent personal ambition for college. I went because Father had gone, because he had trained me with years of personal concentration. And because it was the cultural convention of New England—to which I acceded as I did in most things. Up until Harvard.

College in those days naturally meant Harvard. It was an intoxicating experience to enter a great university. I studied reasonably for my classes but for a restrained encircled son of a Methodist minister there were so many other things than lessons to study. My escapades certainly brought me no credits—but I am not sure they were not the most important part of my college courses and of the most lasting benefit. From my cloistered life I had come to the Tree of the Forbidden Fruit. I climbed that tree to the top.

I am glad to have had the milling with several hundred other boys, an experience of deep value to one who had been alone as much as I had been . . . and [the years at Harvard] thoroughly grounded me in the most useful form of athletics, boxing, wrestling, walking and running.[6]

The development of his undersized body became almost a compulsion. He worked on the track until his legs could carry him through a twenty-mile marathon. With the feistiness of a small man he would frequently box with far heavier partners, willingly taking a beating on the chance that he could slip in a bone crusher and end the match.

His mother's prayers for her innocent Charlie Bird were hardly fulfilled in the kind of college career he undertook.

What I needed, you see, was not so much to learn books as to Find Myself.

Classes and wrestling and boxing ordinarily filled a pretty good day. At night there was generally a little

[6] *Ibid.*

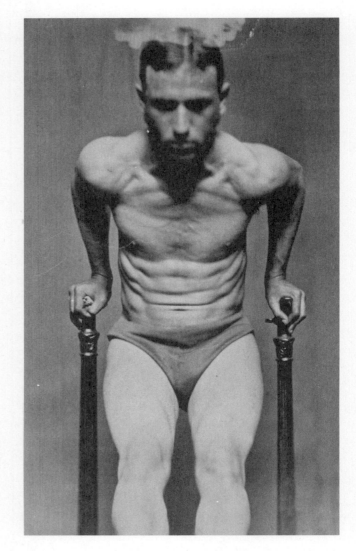

Body building at Harvard.

study and not infrequently plenty of poker. But the real fire was poetry. . . .

I got a big old-fashioned German-English vocabulary of 3600 words and swallowed it nearly whole in four days. Paying no attention whatever to grammar or conjugation, I trusted to my faithful drill in Latin, Hebrew and Greek grammar (never in my life did I study English grammar) to lighten me over the shoals. I passed that entrance examination with 7% to spare.

This brief initiation into German gave me a certain appetite for that majestic tongue. In the first three years of my college course I translated a large number of poems from Schiller and Goethe and

Heine—in fact practically all the Classic Deutche Lyrik. Juvenile enough but it was good practice both in translation and prosody. This meant sitting up practically all night. It was in Harvard that I first acquired the lifelong practice of nighthawking—a nocturnal habit confirmed in later years.

Perhaps the most extraordinary friendship of my life (it would be more exact perhaps to call it an alliance, for we had no real affection for one another that I know of and disagreed in all our ideals, standards and ambitions) was with Boies Penrose, later Senator from Pennsylvania, and for years one of the four or five men that largely ran this putative democracy.

Penrose had in many ways the most astounding mind I have ever encountered. His ability to grasp a big subject swiftly and in one handful was almost superhuman. Ethics he had none. He was cold blooded, a materialist and a cynic. I was the reverse. What attracted one to the other was something outlaw. Neither could "stump" the other. I fancy it was our unconscious realization of this fact that kept us from getting into irremediable devilment.

Boies was always ready for any devilment I could think up. Not much of an inventor in those lines, he was an enthusiastic backer. I do not remember just which form of brigandage began our association, but I imagine it was the Thanksgiving Tramp of our Sophomore year, when we decided to beg our way through New England, dressed as disreputably as possible. We would go without a dollar, along as extensive a route as we could compass; and above all like proper tramps spend at least one night in jail.

With ragged clothes and crownless hat, I made up fairly well. But when I met "Pen," I blushed. He had taken a leg of each of two pairs of heavy woolen drawers, one crimson, the other navy blue, and sewn them together. To this he added a ragged undershirt, a long-tailed coat with holes at the elbows and one tail gone and a plug hat with half the top missing. . . .

People were very good to us. In those days it was all old New England farmers, not the aliens that now possess New England; and while they looked rather scandalized at our appearance, nobody refused us a handout and several gave us good warm meals in the kitchen. We travelled up beyond Manchester, New Hampshire. When we got to Nashua on our way back, I said, "Pen, how about that jail?"

"All right Charlie, if we can break in."

There was no trouble about that when I knocked the cap off a stately policeman and laughed in his face. I admire the self restraint of that big red-faced gentleman from Cork. Instead of clubbing us he got each of us by the collar and marched us down to the lockup.

But our pact was made in total ignorance of what some jails are. The Nashua lockup was the basement room which had been the city morgue. About a quarter of it was occupied by a brick tank in which they had kept the corpses in water. We sat on the rim and thought complacently that the interior looked good enough for a bed. In the dim gaslight, however, it seemed to waver. No wonder. It was marching. When we sat down the milling multitudes below began to come up our way. I don't know that these beasties have a sense of smell or keen vision. But they certainly can find their way to meat. There were seven or eight real tramps in the place. We hadn't dreamed that human beings could be so much lower than beasts.

The next day "Pen" and I were hauled before the Police Judge, accused of being Harvard students, couldn't lie out of it and were dismissed with sneerness. It was bitter cold but as soon as we got two or three miles outside of Nashua we climbed a fence and spent the next two naked hours picking over our clothing with blue fingers.[7]

A generation later offspring who had been allowed little latitude and knew their father as a serious, preoccupied scholar were amazed at the glee with which he recounted his college escapades and machinations. Nevertheless they were impressed by his scope and originality.

Our real consanguinity of devilment [Boies and Charlie] was more organized and elaborate and had far more thrill. Signs had been stolen in amateur ways before by Harvard undergraduates but never had there been such a Napoleonic campaign as we conducted in 1878–80. Penrose hadn't a touch of the Collector's Fever. All he wanted was the fun and the risk. I had the Fever on both sides.

Nothing was too difficult or too dangerous. Right in Scollay Square hung a marvellous blue and red and

[7] Ibid.

8

gold scroll work sign about 4x2½ ft., ribbanded and convoluted in the highest of Germanic art and swung on two strong wires. There were no wire cutters in those days . . . but I climbed on Pen's shoulders and filed the wires off. We got the sign down, aboard in front of me and started for Harvard on the horse car. The sign reached up to my shoulder against the front window and when a huge cop swung aboard ahead of me I felt like a straw trying to conceal an elephant.[8]

A five-foot cigar in gold leaf, a four-foot wooden key, a Punch of "great artistic worth," and a twelve-foot wooden shotgun were among some ninety "objects of art" treasured in the attic museum above Boies Penrose's quarters.

[8] *Ibid.*

2

The First Printing

A CASUAL campus contact between two young men was unimportant at the time; later the effect was far-reaching.

There was an odd looking chap at Harvard. He was flat-chested, thin-necked, hatchet-faced, lantern-jawed. He wore funny thin Dundreary side whiskers, silky but innumerous. His name was Theodore Roosevelt.

I shall never forget the looks of him in those early college days. No photograph I have ever seen of him confirms it, the retouched Freshman picture at 18 mildly suggests it. My own mental photograph is sharp as a cameo. About this stringy bantling, not more than an inch taller than my 5-ft-6 and much lighter than my 120, there was nothing whatever to suggest the powerful frame and world-known forceful face of later years except the same glasses and the same teeth! . . .

Our contact began when he grinned at me across the Unfathomable Abyss. I sometimes wonder if the gulf between us now—the dead and the living—is so profound as that was, half a century ago, when he was a Harvard Sophomore and I a Freshman. But he was a human Sophomore. It was in the early weeks of my Freshman year, 1877. I was very green. My abundant hair was much lower than my ears. One morning as I came to the old University (the Administration building with class rooms below) a laughing crowd was in front of the sacred Bulletin Board, on which some profane hand had printed:

"NOTICE—
If Freshman Lummis doesn't get his hair cut, '80 will do it for him."

Half an hour later, side by side with the above, was this:

"NOTICE—
Lummis '81 will be glad to meet the tonsorially inclined of the class of '80 individually or collectively at any time at 18 Holyoke."

Childish—but it started something which wasn't so trivial.

A day or two later, passing exclusive Beck Hall, I met Roosevelt. To my inconceivable astonishment he grinned amiably, clicked his teeth and said, "Bully! It's your hair—keep it if you want to. Don't let 'em haze you!"

I was too embarrassed to thank the mighty Sophomore, but I fancy that I grinned back in a timid way. Anyhow, he always grinned at me when we met thereafter.

Roosevelt wasn't spectacular in college in any way. He was neither a "mixer" nor a "limelighter." He was rather too deadly in earnest and methodical to be of universal interest. To those "in the know" his almost puritanical schedule was respected rather than understood; his tireless study and insatiate reading, his boxing with his glasses on (a deadly risk, but without them he couldn't see the other fellow's eyes, which is all that a boxer needs to see) and all the rest. It was not a rare cynicism, as I remember in the later years of college: "Say, Teddy must be studying to be President!" Whether that dream ever entered his head in those days I have no idea. I rather doubt it. But I do know—as do all students of our history that no president of the United States ever came to the office so deeply studied and experienced in so many and varied things that would qualify him for it.

Charlie in 1877, as a freshman at Harvard.

Of course, there could be no companionship between a Sophomore and a Freshman, even if the one had not been rich as then rated, an intense "dig," a patrician who chummed with the Minots and Cabots and Lowells (if not with their only other Social Peer), and the other a callow pauper whose sole wealth was Latin and Greek, whose concern was poetry, boxing, wrestling and long distance running and particularily seeing to it that no artistic sign in Boston should fail to find its way to a certain vacant room in Holyoke House. But my turning the laugh on the hazers (he always hated hazing) was a seed which was to sprout. . . .

When I was 12 years old Granpa Fowler gave me a little handprinting press, 8x8, and several fonts of type. The wholly unexpected gift made me a printer

the rest of my life, incurable, although not always active.

If it had not been for Granpa's printing press I probably never would have known the White Mountains of New Hampshire and the lifelong joy they brought me. Without it I would never have known Echo and Profile Lakes, Cannon Mountain, the Presidential Range, the Great Stone Face and Franconia Notch. . . .

In 1878 with my first Harvard summer vacation . . . I secured the job of printer in the Profile House, Franconia Notch, N.H.

Among the things which have changed my life's trend was unquestionably my encounter with the Old Man of Cannon Mountain. One day when out exploring I looked for the first time into the Face. Nowhere have I seen anything to compare with the awful majesty of this mighty outline 90 feet from brow to chin, 14 or 1500 feet above the jewel of Profile Lake and framed against the sky where no obstruction can hide it. The lure of Pemigewassett, the peace of the great pass in the mountains, the jewel lakes, almost always unruffled, the Old Man of the Mountain looking down while I lay in my birch bark canoe, all of this worked to balance and to deepen and if I may say it, half way to consecrate my impetuous boyhood.

As the young man sat in his birchbark canoe watching the sunset over the crags, his emotions flowed into verse.

The westward sun has left a wake of flame
    Across the silent lake, upon whose breast
The stern still Face, by wrathful tempests scarred
    Looks down impassive from the cliffs that frame
The crystal waters as they lie at rest,
    Secure and trustful in his sleepless guard.[1]

It was all enough to make anybody a poet—as much a poet as the raw material would allow! I had been writing verse from 11 years onward. But here at the Profile there was a new vision And a new urge. Of course, I had known the birch tree ever since my youngest childhood but I had never experimented with such birches as these nor found how fairy fine

[1] Charles F. Lummis, "Sunset on Profile Lake," Birch Bark Poems, original ed., 6.

the bark could be split—into from six to a dozen films.

It wasn't much of a gulf for a Yankee boy to bridge, from poetry in your head to the loveliest page that ever poetry was printed on. In my first summer I gathered many thousand sheets of birch bark and split it into its last denomination and set up Birch Bark Poems, 2⅞ inches high by 2⅜ wide. I sold nearly a thousand of them that summer at 25 cents each, nearly all at the Profile House newstand.

The little book was a beautiful adventure, the first significant thing I ever did. In all it sold over 14,000 copies and that paid most of my way through Harvard. Far more important it brought me a host of golden and lasting friendships.[2]

Charlie sent copies to all of his literary idols, and he was rewarded by letters of thanks and commendation from Walt Whitman, Henry W. Longfellow, Ralph Waldo Emerson, Charles Dudley Warner, James Russell Lowell, Oliver Wendell Holmes, and, best of all, Captain Mayne Reid.

Charlie was always as modest about his verse, which came naturally, as he was arrogant about his physique, wrested from a weak body by years of determined effort. Confused with dreams and poetry was the wild urge to flirt with self destruction that boils in the veins of the young male. It was this urge that forced him to take the long trail over the Presidential Range in New Hampshire late one afternoon. Soon it was dusk and a violent snowstorm made it night.

The trail at best was dim and the snow was blinding. But I had only a light shirt and light knickers and this was no place to stop. Hurrying along I caught my foot on a shelving rock which pitched me forward with a jolt that half stunned me. As I lay there collecting breath and sense, I was annoyed and puzzled by the eddy of snow in my face for my face was downward. I reached out and felt first a ledge of rock, then nothing. I rolled a big rock over the brink. A few seconds later far below, a faint click.[3]

He spent the rest of the night dancing up and down, swinging his arms to keep from freezing. But it takes a long time to cool some fires.

It was strictly forbidden to go down Mt. Washington with the sliding boards, pine boards about 4 feet long and a foot wide, with lengthwise cleats to fit inside the flanges of the 6-inch cograil with which the train came up. The brakes were merely a pair of wooden levers hinged to the sides. Several people had been killed within a few months by "shooting the rapids" on these contraptions, especially at the steepest part of the track called Jacob's Ladder and the boards had been broken up.

But a fool has to! I hunted around until I found a pretty good pine board of about the right size. It had no cleats to hold it to the rail, no brakes to regulate it. But it had Youth for a rider and I knew how to use my body and keep my balance. For brakes and also for guide I set my stout brogans against the outer flanges of the cograil and off we went.

When we came to Jacob's Ladder I was somewhat scared but there was no way out of it and I ground my heels against the rail and tried to hold my breath so as not to weigh too much and we made it. Before we got quite to the bottom where there was a sort of lap in the track, I managed to stop. I chucked that board and clambered down the ties to the foot of the incline. The heavy soles of my boots were cut through, my stockings were cut and on each instep there was a hole in the flesh an inch and a half long and a half an inch deep. While I was lame for several weeks and while a new pair of $2.50 boots was a serious drain on the treasury, this was really a better bargain than breaking my fool neck as I deserved.[4]

There were also numerous attempts to break the fool neck climbing around the Old Man of the Mountain, a celebrated natural feature, without benefit of belay or any aids except perhaps luck and the support of some overworked guardian angel. Surviving several physically hazardous summers in the mountains, Charlie made a successful try for real trouble in his personal life.

[2] Lummis, "As I Remember."
[3] *Ibid.*

[4] *Ibid.*

Enter Dorothea

"L'amour est l'histoire de la vie des femmes, c'est un épisode dans celle des hommes."

It was a French lesson that introduced the vicious, naked little character with his bow and arrow to Lummis. A young medical student, Dorothea Roads, with "a pair of marvellous blue eyes and a wealth of golden hair," seems to have been stung somewhat more severely than the tutor, young Charlie Lummis, who sported quite a bit of hair himself in those days.

Dorothea's story of love and heartbreak is told in a box of letters, salvaged from the attic of the stone castle by the Arroyo Seco.[1] The first, dated March 25, 1879, began, "Dear Mr. Lummis," and ended, "Shall I be so unwomanly as to close without a postscript? Never!—Ah! I have it—Forgive me for answering your business note with such a rambling and lengthy epistle, or forgive me for writing at all."

On April 1, there was an outpouring of four hundred words to "Dear Mr. Lummis." On April 4 we find, "Dear Mr. Lummis: I had a vague unreasoning hope that I would hear from you today. . . ." another four hundred words and ". . . Now I shall stop and pray for warm weather, so that I may see you on Sunday. Most truly M. D. R."

So the young scoundrel would only visit her if it was a nice day! In any case by June 27 the eight-hundred-word epistle began, "No I cannot! I really cannot! Call my august and reverend tutor C——? Perish the thought. This is an irreverent age, but there must be a limit somewhere."

Nevertheless by the middle of July she was ready

for that fatal step. Beginning "Dear Charlie," she ended, "Will you not write me soon? *Please do.*"

The little golden barb kept working its way in deeper and deeper.

Dear Charlie,
Won't you tell me whether you are awfully busy, or sick (the gods forbid) or married, or dead?
Yours truly,
Thea

My dear Charlie,
(I am surprised at the absolute audacity of my beginning) I have just five minutes to tell you what a good boy you are to write, how horribly your letter smelled of tobacco and to assure you that I was delighted with the tobacco and you . . . If I do not stop now I will tell you how much I love you.
Thea

"If we have not time enough to become wise, we have time enough to become refined."
Put that in your pipe and smoke it, and don't swear such awful swears.

Dorothea Roads had a fine mind and an outlook far wider than that of the average woman of her day. Just the choice of the profession of medicine in her time took intellectual courage. Male students were not only scornful but abusive of female colleagues. The budding doctor, however, was also vital and thoroughly feminine.

If the preceding letters suggest that she was angling for Charlie Lummis, the following indicate that she was the one on the hook. (And alas, other letters in the box indicate that he was doing equally well with Ellie and Mattie.)

[1] Dorothea wrote hundreds of letters to Charlie. Though seldom dated, they cover the years 1879 to 1891. The several hundred letters still intact are in the possession of the author.

April 4, 1880

Sunday
Forgive me for writing but I want you to know and I'm afraid I can't tell you any other way. I am a coward anyhow and don't deserve happiness, but I want it "all the same." I knew when you had gone that I should imagine and create all sorts of horrors and I have done so so successfully that my brain is utterly unable to see things straight so now I am not even sure it is right that we should be happy. And I must feel that way with all my soul first.

Quaintly then:

April 14, 1880

My Dear:
It is a lovely afternoon and the horses and phaeton are at the door. Won't you come and indulge in the mild dissipation of a drive into the spring woods for wild flowers?

Good-by,
Your Thea

After a year and a hundred and fifty letters more we come to this.

My darling boy:
Will you please buy you a bicycle with the enclosed to remember our first anniversary with—I wish I could have gotten a fine one for you, but you will understand and suit yourself better. I wish you could know how much pleasure I take in being able to do this and how long I have planned it. Please make me happy by getting one soon. I so want you to have it.

Thea

He bought the high wheeler and made a one-thousand-mile trip around New England while his love remained in Boston. "We are a peculiar couple and need our own laws and customs," wrote Dorothea many years later. With another letter it becomes apparent that the anniversary was not in celebration of any formal sacrament.

North Sandwich

Aug. 30
If I do not just oblige myself to write down the facts and leave feelings quite out of the question, I shall go quite insane. Please read the enclosed letter and let me tell you the rest. . . . Then this Quinby, when he came here to spend a weeks vacation, told

his cousin Mr. French and he told it in confidence to Miss Faie McCrillis and she to her sister. Francilla being one girl in a thousand and wholly true to me went down to the house of this French and got the letter, telling him to keep perfectly quiet and say nothing. Then she brought it straight to me with a hearty assurance of her entire faith in me, which hurt me more than suspicion. I totally declined to make the slightest explanation to either the Messers Quinby or French—but I told her that we had been married for some time and that I had foolishly stopped at the Flume House thus giving rise to these guilty appearances. She is kindness itself and yet it almost kills me to think what she would believe if she knew the truth.

I am almost ready to believe I am an outcast. . . . Can you in your rough and tumble fight with men and things, even imagine what such an experience is to me who have been so carefully sheltered from any breath of scorn or shame? Shame! Ignominy—do they really belong to me? Help me some way if you love me. I will do nothing until I hear from you . . . I am so utterly weak without you.

They were married immediately. Years later scandal mongers claimed that Charlie married Dorothea to escape a more pressing but less attractive obligation.[2] This is possible; he had other attachments, but it was the letter that forced his hand. Dorothea was wildly happy and deeply in love. Two weeks later she wrote:

Do you know the pretty song, "Bid Me to Live?" My heart has been singing two lines of it over and over, 'Thou art my soul, my life,
my heart,
The very eyes of me—'

Thea

Presently they broke the news of the wedding to their respective parents. All was accepted, all was bliss. At this point the man who had passed his entrance examination in German by memorizing a dictionary in four days achieved what would have seemed impossible—he flunked out of Harvard.[3]

[2] Mary Austin, *Earth Horizons*, 292.
[3] According to records at Harvard University, Charlie failed trigonometry and analytical geometry. The degree of Bachelor of Arts was conferred on Lummis on the twenty-fifth anniversary of the Class of 1881. In 1903, Santa Clara College, Santa Clara, California, conferred on him the degree of Doctor of Letters.

A Yankee Turns West

THERE soon began one of those numerous and lengthy separations that contributed to the eventual failure of Charlie and Dorothea's marriage. Charlie went to Chillicothe, Ohio, to manage his father-in-law's farm; Dorothea remained in Boston to complete her medical education. It is unfortunate that the father-in-law, or "Pater" Roads as his children called him, did not leave a record of his association with his unanticipated son-in-law, the new and inexperienced manager of his farm. We have only the manager's words in an unusual job description.

I had never managed a farm in my life. I knew nothing about farming. But nevertheless I decided that managing Pater's 600 acres was exactly my job. I proved it too by getting along with suspicious Pennsylvania Dutch farmers, by getting the Jerseys to follow me everywhere, or the bull to carry me on his back as though it were a privilege, or by selling a large number of walnut stumps for something that seemed beyond the dreams of luxury or by improving methods a little.[1]

Shortly thereafter his father-in-law was startled to hear that his manager was giving it all up and moving into Chillicothe. "The mastery of the thing was fine, but the printer's ink was in my blood."[2]

In Chillicothe was published the oldest newspaper west of the Alleghenies, the Scioto Gazette, *a huge four-page weekly founded by the grandfather of N. P. Willis. When I moved to the city from Pater's place it was no trouble for me to get the job of city editor nor any long drift from that to Editor-in-Chief. I signed myself Lum—the name by which the old-*

timers there (and later in Los Angeles) called me for years.

Enormous fun! I suppose the weekly newspaper is as near heaven as man may come who is punctured with the serum of printers' ink.

I became the local staff, the editorial staff, the literary editor, the funny-column man, the proof reader and whatever else came to hand.

In addition I had time to box and wrestle, go hunting and fishing, give physical training to the friends of some of my friends, hunt archaeological specimens and play baseball.[3]

It was during Charlie's three years in Ohio that his love of archaeology, which he attributed to his scholarly father, had a chance to express itself. The Scioto Valley was a seat of aboriginal culture, and many "artifacts"[4] were turned up by the plow or the heavy rains. After one cloudburst he discovered the evidence of a prehistoric massacre involving some forty skeletons. He treasured a 2½-inch spearhead or flint knife which he found embedded in the breastbone of a woman, within whose ribs were the traces of the bones of an unborn child.

Chillicothe in the 80's was a beautiful old town of 5,000 people, nearly all of them F.F.V's:[5] *courtly,*

[1] Lummis, "As I Remember."
[2] *Ibid.*
[3] *Ibid.*
[4] Lummis insisted on this form of the two Latin words: *ars fecit,* instead of the usual *ars facere.* There were other notions that he defended while life and breath were with him: that the shape of an individual's skull could be altered by intensive mental activity and that man was indigenous to this continent. Less well framed arguments have received more serious scientific consideration. An article in *Time,* dated April 29, 1974, suggested that the latter idea may find some support. A professor of Marseille University, Prehistorian Henry de Lumley, commenting on his years of study of Le Trou du Tachou near the Riviera town of Roquebrune-Cap-Martin, is quoted as speculating, "Perhaps man had several different cradles. . . ."
[5] First Families of Virginia.

loveable, slow. . . . Passing people on the street going in the same direction I went by as though they had been hitched. The old valley was a hotbed of malaria. In the three years of greeting acquaintances it never once happened that anyone said: "Fine!" or "First rate!" The average was "Pretty miserable, thank you!" or "Can't complain, I guess!" The brakeman on the old Marrietta and Cincinnati Railroad used to call the station, "Chill-i-coth-e-! Fifteen minutes for quinine!"

It never occurred to me that I could slow down to the Chillicothe gait. But one night without warning the Old Familiar of the region made me an unexpected call—old Fever-'n'-Ager. I burned and tossed and leaked at every pore. In the morning I was pounds lighter and weak as a drowned rat. The bed was as though I had turned a hose on it.

I am not abrupt nor impetuous, but that one night's lesson that even I was mortal, was enough for me. I was fond of Chillicothe and its courtly people, but before night I decided that I was going to move, that I was going to move a long way, that if I could arrange it, I would make it California. And I was going to walk there.[6]

Some of the newspapers admired the editor who made up his mind to walk to California "with about as much ado as you make up your mind to go for a sleigh ride." "If we have ever said anything about Charlie Lummis' poetry, we take it all back now. We always thought it was pretty good poetry anyway." "Juneman gave Charlie Lummis a cigar when he left town big enough to last him till he gets to Los Angeles."

Others scoffed. "I was just thinking what a picnic those fellows out in the plains will have with the seat of Lummis' breeches. . . . I can tell you one of those fellows can take them off Lummy with one stroke of the bull whip. . . . Why they will have more fun with the seat of Lummy's pants than they have had before for a year."

Charlie set forth in his own unique outfit—low, light shoes and the tight-fitting, knee-length trousers worn by baseball players. It was perhaps the first demonstration of his notion that each new office must have its appropriate vestments.

For three decades there were Chillicotheans who liked to talk about Lum's exploit; he was the spaceman of their earthbound era. Seventy years later there was an old-time Ohioan who still remembered the thrill of his hero's progress.

My choice of California as a goal was due largely to Colonel Harrison Gray Otis, editor of the Los Angeles Times, *who had promised to print a weekly letter as I Walked Across and to give me a position on the local staff. My letters were printed weekly in the* Times *as well as the* Chillicothe Leader.[7]

And he was paid the handsome sum of $5 for each letter!

Charlie Lummis was twenty-six years old and hardly known outside the state when he set out from Cincinnati on September 12, 1884. The undertaking was mainly an adventure, but he could hope now to be able to make a living for himself and his "Little Doctor."

Charlie was under contract to produce an interesting letter every week. With a keen eye for a story, he found no difficulty in fulfilling his commitment in this new West which had been so sketchily reported. His letters began to be reprinted by other papers. By the time he reached Indiana the whole region was talking about him. His passage through Seymour, Indiana, wrote a local reporter, "just tore up the burg. Six hundred or more people witnessed his entrance into the town, and since his departure he has been the leading topic of conversation."

It is not easy to visualize in these days of push-button transportation what it was like to cross the country on foot in 1884. Lummis had to brave almost trackless expanses—desolate plains where the bones of pioneers told of starvation and Indian massacres, mountains swept by freezing winds, and blistering deserts with temperatures to 130 degrees.

He slept on the floors of solitary section houses or on the ground in rain and in blizzards. When he didn't have his sleeping bag, he slept without one; it was all part of the game. His outfit consisted of writing material, matches, a small revolver (changed later for a .44), a strong hunting knife, three hundred dollars in "quarter eagles" in a money belt strapped against his skin. He also carried his beloved fishing tackle, although his later life hardly bore out his

---

[6] Lummis, "As I Remember."

[7] Ibid.

statement about fishing, written later in his reminiscences "As I Remember":

If I had ever met up with a mermaid, I am sure we should have lived happily ever after—she would have fulfilled my complete Ideal. Women are adorable while they are—and if. But fish, Always. I have loved many women, and do yet. I have known a marvellous proportion of noble and lovely ones. But if all the lovely ladies in the world were piled up on one side of the path and all the gold in the world were piled up on the other, and I could see just beyond a brook with the flip of a trout in the sunlight, I should beg hasty pardon of both waysides, get to the singing water and proceed to courting trout.

No matter how far Charlie had walked, wherever he camped, whatever the weather, he never failed to do his stint of writing, by a brush fire if at night and in the open, under the corner of his sleeping bag if in the rain.

His letters proved "a bonanza to the newspapers." "Somehow," wrote one editor, "the articles have a strange, indescribable interest and people have got to talking about Lum all over the country. He is the most noted man in the West just now and carries in his shoes a pretty fair-sized circus."

The circus, it may be said, was to maintain the same office for a good many years.

In his youth, canoeing, bicycling, and marathons had made Charlie more intimately acquainted with New England than most young men of his age. But nothing of its gentler loveliness had prepared him for the land which began to open out to him some two hundred miles west of Kansas City.

The Great Plains seemed to be all there was of the world. The buffalo wallow, the prairie dog, the slow-wheeling vulture were the only signs of life. In the presence of such limitless solitude, Charlie began to be aware of what "travel, elbow room, climate and other evolutionary forces of the first magnitude" do to the soul. "[Man] who feels himself the Lord of Creation [comes to admit] that he did not invent it."[8]

He did not reach Denver until October 23, and there, "after weeks of corned beef tougher and older than Samuel J. Tilden, bread as appetizing as Illinois

mud and coffee like the Ohio river on a raise," he sat down at last to real food. The waiters stood along the wall in respectful awe, as he put it, to see that wilderness of dishes before him explored and conquered.

Although he still wrote with the newspaper irreverence of the day, no man who had once quickened to the ethereal possibilities of silver birch and moonlight in a canoe could be the same after he came face to face with what the Hewer of chasm and plain had wrought on the earth. On Pike's Peak he looked up at stars that seemed to bite their way through space; he trod on snow that had fallen perhaps before recorded history.

Late in October Charlie still had the Rockies to cross. More than one of his readers wondered if he would not finish his journey by train. He kept on walking. He sent twelve of the thirty-seven pounds he had been carrying, including a blanket, ahead by express. The package was usually ahead of or behind him, and the nights were freezing. One day near the top of the Continental Divide a blast of wind whipped him through the ice of a shallow pool. With his clothing frozen to his body he walked eight miles before reaching shelter.

At Harvard Charlie had engaged in lawless pranks with Boies Penrose—just for devilment. In the West he found men driven by desperate compulsion who ignored the law and risked their lives and fortunes. Here for the first time the minister's son rubbed elbows with toughs, sharpers, desperadoes, and women of wit and warmth, all ready to hazard everything.

In Colorado Charlie stayed in a shack whose Yankee owner had gone through the seven years of the grasshopper plague. One July evening in 1875 this farmer had returned home from an overnight trip to find that the grasshoppers had eaten his twenty acres of corn down to the bare earth, his cattle range was gone, and not a straw was left of his hay. The grasshoppers had even eaten half through the sheathing at the bottom of the outer walls of his house. He started all over again, and when Lum found him nine years later he was still there battling it out.[9]

There were pioneer children staked to long ropes to keep them from wandering away to their death in

[8] Charles F. Lummis, *Land of Sunshine*, Vol. XV, No. 2 (September, 1901), 158.

[9] Charles F. Lummis to the *Los Angeles Times*, from Platte Canyon, Colorado, October 30, 1884.

the wilderness. He met men such as old Monny of Dead Man's Canyon, who, crippled for life in a fight with a cinnamon bear, still carried on as a trapper. There was rollicking "Judge" Baldwin, the Irishman who once owned and was swindled out of the land on which Colorado Springs now stands. Scalped twice by Indians, "Judge" lived to tell of it, only to be drowned later in two feet of water.

And now Charlie began to hear the tales of the men who sought for gold.

We hear of the few mining kings—the golden accidents of fortune—but who shall tell the epic of that great heart-break, that myriad suffering of the unrequited multitude? Beside that wild story, if it ever be written, the wanderings of Ulysses will seem a schoolboy's recess. These men left wives as faithful as Penelope and never returned. . . . They pierced a stranger and wilder land than Caesar ever dreamed. . . .

How they ran hither and yon as delusive hope blew her golden bubbles about them; how they tore up the channels of the wild mountain streams and grew bent in handling the long rocker or flaring gold pan. How young men became old in the chase, and old men laid their weary bones to rest beside the lonely claim, the little buckskin bag of dust still clutched in their bony fingers. How paupers became princes and princes paupers; and the man whose claim today was worth its hundred thousands, tomorrow turned, a beggar, to strike out again for the hills. How that heterogeneous mass of humanity battled with cold and hunger, disease and death, with beasts thirsty for blood and desperate men still thirstier for gold— ah, that was our greatest, longest, strangest tragedy.[10]

Men and episodes like these proved for him what a frontier means to a nation. He was looking far into the coming century when he said:

Very much as the sea is to this slow-perishing planet, so the Frontier has been to mankind. . . . [The sea] is as it were the earth's liver and our salvation. Without it we should long ago have perished from off a reeking footstool. . . .

To that great filter all unhindered rivers lean. Unless they are to stagnate, they must find it at last and in it be born again. Their acquired impurities it lays

down in quiet rocks to be upheaved, with time, in new and more rugged continents. . . .

In the like fashion, and quite as indispensably, the wilderness has been ocean to man. Civilization . . . is a tremendous river, heedless of the drops it can no longer count, polluted with its own mills and slops, arrogant and forgetful of its source as of its destiny. . . . But . . . imagine it cut off from the outlet. . . . Presently it must die, and its parasites before it—its fishes and tadpoles and mosquitoes and men—unless it may come at last to precipitate its mud and release its ascending vapors.

Ever since that ingrowing of man which we call civilization, the Frontier has been its remedy. It is the only ethnic Fountain of Eternal Youth yet discovered. . . . The real meaning of the Frontier is merely Room and Nature. It is the coming home to Mother Earth . . . we are all sons of the Brown Mother and from her breast strength cometh.[11]

New experiences included a duel in the dark with a wildcat, a narrow escape from a stone hammer in the hands of a convict, and a quaint style in family prayer. In a canyon ranch house in the Greenhorn Range a fortnight after the presidential elections of 1884, a blind, old mother got the family members down on their knees:

We do not know yet, O Lord, how the tide of our country's affairs has turned, but we fear those nasty Democrats have seized the reins of government. But we beseech thee, great Ruler, that if it be consistent with Thy Will, Mr. Blaine may be our next President and that wicked man Cleveland be rebuked.[12]

At a tiny station west of Pueblo, Colorado, Charlie first met and set out to win over a homeless four-month-old hound who had become nearly wild through abuse and neglect. It was a long struggle, but gradually the pup began losing his terror of the man and the rope. Turned loose halfway up the Great Divide, he did not run away, and a little later crept near, trembling, to be petted. From then on for fifteen hundred miles, rain, sleet, or snow, they plodded on together. His master named him Shadow and declared that he was as true a shadow as ever followed.

[10] Charles F. Lummis, *A Tramp Across the Continent*, 52–53.
[11] Charles F. Lummis, *Out West*, Vol. XVII (September, 1902), 269–75, 286.
[12] Charles F. Lummis to the *Los Angeles Times*, from Pueblo, Colorado, November 13, 1884.

As CHARLIE LUMMIS strode across the western plains, thrilling to every minute of the adventure, the beauty, and the hardship, a small-town editor was becoming something of a celebrity and a young Yankee was being exposed to a new way of life.

Never having known any but his own race, Charlie at first distrusted and avoided the dark-skinned natives. Arriving at the little hamlet of Carnoe, New Mexico, hungry and exhausted from fighting through the waist-deep snows of the mountains, he found only two families living there, both Mexican. He was driven at last to ask for help at the home of a poor laborer, Ramon Arrera. Unknown, unshaven, suspicious as the traveller was, the Mexican welcomed him wholeheartedly to his home and scanty rations. This first close contact with a native made a good story for the letter to the *Los Angeles Times* that week and was later rewritten by him for his book *A Tramp Across the Continent.*

Upon a lonely looking table was only a cup of coffee, a dry tortilla and a smoking platter of apparent stewed tomatoes . . . but I was too hungry to be fastidious. . . . I swallowed the first big spoonful at a gulp. And then I sprang up with a howl of pain and terror, fully convinced that these "treacherous Mexicans" had assassinated me by quick poison—for I had very ignorant and silly notions in those days about Mexicans, as most of us are taught by superficial travellers who do not know one of the kindliest races in the world. My mouth and throat were consumed with living fire and my stomach was a pit of boiling torture. . . . I rushed from the house and plunged into a snowbank, biting the snow to quench that horrible inner fire. Poor Arrera followed me in astonishment but smothering his laughter. What was the matter with the Señor? I came very near answering with my six shooter but his sincerity was plain and I listened to him. Poison? No indeed, Señor. That was only chile colorado, chile con carne, *which liked to the Mexicans* mucho—*and to many Americanos tambien.*[1]

By the next morning hunger had toughened the tender New England palate to the extent that it was able to endure a platter full of the concentrated fire, but his writing in later years demonstrated that these meetings had made a more important change.

Why is it that the last and most difficult education seems to be the ridding ourselves of silly inborn race prejudice? All start with it, few of us graduate from it. And yet the clearest thing in the world to him who has eyes and chance to use them, is that men everywhere—white men, brown men, yellow men, black men—are all just about the same thing. The difference is little deeper than the skin.[2]

So for the first time Lummis began to learn how

[1] Lummis, *A Tramp Across the Continent,* 136–38. Eventually Lummis became not only an addict but a "pusher" of the chili pod. Some ten years later, having an editorial page to fill and being at the moment without a greater cause, he wrote: "The use of *chile* is just as much a hygenic necessity in this country [arid southern California] as salt is elsewhere. No universal habit of a simple people is vain. The Californians did not know by definition why they ate *chile,* any more than a cow knows why she prefers alfalfa to salt grass. God knew and He gave them both sense enough at the outset to eat even without a doctor's prescription.

"Briefly speaking . . . the tendency of the liver to become torpid in an arid climate can be permanently counteracted in a population only by the use of some such stimulant. And it isn't any hardship to take the medicine, as all who have ever learned it know that nothing is more genial to the intestinal economy or to the palate." See *Out West,* Vol. XXIII, No. 2 (August, 1905), 173–74.

[2] Lummis, *A Tramp Across the Continent,* 75.

unlike his Yankee preconceptions was the spirit of the dark-skinned people with their alien architecture. Sitting around midnight campfires with Mexican shepherds, smoking their thin, brown cigarettes, taking part in the happy-hearted Mexican *baile*, he became interested in Spanish speech and customs. There was many a chat in the friendly adobes while all the members of the family—grandmother, mother, and the small boys—puffed on their cigarettes. Even the swearing of the New Mexican paisanos delighted his classical taste.

They swear methodically, gracefully, fluently, comprehensively, eloquently, thoughtfully—I had almost said prayerfully . . . there is nothing brutal about it. It is courteous, tactful, musical, at times majestic. It carries a sense of artistic satisfaction:

"Maldito Bueyes! ["damned oxen"] That the Evil One take away your sisters and brothers—that the coyotes may eat your uncles and aunts. Diablos! Get out of this . . . the fool that broke you, would that he had to drive you in Inferno. . . . Ill-said family that wear out the yoke with nodding in it! Anathema upon your grandfather and everything else that ever wore horns and curse everything from here to Albuquerque and back four times. . . ."[3]

Not until he and Shadow had reached the Río Grande Valley did Charlie see the typical New Mexico, forever after dear to him.

Wee peach orchards and tiny gardens, each enclosed by a breast-high adobe wall; neat adobe houses under the giant cottonwoods, cattle and burros grazing in the brown meadows, primitive little mills, and now and then the greaseless shriek of old carretas whose wheels were carved in one block from cross sections of huge sycamores.

Charlie's introduction to an Indian pueblo was at San Ildefonso. Grimy and unshaven, loaded down with two guns, a hunting knife, and belt full of ammunition, he walked in with his half-wild dog companion. But old Alonzo, governor of "the strange little aboriginal republic," met them with simple friendliness and gave them a place to sleep on the adobe floor in the midst of his own family.

The pueblo was a revelation to a New Englander

[3] *Ibid.,* 177–78.

reared on impressions of war-whooping Fenimore Cooper savages and cartoons of "Lo, the poor (and indolent) Indian." Here were Indians building churches, tilling farms, and living in temperance, dignity, peace, and prosperity. Moreover, far from learning these virtues from the European conquerors, their civilization was flourishing long before the first colonists left England.

From the Harvard campus to the dusty streets of San Ildefonso had been a long journey. The preacher's son had passed through many stages of the hurrying westward drive of population and "civilization." He was one of the few who realized that the ways of the Indian, the Spaniard, and the frontiersman were soon to be swamped in the great wave that was following. There before his eyes was history and archaeology alive. He felt that he was one of a generation that had been misled about the Indians and the West, and he resolved to set the record straight.

Late in November, 1884, Charlie reached the capital city, Santa Fe. He had come to stay two days, but, despite the pressure to meet his schedule, he stayed a week. The fascination of the City of the Holy Faith was not solely that of its prehistoric beginnings, its rambling streets, and crenellated walls of a style as old as the patriarchs. There were also the relics of a storied past and the impress of bygone adventurers. But what held him most was its people.

For generations the Lummis strain had been in New England. Charlie, though always grateful that he had been born there, was doubly grateful that he had escaped in time.

I loved New England in all its hardness and all its humanity. It was marvelous how human the hardest could be and how hard the most human! I have never known either finer or tenderer hearts than I knew in old New England. But I have seen many other temporary suspensions of the Attraction of Gravitation.

Then I came to Santa Fe. And once I had reached Spanish America and the hearts of its people, I realized that this was where I belonged.

Though my conscience was Puritan, my whole imagination and sympathy and feeling were Latin. That is, essentially Spanish. Apparently they always had been, for now that I had gotten away from the repressive influence of my birthplace I began to see that the generous and bubbling boyish impulses which had been considerably frosted in New England were, after all, my birthright.[4]

One of the first to help in this awakening was Amado Chaves, speaker of the House of Representatives of the Territory of New Mexico. Lummis' friendship with Don Amado was his first and most enduring friendship in the West. Don Amado had recently discovered on his ranch a buried stone city that had never been described nor even visited by scientists. He invited Lummis to be a guest at San Mateo and there to have his first experience in the exploration of the Southwest. Lummis could not get enough of those eloquent ruins. From their fallen upper stories, scattered skeletons, and broken and blackened utensils he read an aboriginal tragedy.

The Chaveses were among the noted families of the New Mexico Territory. In their patriarchal home Lummis took part in a life different from any he had known in New England. To these New Mexicans of ancient lineage it was not enough to fulfill civic and religious duties. One must also have fun. All ages joined in laughter at noses dipped into flour to find hidden bullets and enjoyed dinners of rice and mutton stew, roasted beef cubes, frijoles, and *galletitas* (little cakes of white and graham flour) followed by dancing and singing the songs of old and new Spain.

The beauty of the Spanish women charmed him.

If there is any type more seductive, you may keep it. Blue eyes are sweet and alluring but for solid magnetism it takes two orbs of jet, framed in lashes of brown still darker showing the sparks of a fire that may blaze up at any minute. There is un diablo chiquito *in the corner of such eyes and I suspect that part of their attractiveness is due to the hint of danger lurking in their depths.*[5]

Don Amado's father, Don Manuel Chaves, was a straight-backed warrior of sixty-eight whose body was literally covered with the scars of ghastly battles with Apaches, Navajos, and Utes. From him Lummis heard many a story of those bloody days. On one trading expedition Don Manuel and eight of his men were surrounded by three hundred Navajos. For

hours the traders fought off the rain of bullets and arrows. By nightfall when the Indians withdrew, all of Don Manuel's companions had been killed, and he was almost dead.

The only thing that saved him was the arrival of a friendly Navajo, a former servant of his, who got him to Fort Wingate. There he lay near death for three months. When he finally set out for home, he was again attacked and wounded and his Navajo rescuer killed. After further great suffering, Don Manuel managed to make his way alone to the top of the San Mateo mountains, and here another friendly Indian found him and carried him unconscious and bleeding to the Chaves hacienda.

It was hard for Lummis to leave Santa Fe and harder to leave the Chaves way of life, but his agreement with Colonel Otis required him to be in Los Angeles by a certain date. He tore himself away from the place but never from the memories or the lifelong friendships.

Continuing the march, Lummis found many causes to champion. In 1884 the men with big holdings in mines, farms, or cattle west of the Rockies were trying to take everything that the man with little had struggled so hard to make his own. All the way across the western half of the continent the young crusader saw what was being done to the miner, the cattleman, the farmer. Ruthlessly the largest owners were swallowing them all.

Great companies owned the canals and most of the crops went for water rentals. . . . Here where in nine-tenths of the region land was worth nothing and water was life . . . syndicates bought and fenced the rare springs and water pockets and the small man's cattle could die of thirst.[6]

The prospector who braved loneliness, heat, thirst, and the madness that comes from solitude struck it rich, only to be brutally frozen out by the big companies. The railroads set freight rates so high that the small miner could not afford to ship his ore. Worn out by the unequal struggle, he sold for the little he could get. The big companies, able to secure a favorable rate reduction, made a fortune from the same mine which the small miner had risked death to find.

Wealthy men who could get possession of a spring

---

[4] Lummis, "As I Remember."

[5] Charles F. Lummis to the *Chillicothe Leader* and the *Los Angeles Times*, January 1, 1885.

[6] Lummis, *A Tramp Across the Continent*, 78.

commanded the range, sometimes for as much as a thousand square miles. Although they had not bought the land, they fenced it with hundreds of miles of barbed wire. Shut out, cattle whose life depended on those springs fell dead of thirst. Frontier hatred was aroused and men paid with their lives.

Lummis found spots where the bleaching bones of cattle lay as far as fifty miles along the wrong side of the fence. In retaliation, fences were down, their wires cut and nothing left of the fence posts but ashes.

In his letters Charlie spoke of the ring leader as

the boss thief of the big ring of wealthy scoundrels who have for years had everything their own way and their way came near being the ruin of this great . . . territory. Many of them were officers in the Rebel army but they have become Republicans out here because it paid. . . . [He] is universally detested throughout all New Mexico and his life wouldn't be worth much if he were to venture into this part of the country. The Chief Justice of the Territory is his ready tool and some of his acts are almost incredible. I am glad to see that the government is making tardy amends and that this thief's resignation has been called for and his successor selected. I couldn't stop to name all who are in this ring—whose crimes are countless and cover the whole list from larceny to murder. Suffice to say that the "Santa Fe Ring"— including the Chief Justice, the Attorney General, the surveyors, lawyers and many more—with a few outside monopolists . . . have been trying to steal the whole Territory and carry it off in their vest pockets. They came pretty near succeeding too but the late election knocked them crazy. That is my one consolation in Blaine's defeat.[7]

Among the crimes of the Santa Fe Ring was that against Golden, New Mexico. Here in this storied mining town it was not the chance for power and fortune which gripped Lummis' imagination. It was the stores of those who were fighting the ring.

The Ring's politicians had suborned surveyors, bought judges and juries, manipulated Spanish grants and true lines of survey until they had grabbed tens of thousands of acres of the richest mining lands in New Mexico. For a long time the true owners were patient. Then the Ring actually threatened to shoot them if they did not leave their own land. One day when the Ring's 100 imported laborers came out of the shaft for lunch, eleven quiet resolute men stepped up and said, "Guess we'd better run this thing for a while now." There was no fighting. The eleven quiet men took possession of their own.[8]

Among the citizens defying the ring were Colonel R. W. Webb, a pioneer journalist, and his young and lovely wife. For years Colonel Webb had fought the group with his paper, the *Golden Retort*. Although he knew he was risking his life, Colonel Webb never ceased his attack. Finally he went to Washington to arouse the government. His wife elected to stay behind to keep up the fight.

"A charming little Louisianan with a pound of dynamite in each black eye," Mrs. Webb knew nothing about running a newspaper, but "she learned how to stick type herself and taught a green young miner. Between them they got out a paper with burning editorials and never missed an issue during the Colonel's absence."[9]

The Webbs' fearless campaign awoke public opinion. The government stepped in and returned the stolen claims to their owners.

The exploits and courage of such frontier personalities as the Webbs, the Chaveses, and the Arreras, bound Lummis to a land that could breed such stalwarts and made him a lifelong champion of the West.

Although he never lost his fondness for the land of his birth, for the rest of his days he took good-humored pokes at New Englanders and the East. The motivation of much of his writing, be it in the breezy journalistic slang of his youth or in the vigorous style of his mature years, was the secret filial desire to make other Easterners grow out of their timidities and restraints and to shake them out of their sacred pantalettes.

He coined the phrase "See America First," and he knew now how much he belonged in this "fascinating land of blood-red mesas, strange sentinel buttes and

[7] Charles F. Lummis to the *Los Angeles Times*, from Golden, New Mexico, December 10, 1884.

[8] *Ibid.*

[9] Charles F. Lummis to the *Los Angeles Times*, from Albuquerque, New Mexico, December 19, 1884.

rifted canons, the land whose very atmosphere is an enchantment and its erosion the playground of the giants."

Dorothea, meanwhile, had proceeded to Los Angeles by regular transportation. She wrote,

Los Angeles, Nov. 9, 1884. Here I be at last sweetheart. We found the trip down the coast longer and harder, comparatively, than all the rest. The way lies through a dusty, sandy, hot desert and the scenery is nil. They talk big out here, you know and the reality is apt to be small. We reached here about 2:00 P.M. and as soon as we got into the air we felt its charm. Soft and warm and sweet. The town is not a bit imposing but I think it is going to prove a nice one and I think we will like it. It is a kind of irrigated oasis in the sand, however, and one must resign once and forever all hopes of what we call greenness and fertility, except right in the city. . . . You will want to ask good wages here or we can't live. Prices are so fiendish. Virginia has one small back room, without heat and light, and has to pay $12 a month, unfurnished, so I tremble at what I will be asked for two good rooms . . . four dollars a week here is low for meals. Jim says Mr. Otis is smart, but not considered any too good principled. . . . Just think, I have to send my diploma up to S.F. to be registered before I can practice here at all. It's good though for it keeps out quacks. . . .

You don't know, sweetheart, how much of the old and marvelous light of our early love and marriage still lives and lightens my sometimes weary and often worldly heart. I know I was too romantic then . . . must I let it go? It is for you to say.

6

The Last Hard Miles

On leaving Golden, Lummis faced the worst of the winter and more than a thousand miles of walking. Christmas Eve was spent in a tiny section house. The section boss was impressed. "Stumpin' to Californy, hey? Banged if I don't stump it with you!" Whereupon he quit his job and the two started off together. They arrived at the pueblo of Laguna while the Indians were celebrating their remarkable holiday dances which Lummis described for his readers in detail, adding:

> . . . Those eight hundred men, women and children all stood looking in decorous silence, never moving a muscle or uttering a sound. Only once did they relax their gravity and that was at our coming. My . . . appearance, as I climbed up a house and sat down on the roof was too much for them as well it might be. The sombrero with its snake skin band, the knife and two six-shooters in my belt, the bulging duck coat and long-fringed leggings, the skunk skin dangling from my blanket roll . . . the stuffed coyote over my shoulders looking natural as life made up a picture I feel sure they never saw before and probably never will again. They must have thought me Pa-puk-kewis, the wild man of the plains. A lot of the children crowded around me and when I caught the coyote by the neck and shook it, at the same time growling at them savagely, they jumped away and the whole assembly was convulsed with laughter. . . . For hours we watched the strange wild spectacle until the sinking sun warned us to be moving and we reluctantly turned our faces westward.[1]

A short time later Lummis arrived in Defiance. There he met the sort of Indian trader who has helped to make the history of our dealings with the Indian a black and shameful chapter. A card sharp, braggart, and bully, his talk was of the "jesusly" time he had cheating the Indians and killing off enough Navajos to keep the rest cowed. He had more than a hundred revolvers lying at full cock in hiding places all over the store and had been known to murder at least one Indian.

> We talk of the cruelty of the Spanish conquests but they were far less cruel than the Saxon ones. The Spaniard never exterminated. He conquered the aborigine and then converted and educated him and preserved him with a scholarship, humanity and zeal of which to our shame be it said our own history does not furnish the hint of a parallel. The proof is in living flesh and blood. If we ever reach as humane and honorable an Indian policy as the Spanish had firmly maintained for 300 years, it will be a most creditable national achievement.[2]

Leaving Defiance, his companion having given out, Lummis slogged on alone, now sinking into mud at each step, now pushing on through snow. "If a man knows how to use the lemon-squeezer of philosophy he can punch a power of good juice out of adversity," he was pleased to disclose to his readers in the *Los Angeles Times* and the *Chillicothe Leader*. Then he crossed the New Mexico line into Arizona. "Thenceforth the whole Tramp was an experience one would not care to repeat though it is well to have had it once."[3]

His weekly letter told how, climbing a mesa a little after dawn one day in pursuit of a deer, he fell and

---

[1] Lummis, *A Tramp Across the Continent*, 158, 164–65.

[2] *Ibid.*, 95.
[3] *Ibid.*, 223.

fractured his arm two inches below the elbow. He could not pull the jagged bone into place by tugging at his hand while he held it between his feet. So he wrapped one end of his canteen strap around his wrist, buckled the other around a cedar, threw himself backward as hard as he could, and yanked.

The next fifty-two miles to Winslow, Arizona, were torture. And there were still seven hundred miles of walking through desert and mountain in the dead of winter if he was to go on with "the Tramp."

"It is not pleasant to walk with a broken arm but neither is it pleasant to be in bed with one." Never one to give up anything he had once started, he decided to keep on. Getting back to the railroad track, he replaced the rude branch splints he had made with the staves of an old spike keg and set out on the last seven hundred miles.

Charlie never was very clear about the long trek to Winslow. Snow and mud, howling coyotes, drenching rain by day, a track walker who looked at him curiously and spoke kindly, an occasional section house, the throbbing ache of his arm—until after more than thirty hours of continuous walking he reached the town.

In those days Winslow was a tough frontier community without a doctor or even a church. Only the Mexicans and Indians had churches in that part of the world west of Albuquerque. According to Lummis, the solid businessmen of Winslow "built and furnished a house and gave it to a prostitute and are even now cursing the ungrateful thing because it burned down in eight months and left them desolate."

The pain of a broken arm could not keep him from enjoying a stronghold of characters such as these and the pioneer merchant whose handbills covered the town.

Not many years before Lummis walked into the West, many men of great vision knew nothing of it.

The First Statesman of New England—a giant anywhere in American history and the very Jove of Tenderfeet—Daniel Webster, towered mighty in wrath to protect his home against contamination by the threatened national acquiring of the Far West.

"What do we want with this vast, worthless area?", he asked the Senate of the United States, "This

STOP AND READ

J. H. BREED

Having returned from Chicago with the largest and

FINEST STOCK OF GOODS

Ever brought into Arizona,
is prepared to give the people of

WINSLOW

And surrounding country the

DAMNDEST BARGAINS

Ever heard of in this part of the World!

I CARRY

A HELL OF A LARGE ASSORTMENT OF GOODS

Which space will not allow me to enumerate here but if you will hitch up and call on the "Old Man," you can bet your shirt tail he will treat you right— and sell you anything you may want in his line.

J. H. BREED
WINSLOW, A. T.

Handbill from Winslow, Arizona Territory.

region of savages and wild beasts, of deserts, of shifting sands and whirling winds, of dust, of cactus and prairie dogs? To what use could we ever hope to put these great deserts or those endless mountain ranges, impregnable and covered to their very base with eternal snow? What can we ever hope to do with the Western Coast, a coast of 3,000 miles, rockbound, cheerless, uninviting, with not a harbor on it? . . . Mr. President, I will never vote one cent from the public treasury to place the Pacific Coast one inch nearer Boston than it now is![4]

But to Lummis, "the World's Wonderland is not in Europe, not in Egypt, not in Asia, but in the West of our own United States. Area for area no other land on earth is half so crowded with marvels of the first magnitude and of such range—of antiquities, scenery, anthropology and picturesqueness in every sort. . . ."

Not long after Lummis broke his arm, he came

[4] Charles F. Lummis, *Out West*, Vol. XVIII (February, 1903), 139.

upon what was ever after to him "The Greatest Thing in the World," the Grand Canyon of the Colorado. If he were dictator, he said, no American should be allowed to hold office, no American should even be allowed to vote who, by the age of maturity, had not visited that "incomparable chasm, that Geology-on-End, unforeseen as death tomorrow, this Cosmic Intaglio, God's chiefest wonder-vision on earth." How could a man call himself travelled who had never seen how

. . . with each degree of the sun's course the great countersunk mountains fade away and new ones, as terrific, are carven by the westering shadows . . . like a disection of the whole cosmogony. And the purple shadows, the dazzling lights, the thunderstorms and snowstorms, the clouds and rainbows that shift and drift in that subterranean area below your feet! . . . such square leagues of inverted and captive skies, of rainbows in solution . . . brimming fogs that flow with the moon and with dawn, ebb and ebb—till one by one the wide voiceless tide reveals the glorious "islands" of glowing peaks.[5]

After the glories of the Grand Canyon came the long march down to the desert. The January nights were bitter, the days dry and hot. Suffering with his arm and overburdened with gun and other equipment, Lummis gave up his blanket, thinking to take what shelter he could find in section houses and barns.

At Yucca, Arizona, the boarding house mistress refused to take him in or rent him a blanket, and he and Shadow spent the winter night huddled together in a leaky shanty under a few gunny sacks. Shadow had seemed discouraged for some time, and all that long night he quivered and moaned. The next morning, some miles below Yucca, he suddenly attacked his master, growling strangely and frothing at the mouth. In self defense Lummis had to shoot his faithful companion. In the years of train travel that followed, he never passed that spot without pointing to a mound under a certain yucca and saying, "That's Shadow's grave."

Lummis moved into the Mojave Desert, "the loneliest and most beautiful place on earth," but not the place to cross afoot. By nature too stubborn to quit,

he pushed on into "the color, the life, and the lack-life, the terror and charm of this bewitched land."

It was impossible to carry enough water. He walked until noon without drinking and carried a pebble under his tongue to stimulate the saliva. Often when he came to a station his tongue was swollen, making the first drink painful. Still he continued to step off his thirty or forty miles a day.

On one stretch of 160 miles, the largest of the three settlements had only three houses. Each mile looked so much like the one that had gone before that it was as if "the Lord had picked up the very same ground and set it down again in front of you."

It was hard going, but it made good copy. Lummis told of his diet—one square of chocolate and one quart of water a day. And he described the torment of the mirage to a thirsty man and the misery of shivering through a desert night with only sand for a blanket.

Once, travelling by night to escape the heat, he stumbled over the chalky bones and flinty skull of one who long before had attempted the same crossing. Kneeling in the moonlight with the skull in his hands, he seemed to see the slow ox team of a little band of emigrants toiling across the plain, its drivers crazed by the sun. He imagined the piteous bawling of the oxen while the blood-warm water in the kegs fell lower and lower. Then one desperate man set out on the hopeless search for a fresh supply.

It made more good copy—excitement for those who, from the comfort of their homes, had been eagerly following his travels. After his intimate contact with the desert, Lummis was able to write with special understanding of the pioneer trail breakers.

Taking up the march again, Lummis' thoughts turned to the men of Spain who centuries before had walked the same ground, and he reaffirmed his decision to do justice to their "brilliant discovery, unparalleled exploration, gallant conquest and heroic colonization."

Long before a Saxon had raised so much as a hut in the New World or penetrated a hundred miles from the coast, the Spanish pioneers had explored America from Kansas to Cape Horn and from sea to sea and had far inland a chain of Spanish cities five thousand miles long![6]

[5] Charles F. Lummis, *Mesa, Cañon and Pueblo*, 26–29.

[6] Lummis, *A Tramp Across the Continent*, 95.

In his letters he made light of his hardships and reproved those readers who warned him that many a traveler walked in circles and died of heat and thirst madness. "A hunter doesn't walk in circles. A dude might and there are some I know who would be as useful swinging around in a circle as anywhere else. Even a clever fellow without experience might. But I am related to neither."[7]

At Daggett, California, Charlie decided to save time by leaving the safety of the railroad and striking out across the sands. The townsfolk warned him that he could not make it. This only added to the challenge.

On this stretch he had a companion, a green, young Swiss named Albert Munier. What they had to face together was more than they had known men could survive. They ploughed through heat like that of a blast furnace. That night at Stoddard's Wells, they were refused shelter from the bitter cold. Young Munier had the only overcoat, which they shared.

The next day the lad's feet were covered with blisters, but, joking, he trudged on. Late in the afternoon he fell exhausted in front of a house on the far side of Cajon Pass. There Lummis bade goodbye to this boy who had won his lasting respect, gave him all his provisions, divided what money he had, and made his way down Cajon Pass, feasting his eyes on green fields and orchards. That night for the first time since breaking his arm Lummis was able to undress fully, take a hot bath, sleep in a bed.

The next day, January 31, 1885, he walked into an area of wild flowers, meadow larks, butterflies, and orange groves. Though it was the middle of winter the air was like June. Along the banks of brimming brooks were orchards and homes and gardens. All over the San Bernardino Valley he saw springing grass, heard the hum of bees, and the songs of birds.

There was nothing in life for which Lummis would have exchanged that three thousand-mile journey. "It taught me more in its 143 days than all my years at Harvard. More in mental equipment. . . . As a course in physical training it did me more good even than my years of college boxing and wrestling. . . ."[8]

The imagination of the country had been cap-

[7] Charles F. Lummis to the *Chillicothe Leader* and the *Los Angeles Times*, February 8, 1885.
[8] Lummis, "As I Remember."

The *Chillicothe Leader* sold this souvenir picture of Charlie following his trek from Ohio to California.
You Can Secure
A Handsome Photo of
LUMMIS
In full traveling costume, just as he appeared when he entered Los Angeles, after his trip across the continent, either at the *Leader* office or Horney's Book Store, opposite the Postoffice. Price 50 cents. All mail orders for Photos sent to this office will be promptly filled.

tured by his letters and Los Angeles was especially curious to see him. Colonel Otis was the most curious of all.

He [Otis] had got word to me enroute and when I reached San Gabriel, he was there to meet me. We had dinner together under the famed giant grapevine. After the meal had settled, we walked the eleven miles to Los Angeles. I imagine it was the last long tramp the veteran ever took.

We reached Los Angeles a little after eleven that night. The memory of the earlier dinner entirely effaced by the walk, we had at Jerry Illich's on Court Street one of the famous meals that fine old Hungarian knew how to cook.

The night was largely passed in domestic pursuits in the New Hollenbeck Hotel—delousing, cleaning up, extricating my arm from its home-made splints and getting acquainted again with my wife. At ten the next morning, I was on duty as first city editor of the Los Angeles Times.[9]

And the West had a new spokesman.

[9] *Ibid.*

7

Antediluvian Southern California

LOS ANGELES, as it appeared in 1885 when Charlie first arrived, was a city that had little to brag about.

When I walked into Los Angeles that winter day of 1885 it was a dull little place of some 12,000 persons. There were perhaps six buildings of three stories or better. The street railway had a few doleful miles of "bobtail" horsecars (like those which still served parts of New York City as late as 1903). I used to shoot quail and jackrabbits in the center of such a residence district as no other American city has quite the likes of.

The Los Angeles of my day was preponderantly of adobe, and the Spanish-speaking population outnumbered the Gringos two or three to one. The Pico House, the Baker Block, Nadeau Hotel, the Downey and Temple Blocks were the outstanding buildings. The streets were narrow and crooked, with an infinite capacity for mud. It was a fond joke to erect a pole at the intersection of Spring, Main and Temple Streets (where the Federal Building now stands) recording that a hack had sunk there beneath the surface.

Third Street was pretty near the southerly urban limit—beyond that were gardens and orchards and embowered residences. The Times Office was in the Downey Block. So was the Los Angeles Public Library—what there was of it—in a narrow room presided over by a graduate of the first L. A. High School class. (I had no premonition about this institution.)

The first City Hall was a long, one-story adobe across Spring Street from the present magnificent City Hall. The police headquarters and some other city offices were still in the aforesaid adobe. In the high-fence backyard I saw three notorious gentlemen

suspended from their necks for various offences, chiefly killing wives.

The Council Chamber was over the Fire Engine House on Second Street in a two-story brick building. I had to report the council meetings, which was not so bad until dear old Dr. Sinsabaugh became president and ruled out smoking. To report a council meeting without smoking would tax the sainthood of any reporter. Chewing of tobacco was however sanctioned. I tried to learn the mastication but could get nowhere.

Just beyond the Council room and fire house was the office of the Los Angeles Herald, our Hated Rival. It was a paper of great influence and ability. One of the editors was Joseph D. Lynch, a vigorous booster, an ardent Democrat, and a man of many fine qualities. He gloried in his physical strength. I remember one midnight as I came by the City Hall, "Jodie," as they familiarly called him, came from the Herald office with two young reporters and some warmth under his belt.

"I sometimes think," he said, "that I am the strongest man in the world. There is no way of proving that, but I have many reasons for my belief." And then he sighted a horse. The gutter was wet, but he knelt in it, caught the horn of the saddle with his left hand, got his massive shoulder under the horse's belly, and lifted it bodily over the curb onto the sidewalk.

I think no one who was in Los Angeles in the middle Eighties will challenge my belief that in those days no one going in the same direction ever passed me on the street. I was in perfect physical training from the Tramp, and I was "sent for" by a passionate

Los Angeles in 1888, looking up old Fort Street towards the *Times* building. (*Courtesy Bancroft Library, University of California*)

interest in my work. Lynch also was proud of his walking. At two one morning as I came pattering along Spring Street, I saw someone ahead of me making pretty good progress. When I came closer he let out his links, but my gait was the faster, and this large man broke into a run, to keep from being passed by a walker.

I am glad to remember that our long newspaper rivalry ended long after with a friendship. In an accident this splendid powerful man lost his right leg by amputation. I could realize a little of what this meant, and one day I ventured with a good deal of timidity to the lonely room where the crippled giant, mostly deserted by the "friends" of his big days, was living by himself. He came on crutches to my knock, and looked at me in a way I shall never forget. I had fought him pretty hard not only in the newspaper business, but in his political aspirations.

"Col. Lynch, what's the War, anyhow?" I said. "You and I are both out of the newspaper scrap, you and I both care for this little old town and for California. And I was mighty sorry to hear of your accident. I know what a blow it was to a man of such magnificent physique. I have always admired your mind and its independence. What's the matter with calling it friends?"

His glaring eyes changed, a couple of big drops ran down over the rugged cheeks. He gave me a fist that nearly crushed my reasonably hard one and asked me in. We had a long and beautiful talk about the Old Days—"old" even then.[1]

In that Santa Clara River Valley region which Lummis called "The Land of the Afternoon" there was a Spanish hacienda named Camulos. No story of

[1] Lummis, "As I Remember."

30

his life would be complete without including that part which was bound up in this bit of Mother Spain. It was to this Spanish Eden that the Chaveses had sent him shortly after he had crossed the Mojave. There could hardly have been a greater contrast to the desert than these thousands of green and fruitful acres planted and maintained by the aristocratic clan of the Del Valles.

There were whimsical stories about Camulos. Of the children of Don José and Doña Ysabel del Valle, the last three were born in the same bed, in the same room, but in three different counties. Uliapano came in Los Angeles County. By the time Ysabel II arrived, much of Los Angeles County had been taken over into Santa Barbara County. And a few years later when Ygnacio was born, Ventura County had been created and included the beautiful rancho.

Perhaps one of the reasons Lummis felt so close to the Spanish was that their warmth gave him something that he had missed ever since his "Little Mama" had died. For there was always a certain loneliness about him, and in Camulos, with its slow,

The Del Valle girls, with Lummis tripping the lens. (*Courtesy Southwest Museum*)

Charlie and Nina del Valle dancing the *cuña* ("cradle") on the porch at Camulos. (*Courtesy Southwest Museum*)

sweet days, its old-world friendliness, its perfume of sage and orange, its nights of song, his heart found a home. From the well-loved and remarkable matriarch of the family, Doña Ysabel del Valle, down to its humblest retainer, all who lived there proved to him again what the Chaveses and Ramon Arrera had first demonstrated.

Human touch is the real characteristic of the Latin races as compared with the Germanic. The charm of the Spanish in particular is that they are still of the child heart.[2]

In verse he glorified the dark eyes of Doña Ysabel's beautiful daughters. To him the most beautiful of all was Susana Carmen. He called the girls his little sisters, and it was they who taught him some of the love songs of Spain.

Oh, Love! Your passion passes understanding,
I understand it, but 'twill not be expressed
I go to hide your sighing and your anguish
There in the tomb, where only can I be at rest.[3]

For almost forty-five years Camulos was his second home. Again and again he went back to it. The spell

[2] Ibid.
[3] Charles F. Lummis, "Angel De Amor," *The Land of Poco Tiempo*, 221.

he found there swayed his pen and witched his dreams. He used pictures of the Del Valles and their rancho many times. They were the inspiration of innumerable articles and poems.

A Sentry star peers off the dark sierra's parapet;
Across the almond-blossomed league the breeze is loitering yet;
And in the dim placita, where Castilian roses blow,
The cypress beckons on the dusk, the fountain plashes low.
Along the old veranda creep the bolder shadows on,
Where wistful with the gloaming sit the daughters of the Don—
Their daylong tuneful laughter mute, their maiden hearts beset
With all the twilight's vague desire, with all its vague regret.
Tomorrow—'tis another day!
Again their laugh shall wake
What echoes live forever young to laugh for life's young sake;
For gloom dare not o'erstep the night, nor wolfish care may roam
In this, the patriarchal life—the very home of Home![4]

[4] Lummis, "At the Hacienda," *A Bronco Pegasus*, 112.

8

The Times of Los Angeles

WORKING for Colonel Harrison Gray Otis, the chief of the *Los Angeles Times*, was an experience Charlie never forgot.

Col. Otis and I had hit it off from the first. The owner of the Times *was a large paunchy man with a fine head and a gray imperial. After the Civil War he had been in the Federal Service in Alaska, then a newspaper man and printer for many years. He had a deep gruff voice and a brusque manner.*

He hated anybody who was afraid of him. Because of his dominant and overbearing way a great many good people were afraid of him. One of the reasons he liked me was that I wasn't. In my judgment, all the heartbreaking toil I put in on the Times, *all the scoops I got and all the material help I gave toward making it a metropolitan daily—nothing did so much to clinch the old man's liking for me as this finding out that I wasn't afraid of him when I thought I was right.*

The Times *had been supporting the Chief of Police, a charming Irishman, in one of the periodic police fights that have characterized the city through all the years I have known it. I was greatly taken with Mac myself and fought valiantly for him. But one day I found out that he wasn't straight. "Colonel," I said, laying some revealing papers before him, "We'll have to fight the chief of police."*

The Colonel shuffled over the papers. "Lummis! Don't you know this is contrary to the Policy of the Times?"

"To hell with the policy of the Times! *I'm understanding that it is the policy of the* Times *to tell the truth and to be in the right. If it isn't, take it and go to hell!"*

Dear old Bates, the telegraph editor, was fumbling his "flimsy" at the telegraph table, and Clarence Eddy, Foreman of the composing room, stood in the door thereof. Having seen the "Old Man" explode before, both looked to see the furniture fly.

He looked at me steadily for a moment and said very quietly, "Lummis, do you think that is the proper way to speak to your superior officer?"

It wasn't and I said so. But I also stuck to my guns.

The Old Man wasn't afraid of anything. Few people in Los Angeles realize today what they owe him. I don't exaggerate when I say as one who has known and studied this town for 44 years that it owes no other man so much as this rough old soldier.

The first fight of the Times *was for High License [for the purpose of limiting the saloons]. Los Angeles in 1885 was wide open like any good Frontier town. The saloons bossed politics and everything else. They weren't such bad bosses at that! But feeling the urge of progress we made a fight for High License. Everybody laughed at us. We had no real expectation of winning. Both the other newspapers were against us. Yet the* Times *single-handed rolled up a majority of more than two to one in favor of High License. That was the beginning of modern law and order in the city.*

An Angeleño who was probably the most popular man in Southern California, a "Prince of Good Fellows," with a wonderful mother, a beautiful wife and high social connections, ran for Secretary of State on the Republican ticket. The Times *was Republican; but the personal character of the candidate was too much; and we fought him, tooth and nail. Every other publication in the city stood by him and bombarded us; but he was hopelessly snowed under in the* election—the greatest political surprise in California up to that date.

Of course the Typographical Union controlled all the newspapers in Los Angeles. Col. Otis was a printer himself and a relentless worker. The Times was the only newspaper in town that never missed a payday, and it paid higher rates than any other. But the Union got greedy. They held us up time after time, presenting their demands at one or two o'clock in the morning—when to refuse would mean no issue in the morning, and that would have spelled ruin for a young and struggling paper.

We had to knuckle under many times. The Old Man would get purple in the face. I was present, I remember, when the last straw broke the camel's back—if you can call it a straw. You may recall the old patent medicine ads, two columns wide and a full column tall. These ads came to us in electrotype blocks. All the printer had to do was to pick up the block and put it in the "chase." At two one morning, Eddy and a couple of walking delegates came in and demanded that they be paid the same price for the one motion of picking up that block and laying it on the stone as they would be paid for picking up one by one the 50,000 or 60,000 letters and putting them into their printer's stick and unloading stick after stick into the column!

Col. Otis looked the committee up and down, drew himself to his full military stature and said without heat or explosion, "That is an unreasonable request and the Times will not accede to it. You gentlemen have blackmailed the Times long enough. You can get your time at the window tomorrow. Good night."

They stared at him as though petrified. Going to slip an issue in the morning? Was the Old Man crazy? They lingered but he showed signs which they recognized and they hurriedly backed out.

Within half an hour a full force of Union compositors was at work in the Times composing room—but they were not Typographical Union. Foreseeing the inevitable, Col. Otis had imported from Ohio a band of the Typothetae. Quite undreamed of by anyone, he had them in waiting in a quiet hotel. Now at the drop of a hat they came.

So far as I know this is the only case in the United States in which the all-powerful Typographical Union has been defied and defeated. The nationwide organization rallied to the support of their brothers in Los Angeles and the war was taken up by the American Federation of Labor. The Times was boycotted, threatened, attacked. Advertisers were bulldozed, every house at which the Times was delivered was threatened and cajoled to cease subscribing. The ingenuities and the shamelessness of the boycott were almost incredible, but as Americans have a sense of fair play, that same boycott was the making of the Times.

Things looked particularly ugly during the countrywide railroad strike of 1904 when the dissatisfied elements marched around the streets openly threatening the Times. I had long been out of the paper but went up to see the Old Chief (who in the Spanish-American war had become General Otis) and asked him if he needed a man with a scatter-gun to help stand guard. He thanked me and said he thought not. "If they do dynamite the building as they threaten," he said, "I suppose it is about as good a tomb for me as any."

Several years later (Oct. 1, 1910) a little after midnight, I was writing in my den some six miles away when I heard two explosions. To my practiced ear they said dynamite. And though there had been no threats for a year or so, I jumped up and shouted, "By God, I believe they have got the Times!"

At 8 next morning there came to my door a little 4 page Times telling how the Times building had been dynamited, killing twenty men at their work. The Old Chief had not been caught napping. For a year, unknown to almost anyone, he had had an auxiliary plant half a mile away down by the railroad yards. As soon as the bleeding feet and hands of the heroic survivors could be bound up they trudged down to the new plant and got out the little paper.

It was a big thing done without a dramatic gesture and in the plain line of military duty. The dynamiting was the stupidest blunder the Union ever made—which is saying a great deal.

I have lived in many countries; but never in one where human life was so insecure as in this, nor any in which the criminal was so safe as he is here. In Mexico, Guatemala, Central America, Peru, Bolivia and Chile, justice is far swifter and surer than with us and murder much less endemic.

Col. Otis was brusque, rough, suspicious, vindictive, a strange combination of childlikeness, of great practicality in many things—in printing and newspapering he was a past master—very far from worldly-wise in many others. He made innumerable enemies quite needlessly, as well as a large number that were greatly to his credit. It was good that every scoundrel, every criminal, every low politician hated him. It was a pity that so many thoroughly good people disliked him. He could have done a great deal more good if he had not antagonized so many good citizens. However as he did more for the community than all the other newspapermen put together, I presume we may forgive him this loss of further achievement.

The episode which gave me undying admiration and reverence for Col. Otis involved his partner, a polished plausible gentleman known as Col. Smoothy. His ideals of citizenship and public honesty did not at all jibe with Otis's. When the latter found this out unmistakably, the last strand of tolerance broke, and there was open war between them.

Smoothy made an offer which he felt sure would give him the paper. Col. Otis had neither money nor connections. He sweat blood to raise the necessary sum but failed.

One afternoon three gentlemen came up to the Times office. The Chief told me to sit still at my table. Major E. F. Spence, a heavy, stolid, honorable president of the First National Bank, had the congressional bee. There was nothing against him. Indeed there was much in his favor.

"Col. Otis," his emissaries said, "if the Times will give its support to Maj. Spence's campaign we can adjust that financial matter for you on your own terms. Within three days you can be absolute master of the paper."

Up and down the room without saying a word walked the big, clumsy man, the sweat rolling down his cheeks. It was his Gethsemane.

He wheeled at last like a soldier. "Gentlemen, I thank you. Maj. Spence is a good man. He would make a good Congressman. But I don't know what other candidates may appear, and I cannot sell the support of the Times to any man alive. It belongs to the community. I cannot bargain with you."

That chivalric heroism, I am glad to record, was not lost. The Colonel managed to acquire the money in another way and to buy out his partner.

Later on Col. Smoothy started a rival paper. One morning it came out with the phrase, "Otis, the Brute, and Lummis, the Little Liar." I sought out Col. Smoothy and whacked him across the face with my leather cane. Next time we met he reached for his derringer. I laughed in his face. And though for several months he carried the derringer in that pocket and got his hand on it whenever we passed, he never did pull the trigger.

His paper did not live many years. Before it died he brought a violent and sensational libel suit against the Times for $50,000. The jury awarded him the sum of $1.00.

The Southern California Land Boom lasted from the spring of 1886 to about January 1888. The area it covered—though in very varying pitch—was nearly as large as New England. I think there is no doubt that in area of land plotted and sold it exceeded any similar land gamble in history. Lands have elsewhere brought higher prices and in a few other instances been more rapidly sold; but it is probably safe to say that nowhere else (certainly never before this specific instance) did the prices rise so fast nor so unreasonably, and that never has such a stupendous sum in transfers been accomplished with so small an expenditure of cash, nor by such unwonted speculators.

The boom began by purely legitimate "additions" to towns and cities actually extant, of lands whose immediate potentialities were very little exaggerated. It is fair to remark too that counting the average of the Boom there was very little real swindling. Almost all that came after the collapse. In this desperate post-mortem gleaning thousands of the 25-foot holdings were sold in Mexican territory, 150 miles south of the California line, for enough apiece to have bought a good farm. But it is only fair to say that this was pursued wholly by professional sharks and almost without exception through the columns of Eastern newspapers.

Early in 1887 tens of thousands of acres fit only for grain or pasture, if that, were cut up into 25-ft. city lots, thousands of acres purchased from their original owners at $10 to $30 an acre were sold in lots at $1000 to $10,000 an acre.

In 1887 Los Angeles was growing at the rate of at

least 1500 a month, and San Diego was growing by at least half that rate. On an average business day one could not stir upon the street without encountering brass bands, transparencies and other fake sales devices. At the tract office a line would begin to form one or two days before a sale was to open. I have seen men pay $100 for a place in that line. I have seen them serpentine for a block or worse all afternoon and night and until 9 o'clock of the critical morning. There were dozens of cases in which a company or individual sold over $300,000 worth of lots in the first few days and had at least three-fourths of the land left. The barren sandspit that I used to know seaward from San Diego, on which is now one of the fine hotels of the world [Del Coronado] took in for its organized owners two and a half million dollars in cash in one year, and after paying off its debts and making its enormously costly improvements it had four-fifths of its landed property left clear of incumbrance.

Real estate transfers recorded in the county of Los Angeles for 1887 exceeded $1000 for every man, woman and child. Everyone was plunging—bankers, ministers, school teachers, policemen, tramps, judges, servant girls, bootblacks, car drivers, society ladies, counter-jumpers. At then current real estate values Southern California was worth more than perhaps New York State. Yet not one single bank, not one well-established house, not one legitimate enterprise failed in the collapse of that stupendous madness. For with all its greed, its ignorance, its idiocy, the boom was not quite a lottery. Thousands of lots were sold for far more than they were worth, but all were worth something real.

The colossal superstructure of values that upheld a million fortunes came down as fast and as noiselessly as a castle of cards. But its victims were born game. In May 1888, fifty percent more land was plowed in Southern California than ever before. When the bank quietly raked in the chips, the greenhorn victims turned instantly and almost unanimously to developing the values with which they had diced, and from the bursting of that bubble there has not been a day's cessation of steady growth.[1]

[1] Lummis, "As I Remember."

9

Back Across the Mountains

CHARLIE LUMMIS loved his work on the *Times*, but he had the memory of the wide lands in his blood. In a letter to friends back in Ohio he wrote,

I don't believe prosperity agrees with me. Here I am in the land from which it is generally supposed that the Lord got His plans and specifications for Heaven; basking in eternal summer while you poor creatures are building fires under the thermometer to keep it from freezing. I am eating four meals a day, not to count a superabundance of the finest fruits, plugging away at work which fits my intermittent intellect like a pair of dude pantaloons, drawing a neat salary and fixed in just the swellest suite of rooms in the city with all the furniture of domesticity—and still I am not happy. That is, I'm always happy anywhere—but there's a sense of something lacking. It is too soon yet to forget my old exultant careless life in the New England woods, called back so vividly by the experiences of the Tramp, and the full free blood and knotted muscles which grew from that life are not toned down enough yet to lie content between four walls. And so I sit and scratch at the offensive paper as if I owed it a grudge while my thoughts go drifting out of the windows and across the mountains to— well, I call it life. The best that civilization can give is not much more than existence. However, by the time this Indian complexion fades out—as it is doing tolerably fast under the regime of all-night work, I shall have gotten over the edge of my hunger for the wilderness probably.

Early in 1886 there was a fresh outbreak of the Apache wars. Colonel Otis ordered his city editor to cover the campaign. Nothing could have pleased him more.

The newspapers of the country were full of the Apache situation, but Lum of the *Los Angeles Times* was the first bona fide war correspondent to be commissioned to get the truth about it. The articles[1] he wrote for the *Times* and one or two eastern papers were factual reports of what had previously been described only by a "mass of misstatements, exaggerations and genuine lies."

General George Crook, who had been fighting Indians almost continuously since he graduated from West Point in 1852, had borne the brunt of this ignorant or deliberate slander. Yet it was his powerful enemies in politics and those who profited from the presence of the army in Arizona who were directly responsible for the new outbreak.

The Apaches had already surrendered to Crook— Captain-with-the-Brown-Clothes, as they called the great Indian fighter—and the costly war was over. Two days later a white trader named Tribolet, who foresaw the end of his profitable contract to supply beef to the army, managed to get to the Indians with whisky. Twenty dollars a gallon was the going rate. He frightened them with stories of the punishment they could expect, and Geronimo was on the warpath again.

"But," Crook pointed out to Lummis, "if we shot him down like a coyote as he deserved [for selling that whisky to the Indians], it would have raised a terrible row."[2]

The old general was criticized for using Apache scouts to track and fight Apaches, for dealing honestly with the Indians, and for keeping his word to them.

[1] See Turbesé Lummis, *General Crook and the Apache Wars*.
[2] *Ibid.*, 16.

He was reviled because he was not immediately able to capture the elusive natives in their own territory and because when he did capture them he refused to make "good" Indians out of them. Meanwhile the War Department continued to disburse over two million dollars in the sparsely settled Arizona Territory.

Crook never complained of the lies about him. "If ever there was an honorable task in letting in the light on a libelled career it lies before me now," wrote Lummis, and he made it his business to write the truth about "the old gray wolf at bay."

Lummis shared the hard life of the scouts and soldiers. He took so vigorous a part in the actual campaign that, after he had returned to the city desk, Captain (later General) Henry W. Lawton wired him to come back and take a position as chief of scouts. He jumped at the chance. However, because he had become too picturesque a "newspaper property," Colonel Otis was unwilling to let him go. Leonard Wood, with whom Lummis had already begun a lifelong friendship, was made chief of scouts instead.

"Why didn't you come when I sent for you?" General Lawton asked Lummis a year later. "They told me—Al Sieber himself told me—that you were the best tracker short of the Apaches."

"I would have liked it," was the reply. "But you got a better man. Maybe I couldn't have caught Geronimo. Wood did."

More than one contribution to the literature of the West has come out of Lummis' activities in that campaign. The chapter "The Apache Warrior" in *The Land of Poco Tiempo* was quoted by military critics for over a third of a century. His ballad, "Man-Who-Yawns,"[3] the epic of Geronimo, is a biting summary of what one man learned before the passing of the last frontier.

Lummis' three years on the *Los Angeles Times* were lived at top tension.

It was a wonderful game to help lift this small young paper to its feet. I had the satisfaction. of watching "my" paper develop from a little sheet of 2700 daily circulation to a powerful newspaper medium.

The growth of the Times *was being hotly con-*

Charlie as an Apache, 1887.

tested. The Herald *and* Express *were both far older and richer, and had many times the circulation. But I put into my work on the* Times *all the soul and brain I had. I worked without a thought of late hours or of health. Having long before sent off my reporter, or reporters (in the growing days when I acquired any) I would put the paper to bed myself. At 6 A.M. I would get home. At 7 my wife—not daring to disobey my orders, for the smell of blood was in my nostrils—was shaking me violently and weeping. In my three years on the* Times *I never got more than two hours of sleep in the 24 and for the final newspaper year not over one. But I felt like a fighting cock. I was never tired when I went to bed nor even when I got up and doused into my cold bath.*

---

[3] Lummis, *A Bronco Pegasus*.

For several months I had admonitory symptoms. My left forefinger went to sleep and stayed so. And sometimes the same crinkly feeling ran all around my heart. But I laughed to scorn those who warned me to look out.

December 5, 1887, I went home for supper and lay down for a few minutes on the lounge. I couldn't get up. I fought like a tiger. I knew what fighting was, too. Finally I did get up—but only to discover that my left side was helpless. I was paralyzed.[4]

Lummis was his usual stubborn self. In spite of Dr. Dorothea's protests, he limped down to the office and went to work. The office force had to carry him home. For two months his wife managed to keep him in bed, but he would not surrender to the paralysis. His body had never before refused to respond to even the most unreasonable demands. He agreed to go away for a rest, "just long enough to get sufficiently strong to come back to work."

Although Lummis had been putting great enthusiasm into his work with the *Times*, his thoughts long had been "drifting out the window and over the mountains." It is also apparent that he was weary of Dorothea, who was now more of a mother than the romantic figure he desired. In some strange and perverse way the attack released him from these responsibilities.

Don Manuel invited Lummis to return to the land of "the sunburnt mesas and ardent skies" for which he had longed. On February 5, 1888, he left Los Angeles for New Mexico. That day he began a diary which he was to keep for forty years.[5] Its first entry tells of his train being blocked by a slide and how he climbed over three or four hundred yards of fallen hillside, crippled as he was, carrying his luggage. Three days later he reached Grants, New Mexico. It was thirty miles from the Chaves home. He rode there on horseback, determined not to be a helpless invalid and as much as possible to do what other men did.

Lummis would not allow his hosts to coddle him. Every morning he went out into the open country. At first he could only manage to limp a few hundred yards from the house, but as he gained strength, he extended his explorations. He taught himself to shoot with his one good arm, carrying a light shotgun on his shoulder which he would take by the guard and "throw down" as was done with a six-shooter.

He described his hunting in the autobiographical *My Friend Will*: "Every morning he sallied out in the sagebrush to escape himself by hunting. I fear it was a rather ludicrous sight, this tottering, wobbly Nimrod, clumsily wielding the gun with one hand, and missing far more rabbits than he killed, and often dropping under a bush in sheer exhaustion."[6]

Chillicotheans used to say, "There's only one Charlie Lummis." Now New Mexicans began to say it. Two weeks after he arrived, this paralytic tramped ten miles in four inches of snow and the next day climbed to the top of the Peak of the Awl to hunt for a bear's cave he had heard about.

Many did not even realize that Lummis was disabled; he kept his hand out of sight in his pocket. For a long time he went without meat unless he could cut it himself. Learning to roll cigarettes was his hardest task. He told himself that he didn't deserve a cigarette unless he could make his own, so he taught himself to roll them with one hand—a rare trick.

The Chaveses were torn between admiration and dismay. They were unable to confine their guest's activities to those they thought suitable for one in his condition. He told them that he had to get away from himself or go crazy. He pled and battled and beguiled until they reluctantly gave in and let him "ride messenger" from the home ranch to outlying sheep camps fifteen to thirty miles away.

One day Charlie started from the home ranch with a Studebaker wagon loaded with four quarters of beef and six hundred pounds of sacked corn. Everything went well until he came to a shallow arroyo. Both

[4] Lummis, "As I Remember."

[5] The diary which Lummis began on February 5, 1888, is now in the possession of the Southwest Museum. The diary spans the years from 1888 to 1928; there are forty volumes, covering each day of each year. All entries are handwritten, mostly in English, though occasionally in Spanish or coded Greek. Hereinafter cited as Lummis, "Diary." In addition to this diary Lummis kept another daily record—a journal. The journal was begun once Lummis could afford a secretary (or two or three). Entries included detailed accounts of the day, recollections of that date in the past, and letters written and received. Entries were periodically copied and mailed out to friends who passed them around. Those Lummis sent to Marco H. Newmark were later retyped as a WPA project and are now in the Los Angeles Public Library. Others are in the possession of Keith Lummis and the Southwest Museum. Hereinafter cited as Lummis, "Journal."

[6] Charles F. Lummis, *My Friend Will*, 22.

Some friends in the New Mexico Territory. Ramon Liberato Baca, a well-known political figure in the territory in 1888; Fanny Clark Baca, his wife; and Amado Chaves, one of Lummis' closest friends. (*Courtesy Southwest Museum*)

wagon and team bogged down in the sand. It was raining; the water was rising. He had no time to go for help. One by one he dragged the four quarters of beef and the six sacks of corn up onto the high bank for safety. The next day, roaring a Spanish song he drove into the hacienda with outfit and cargo com-plete. "To this day," he said fifty years later, "I look back on it with a warming in my heart."

There were those days when he was very ill. His diary records times when his plight seemed more than he could bear. He was almost shattered by the realization that at only twenty-nine he was paralyzed.

10

Dorothea Moves Toward the Exit

CHARLIE and Dorothea had planned a home and a family. The firstborn son was to be named after her brother, Alfred. These were two of many things they never had.

They longed for each other when apart, but when together, friction soon developed as the two strong and original personalities clashed. Many years later Dorothea wrote to Turbesé, "What monstrous joys and sorrows he caused those who were near." How could an inexperienced young woman understand "that strange, wild, cruel yet deathlessly attractive nature," the enemy of woman and her most ardent lover? Somehow, no matter how much he hurt a person, he always managed "in some way to pull them back to him, now an illness, now an accident, now some winsome impulsive gesture of the old boyhood days, now some alarm." Dorothea continued, "I cannot yet understand why your father did not put down anywhere the bitterness that he sometimes expressed toward me. But it was usually just because I would not do what he wanted—so perhaps it just wore off."

Dr. Dorothea's early letters expressed her girlhood dreams, those later her feeling of failure and sorrow.

If it were wise to look back, I could weep a little to learn how far short I have fallen of your ideal. Had you only not given me credit for far more brain and heart and tact, had you simply treated me like a plain fond fool and explained your need for solitude when you were writing, it might have been so easily avoided . . . I sorrow for the lost work and the lost hours and the lost—everything. But a hungry hearted woman is never sensible and I think I was less so than the general—and so I am sorry again."

In April, 1888, while Lummis was still paralyzed

and in New Mexico, she wrote him in great sadness.

I have shed so many—no not many—but such salt tears that they have literally burnt my eyes out and scalded my face so that I can hardly bear the light. . . . It isn't the 'fight with a straitened purse' that's breaking me down but the loneliness and starvation, the daily grind of my life. I rise every day to go about my work, tired and nervous and irritable, and make my calls on a lot of people who are civil and friendly only when they are not presented with a bill. I come back at night to go to the theatre and report the play [for the Times] *which is by now, a burden only, and crawl into bed and sleep to wake more tired than ever. I have no society; I have no special woman friend and can have no men friends without gossip, and so my days go on. . . . I must get away where I can rest and rest. . . . If you can earn enough to keep you in New Mexico till fall, I think I could send you some money then to take you to Old Mexico as you wish. . . . You need not, you* must not *send me any of your hard-earned money. Keep it and if you wish, save it for the future.*

. . . It seems as if my heart had been bleeding for two years and then it stopped all at once and I haven't felt a thing, not a speck of love or passion for many a long week. You have felt it, of course, and you can't be more surprised than I. However, your letter waked it up and if it's only to sting you I can't help it and you must either forgive it or forget it and me.

That letter is crumpled and sweatmarked as though carried in a man's pocket for a long time. In his diary for the day he wrote, "That letter from Dolly does me." After that the diary is blank for many days. Don Amado's mother had to feed him like a baby. He had suffered another stroke. Then: [1888] "Monday, May 14, 7 p.m. I wake up and recognize everyone after ten days of illness in which I knew nothing and no one."

He sent for Dr. Dorothea. In spite of all she had written, she came. They had another of their bitter-sweet reconciliations. After Dorothea had gone back to her work, she wrote:

. . . We ought to be together somewhere as soon as we can and both try once more the experiment of our life together. Once I thought I wouldn't try again and several times you have made up your mind not to endure it any longer. This must be the last trial . . . this half-way living is useless killing work. We are both young and we must make our bonds stronger now or cut them. I will try—Oh, I will try it if you are willing to experiment with me once more. . . .

Almost daily he wrote her letters of lonely longing. Often in the same mail he would write to his "little sisters" in Camulos.

A few months later he went to Los Angeles to visit Dorothea. They had barely gotten reacquainted when he went to visit the del Valles.

. . . fiesta of San Agostin. Susie, Rose and I go walking . . . they do not even notice when the fog comes in . . . and then I know that my Susie loves me. Aug. 26 . . . Va! how precious a day. . . . Belle teaches me "Love is a Lie." I leave for Los Angeles at 7 having kissed all the girls.
Aug. 27 . . . A great deal of pain in my head and cannot tell Dolly what is in my mind. . . . In the morning, not having slept any, I tell Dolly everything.[1]

"Everything" meant that she whom he had wooed so often and importunately had to hear that he loved another woman.

Dorothea once wrote him that there "must be a place somewhere later where we can carry out all our defeated selves and hopes and wishes."

"Ah, what an Angel! She will sacrifice herself in order to free me."

Charlie did not seem to realize that he was asking an even harder sacrifice when he begged her to go on writing to him. In this, too, she complied: "It is beautiful, not regretful that you are a 'fool boy' over your new hopes. It means that once more can dwell in your heart all the delightful pains, the miserable joys of a fresh passion. I am glad—yes, I am glad, though to think of it seems to make my heart tear its way up into my throat and the very daylight turn to darkness."

When he was dashed by finding that he would have to wait a whole year for their divorce, she urged him to bear with it in patience. He replied that a year was a long time—and turned to her for comfort because Susie did not answer his letters.

It had never occurred to him that he who was welcome as a friend might not be welcome as a son-in-law. At Christmas time the Del Valles told him frankly that his idea was impossible. Their religion forbade marriage with a divorced man. Like a stunned small boy he turned again to Dorothea. Forgetful that he once had written, "Upon that sullen altar Desire no more shall blaze," they had another honeymoon.

[1] Lummis, "Diary."

11

A New Life in New Mexico

RETURNING to New Mexico, Lummis continued his fight against the paralysis. One of his most difficult physical triumphs was in photography. The small, light camera had not yet been invented, though he claimed, "I wouldn't have used one anyhow." He had to manipulate a ponderous forty-pound view camera with five-by-eight glass negatives and a big tripod. To manage this with one hand was not easy, particularly in the violent winds so common in New Mexico.

It was even harder to do my developing. But I made in this time many thousands of 5 x 8 plates, developed them and made my blue prints. For silver prints I had to take my negatives to Albuquerque.

If there is anything that is something of a test, it is to develop two 5 x 8 glass negatives at a time in an adobe room with a big basin bowl for a sink, no outlet except the outside door, no running water, nor other water except what was brought in tinajas [Indian pottery jars] and without any other facility whatever.

I cut myself pretty badly several times where there were reef edges on the glass—for which my chief concern was that the blood spoiled the negatives. But of that host of pictures made at that time, while nearly all are interesting, there are very many that are unique and can never be made again—of types that are dead, buildings that are destroyed, ceremonials that are no more.[1]

In that day most of the people of New Mexico Territory believed in witches. Even as late as 1892, a paisano who dared could point out among the villagers *brujas* who by night roved abroad with animal legs and eyes. Was not Don Carlos' own ailment proof of the existence of Those of the Evil Road?

When Lummis learned that three such witch women actually lived nearby, he naturally wanted a picture of them. In spite of grim predictions as to what would happen to him, he found that even witches were susceptible to the flattery of being asked to sit for their portraits. Of all the photographs he ever took, however, he was proudest of those of the procession and crucifixion of the Order of the Penitentes.

It was early in March, 1888, that he first learned of the Hermandad de la Luz, one of the more fantastic survivals of the Middle Ages. Members of the highly secret and fanatic order scourged their bodies with fiber thongs, lay naked on beds of cactus, and on a certain holy day crucified one of their members.[2]

Lummis took fire on learning that in the enlightened year of 1888, citizens of the United States were re-enacting the awful pangs of Calvary. He could find no confirmation in the encyclopedias. Although most New Mexicans knew something about the Penitentes, scholarship in general supposed the Flagellant Brothers to be as dead as Columbus.

The Chaveses were distressed to hear that he planned to photograph the forbidden rites. It was impossible to get such a picture; the Penitentes would kill him for trying.

Warnings only served to stimulate a man who hungered for danger. Only recently he had gone alone armed with a shotgun into a mountain lion's cave. He liked to maintain that there was nothing

[1] Lummis, "As I Remember."

[2] There is in the possession of the Southwest Museum a "bull" in Spanish condemning the practices of the Penitentes. It is signed by Arzobispo de Sta. Fe., February 7, 1892.

The crucifixion ceremony of the Penitentes. Of all the photographs made by Lummis, perhaps this one, taken in New Mexico Territory in 1888, was the one of which he was most proud.

... more dreamily delicious than to tease a rattler with some object just long enough to keep those grim fangs from one's own flesh. I have stood thus, thoughtless of discomfort, carried away by the indescribable charm of that grisly presence. Perhaps the consciousness of playing with death and as his master contributes something of that spell. ... No one who has ever played with a rattlesnake can disbelieve the superstition that it fascinates its prey. I have felt it ... a sweet dreaminess which has tempted me to drop that stick and reach out my arms to that beautiful death.[3]

Since nothing would dissuade Lummis, the Chaveses were determined to stand by him. Don Ireneo ("Don Amado's brother whose reckless bravery was a proverb in all that country of brave men") chose to accompany him.

On March 25 I learned from one of the men the tune of the Penitentes on the pito, the strange wailing flute of the region. At last came Holy Thursday, the 29th. With Don Ireneo at my side and a peon to carry my big 5 x 8 glass-plate camera with its heavy tripod, I trudged the couple of miles to the village of San Mateo and to a hillock commanding the route of the Penitentes' procession, about 100 yards from their path. Don Ireneo and the peon stood near me, each with a six-shooter cocked in his hand. As I needed my only hand for the camera, my gun lay cocked on top of the camera box.

I got several unimpressive pictures of the procession from the town to the Campo Santo (burying ground). This made a great deal of bad feeling in the

[3] Lummis, A Tramp Across the Continent, 22–23.

village and there were many threats. But that night thanks to Don Amado and his brother, I got the Hermano Mayor (Chief Brother) and some of the Brothers of Light over to the Chaves home. There I plied them with cigarettes and good words, photographs of other strange things I had taken and a good deal of "soft Sawder and Human Natur' " and they were Mine.

On Good Friday Don Ireneo and the peon accompanied me to the front of the Morada, Brotherhood House of the Penitentes. We had to wedge through a scowling and threatening mob. But the Hermano Mayor came out of Morada, shook my hand and marked with his heel on the ground a space 7 or 8 feet in diameter in which I might operate. The peon put the camera and tripod inside that and I hitched them together.

Two Brothers of Light dug a deep hole on the slope. Beside it they laid a huge cross. Out from the Morada, with a Brother of Light holding each arm, came a fellow naked to the waist. He wore white cotton drawers and a black hangman's cap over his head. In his left side was a bleeding wound down which the blood ran to his feet in a stream two inches wide.

Laying himself down on the cross he was attached there hands and feet with a new half-inch rope which cut into the flesh as each Brother of Light put a foot on him to pull tighter. The cross with its burden was then set up and packed into the hole, and another penitente (similarly marked, with a burro-load of buckthorn cactus strapped tightly on his bare back) came and lay with his feet to the foot of the cross and his head on a stone. Thereat the Hermano Mayor gave me the sign and I made my photographs. They showed the procession forming for the march to the Campo Santo, the self-whippers, the Hermano Mayor and the men carrying on their shoulders the arms of enormous crosses. These dragged ten feet on the ground and were of the calibre of goodly telegraph poles.

Through Don Amado and later through the great Bandelier, I learned the derivation of this extraordinary rite still persisting in the United States, tracing it back to the Flagellants of the Middle Ages in Europe.

But so unknown was the Brotherhood then, every magazine in the United States returned the article I wrote about it. They deemed it a fake. It was only when John Brisben Walker ventured with his old time Cosmopolitan *that the matter saw the light for the first time. Since then the pictures of this medieval ceremony have figured in several of my books and the cult of the Penitentes is known the world over.*[4]

To Lummis it was well worth risking his life to get these proofs of an unknown practice of his country, although, even as the Chaveses had warned, he was to pay for it later.

A great factor in my upbuilding was the deep interest I took in New Mexican folk songs. In California I had learned many beautiful Spanish songs. Out here I learned hundreds of others. For months I hung by night around the sheep camps of Don Amado, squatting with the quiet Mexican herders in the little semi-circular brush shelter by a crackling fire of juniper. March and spring nights are chill up there at 7,000 or 8,000 feet on the north shoulder of Mt. San Mateo.

There were no musical instruments, save now and then a mouth organ and more frequently the "bejuela"—a stick maybe a foot long, strung like a little bow with a piece of linen thread and played at the mouth precisely like a jew's-harp. There were few good voices but all had what is much more important than a good voice, the will to sing and express their emotion. And beyond that, an invariable sense of time and rhythm which only our best musicians can match. And they were such human, friendly folk! Glad to sing a song over and over until I had it note-perfect and then to repeat the words while I wrote them down. They were greatly pleased when I could sing their songs back at them....

So we sang and talked and smoked cigarettes under the infinite stars of a New Mexican sky or the even more numerous flakes of a mountain snowstorm. Out in front was the still herd clumped like jack-knives. The two patient burros, relieved of their pack-saddles but handcuffed with hobbles, were hopping gravely about in the farther darkness; and the two great shaggy wise sheep dogs of nondescript breed but with a herding ability of two men, kept guard outside the

[4] Lummis, "As I Remember."

flock or dashed off to repel invaders when they scented the skulking coyote or shuffling bear.[5]

His rendition of the popular songs of his college days was a great delight to the simple-hearted *pastores.* ("Thou shouldst see his eyes in the firelight and the faces he makes as he roars out the words.")

To Lummis, the folk song of Spanish origin had

. . . a peculiar fascination, a naivete, and yet a vividness and life, a richness of melody with a certain resillience and willfulness which give it a preeminent appeal. It has more music in it, more Rhythm, more Grace. It is more simpatica. It not only joys my hearing and tickles my pulses but cuddles my heart more happily than the songs of any of the score of other nationalities to which I have given friendly ear.[6]

Such music, "born of emotion came from the heart and it reaches the heart." He saw that these songs of the drunkard, the virgin, the coyote, the mother-in-law, the foolish shepherd, and the exile were the record in music of a vanishing New Mexico. He set out to capture them before they were lost. In the forty years that followed he secured over 550 songs of the Southwest.

During Lummis' first winter in the New Mexico Territory, he chose to live for a while the life of the shepherds, "the loneliest in the world and the most monotonous." He camped with them in the remote sheep camps, worked along with the *pastores*, and shared their hardships and primitive pleasures. All this was only four months after the onset of his illness. More than once after chasing a wayward lamb, he would fall and lie on the icy ground from sheer weakness. But he kept on rising at five, hunting, bringing food to the shepherds, helping make corrals for the lambs, singing or writing articles until late at night, and joining shepherds in guarding the flocks on the upper heights in five inches of snow.

Up at San Miguel, headquarters for the extreme north of his grant, Don Amado had built a stone cabin of flat thin rocks without any mortar. The windows and door had nothing to close. Charming places for the summer—but this wasn't summer. In *spite of two sheepskins, two folded Navajo blankets and a sleeping bag, it was cold sleeping. So I built fires on the frozen ground, scraping up the reluctant mud with my good hand, and with it as my trowel, chinked the inside of my wall. Great improvement.*

Dr. Dorothea years before had converted me from the old New England tradition of a bath Saturday night "whether you need it or not," to the gospel of a cold bath every morning wherever you are. It had become a prime necessity to me and my greatest luxury. Up here the tiny rivulet in front of the house was frozen over much of the time . . . but a little way down stream was a rock pool 8 or 10 feet long, nearly as wide and 6 feet deep. It was all very well for me to chop a hole through the ice on this pool, until I split the only axe in camp with my one-handed clumsiness. "Cuate" spliced the hickory but I was prohibited any further axe work.

I found a hatchet head and sent it down to Albuquerque 150 miles to a blacksmith to have it welded onto a light crowbar. Until this ice chisel reached me, I had to make shift by rolling in and scrubbing with the powdered snow. When this fine instrument came, it was very easy to fall out at 4 a.m. at 10 below zero, chop my hole, go down feet first into the good, cold water and ramp back to the shack, rub down with a gunnysack and dress.

This regime had more than a mere hygienic value. The ignorant herders were convinced that a man who would do such a thing must be in league with the devil. Word of it spread for me through their kind throughout the territory. In following years when a Big Boss put the price on my head and I was waylaid and shot at on lonely roads, this conviction of theirs that I was devilishly protected seemed to incite a certain "buck fever" so that very excellent shots missed me.

As for the cold baths, I certainly wouldn't be alive at all nor have lived to half my present span but for them. In the upper Andes where there was no other "bath" I have rejoiced in the flour-like snow at 16 degrees below.[7]

Soon the paralytic announced that he wanted a horse, and he wanted to break it himself.

His first bronco was a little Navajo pony which

---

[5] *Ibid.*

[6] Charles F. Lummis, *Spanish Songs of Old California*, introduction.

[7] Lummis, "As I Remember."

weighed but seven hundred pounds. Only slightly used to being led, he was quite enough for a one-armed man's kindergarten lesson in bronco busting. The pony had "a great deal more spontaneity and a much higher range in altitude than any New England pasture colt" he had ever gentled. In a couple of days, however, they were on very good terms.

As I got stronger I wanted a real horse. Now the only way to get a real horse is to make him yourself from the raw material....

So Don Amado sent out with me a score of his vaqueros. After a few miles we split into two parties, each taking one of the ranges that walled a northern valley two or three miles apart. We clattered up dim and stony trails, mile after mile, until five or six leagues lay behind us; then the ends of the lines began to close into one another. There were dozens of wild horses in these mountains—wild as deer or bear. They had never felt a rope and if they had seen a man, it was from afar. As we came near, they broke for the valley. Every now and then we would hear a great crashing in the thick brush or catch a glimpse of a flying mustang. "Cuate" was at the head of my line on the east side of the valley. As we ourselves came down the precipitous slopes without trail, we found whole groups of the wild horses stampeding to our left and backward from the enclosing line. Three miles down the valley was a big round corral. Its V-shaped entrance came close to the low cliffs on each side of the valley. As we rode into the open and approached the corral, dozens of scared horses that were running, doubling, trying to break through our line, were relentlessly chased forward into the V-shaped entrance and they had no recourse but to pass through the narrow gate into the corral. No sooner were they all in, than strong bars were put across the opening. The corral was made of piñon logs about 14 feet long, set four feet in the ground and tamped and lashed at the top each to each and all around with great thongs of wet rawhide which had shrunk until it was like iron.

It was a gallant sight as we climbed to the uncomfortable top of this crude stockade and looked at the 45 or so beautiful wild creatures milling frantically around at our feet. Round and round they went, their heavy tide swinging against the palisades until they

swayed and creaked. Beautiful creatures they were—none of the hammer-heads of the northern cayuse or the common American horse—but the proud, clean cut, small head and noble neck of the Arab Barb. There was no other drop of horse blood in their veins than that of the Arab steeds brought over by Cortez and brought to New Mexico by Oñate. They had run wild and multiplied to great numbers although never into great droves for they always went in harems. A wild stallion always ran with his ten or twelve mares whom he guarded jealously and fought for like a very demon against wolves or man and particularly other stallions who came around on home-wrecking errands. No horse has ever been in the Southwest today ... so fitted for that country. Of the highest intelligence, light, swift, sure-footed with slender legs, they could cover distances that would seem incredible to an Eastern horseman.

As we sat watching them mill, each man picked out the one that suited best his fancy, shouted his choice and, as soon as he could get a chance, dropped his rope over its neck, taking a dally around one of the palisade posts. It was risky business for the lassoed horse plunged and kicked. The others ran into the raw-hide reata and over it, sometimes throwing and trampling him ... so after the first noose was thrown it meant quick work with the others. When six of us had our catch, the men at the bars opened the gate, those on the stockade waved their sarapes and the unroped horses went roaring out through the gate in a wild tumult back to freedom.

The man nearest the gate hopped down into the corral with the rope back around his right hip, got his captive out through the gate into the open valley and then proceeded to minister to him. One after the other, these fighting, screaming animals, rearing and striking with their forefeet, were somehow brought out into the plain. Since I was least able to cope with the corral full of plunging beasts and farthest from the gate, I was last. I managed to bring out the beautiful creature that had been half choked under my reata for 20 minutes. Outside the gate, some of the cowboys grabbed the rope and helped me get my captive to the plain and threw him for me. I tied on the blindfold and let him up to his feet. Two men stood at the reata though there was really no need for being blinded he was helpless and stood trembling. I brought my Navajo saddle blankets and laid them gently on his back at which he kicked and groaned . . . then as gently as a one-armed man could, I placed the heavy California saddle on the blankets. I got the bit in with infinite trouble, laid the reins back on his neck, cinched the center-fire saddle up to the last notch my strength could command, then one of the boys gave me a hand. I stepped into the saddle, got the rein over his neck and reaching forward with my one hand, lifted the blindfold.

But that bandana wasn't lifted half as far as the rider for the wild creature bucked high and hard and came down with his forefeet like stakes. He buck-jumped about twenty minutes and then started off on a dead run up the valley. I was pretty sore and pretty tired but "sitting pretty." When he saw a low-spreading cedar he swerved and made for it like a bullet to wipe me off. I swung down on his farther side and escaped with some hard rakes on my right leg.

Up and down the lovely valley we fought all the afternoon but by sundown I was pretty well worn out and he also began to feel a new sense of proportion toward this strange brute on his back. I had talked to him whenever I had breath and patted him whenever the tempest wasn't too high. The upshot was that I was able to ride him back to San Mateo and shut him up in the corrals there for the night, with a patting rub on the nose, at which he snorted, but not as one that would not be comforted.

He was a stallion, about three years old and of that beautiful brown sorrel which the Spanish call alazan tostado *to which they add* antes muerto que cansado *—"toasted sorrel never tired until dead." And I named him Alazan. He was a very dear companion for many years, not only in New Mexico but in California later.*[8]

During this period one-armed Lummis broke twenty-five wild horses.

[8] *Ibid.*

NOT FAR from the Chavez holdings was the Indian pueblo of Isleta. Lummis felt drawn to this peace-filled village on the Río Grande. In the fall of 1888, he decided to move there and "go to baching it"—just until he was well enough to return to his job on the *Times*. For of course he planned to return.

Isleta, called by its citizens *Shee-eh-wheeb-bak*, the City of the Whib Sticks, had been an independent Indian republic for hundreds of years. Some time after he moved there, Lummis began receiving hints that white Americans were not particularly welcome. However, he had grown to love the pueblo, the sanity and poise of those who followed the old ways, the True Believers. Although he respected the messages the *alguacil* ("constable") kept sending, he had a great desire to stay and learn all that the elders would teach him.

With his knack for making friends, Lummis came in the end to be a welcome intimate. They gave him the affectionate nickname *Por Todos*, because he always had tobacco "for all."

Although he continued writing to Dorothea that he was lonely, to others he wrote, "Baching it suits me down to the ground."

Those were the days when even a poor man could feast. You could get four pounds of beef tenderloin for 24¢, a big leg of mountain mutton or a 6-pound hen for the same price or a beef tongue for 20¢. Juan Rey Abeita cared for and corn-fed my horse, Alazan, for $2.50 a month—the same price I paid for rent.[1]

His eating habits were not the most wholesome. His diary is full of enthusiastic references to pickled pig's feet, fried potatoes, roast pork, sausages, pickled tripe, doughnuts, frijoles, pie spread with mustard, sardines, plum pudding, Neufchatel cheese, and lobster. After a few weeks of this fare, he had a painful attack. He called it angina pectoris.

Mishaps gave Lummis literary material. His description of how he started out with a "few cupsful" of dried frijoles and ended up by "shoveling them out of the kitchen" bought him many dinners. He earned his bread and butter by describing the night he bogged down in a slough and had to be hauled out by the Indians with their reatas. The tale of his home treatment of an ulcerated tooth helped to keep a wolf cub from the door.

In those days even the ethnologists had little information about the Pueblos. Lummis determined to learn the language and the lore of the Tiguas, the Isleta tribe. He made an arrangement with one of its boys who had been educated at the Carlisle Indian School. Twenty-five cents an hour made quite a hole in an uncertain income, but he put every spare cent into the lessons.

The imaginative aptness of Indian names appealed to the poet in his nature. The blackbirds were Seeds-of-the-Prairie, the rattlesnake was *Char-ra-rá-deh*, with the sound of its rattling in the syllables, and the duck was Old-Man-Afraid-of-the-Water.

Lummis was able to tap the most ancient font of knowledge—the wisdom of old men. In the winter when farming was over, the villagers visited one another, and the young would gather to learn Tigua traditions and ethical teachings told in folk tales.

This aboriginal kindergarten was beautiful with the gentle patience of the sages and the respect of the listening boys. Lummis passed many evenings with

[1] Lummis, "As I Remember."

The Pueblo of Isleta, New Mexico Territory, showing the Feast of the Dead. Photograph by Charles Lummis. (*Courtesy Southwest Museum*)

them over the roasting corn. The young men of marriageable age, who were supposed to know the teachings already, would be off in a corner by themselves. Sitting on the knees of a father or grandfather, dark eyes shining, the young pupils drank in the time-hallowed words. "Is that so?" they would chorus in the traditional phrase as they learned that it is well to do thus and so, not "because I tell you to," but because *Nah-chu-rú-chu*, the hero medicine man, thus walked the road of virtue long ago. (You must not put on false colors lest the same thing happen to you as did to the Coyote-children when they burnt themselves with hot coals under their arms trying to make out that they too had the woodpecker's hues!)

Tigua families were affectionate and happy together. All members of the pueblo worked for the common good. There were no suffering poor and, until the coming of the "superior race," no drunkards

and no prostitutes. Children were brought up in a tradition of reverence toward their elders.

Yet under the Indian policy then in effect, children, reared with a direct and unshaken faith in their parents and "Those Above," were dragged off to school by force, there to be taught to ignore and despise their elders and the sacred teachings.

Lummis saw Navajo boys come back to their fellow nomads fitted only to do typesetting, watchmaking, or sanitary plumbing. Sturdy young Pueblos were turned into consumptives by being transported to unfriendly climates and forced into alien ways. He saw white teachers strip children of the names that had been given them by sacred ritual. Though to an Indian his hair is a precious possession, young Arizona Indians were rounded up and tied with baling wire, then shorn with sheep shears.

Lummis saw small children torn weeping from

their mothers' arms and saw the same children come back unfitted for life among their own people. They had learned the white child's impudence toward his elders and had been instructed that their parents were superstitious savages. They had been taught to forget their own language, and mother and son could not even speak to one another. In more than one household he had to translate the very words of greeting for a parent who had not seen his child for several years.

Angered by these things, Lummis was compelled to take action. Yet he found the Indians pitifully patient. The white principal of a government school would not let the Pueblo children go home even in summer. Parents who went to see them were literally beaten up by his orders. The Pueblos held many desperate and sorrowing councils. But they were still patient. It was not until they had gone through three years of such abuse that they felt driven to act.

The three children of Lummis' good friend and landlord, Juan Rey Abeita, were made a test case. Tuyo, the smallest, had been abducted from his home before he was four. He had not seen his mother and father for more than three years. The Indians begged their friend "Por Todos" for help.

It was necessary for Lummis to procure a lawyer and a writ of *habeas corpus* in order that American parents might gain the right to their own flesh and blood. An accredited government official fought that right. There was an attempt to kill or cripple the Indian who had thus dared to question what was done with his children. There was an attempt against Lummis himself.

Lummis carried this dramatic and bitter fight to the columns of the various papers for which he was writing and stirred up publicity in many parts of the country. He had many things in his life to regret, but against them he set the day he took those three boys back to Isleta and the mother whose arms hungered for them. Three days later he and a caravan of Indians went to the school to bring home the thirty-seven other children who had been kept like prisoners of the officials who made a living by "enlightening" them.

Defenders of government education used to point to an Indian named Henry who had been educated at Carlisle. In him Lummis saw the perfect example of the ruthless bigotry of our Indian policy. Taken from the Pueblo as a little boy, Henry came back a grown man alienated from his people, unable to live with them or with the whites. Lummis tried to do what he could for the youth, but it was too late. In the end, heartbroken and disoriented, Henry went to pieces morally and physically. He died a tragic death —a man without a country.

13

Bushwhacked

IT IS PART of the tragi-comedy of their relationship that, at Lummis' own request, Dorothea was still writing almost daily to her peripatetic husband. One day she decided that he was now strong enough to be told the truth—that the *Times* had granted him leave of absence for three months only, with pay for merely half that time. The news brought on a relapse: "Can't walk except with much difficulty. What a devil of a day for me! I have lost all that I had gained and more."[1]

Three days later, March 1, 1888, was his twenty-ninth birthday. He wrote in his diary, "I am 31 (sic) years old and not worth anything." His condition seemed hopeless. He had lost his job, he had no business ability, no money, no prospects. Yet inside the crippled body was a man who had never given up. He decided to stay on and fight things out in New Mexico. Left with nothing, he would make capital out of his very misfortune. The most humorous material he ever wrote was written while he was paralyzed.

My mind was oppressed though I was cheerful and pugnacious. It seemed sometimes as though there were an actual floor in my brain about halfway to the top which I couldn't bore through. It was baffling and irritating for I "had my senses" perfectly and was not noticeably stupid. Kept from any more concentrated application by this condition, I turned to writing humorous verse and paragraphs. It brought in only a dollar or two at a time.

Often I did not even have enough stamps for postage. I began to augment this meager income by selling photographs and by trading in a small way.[2]

[1] Lummis, "Diary."
[2] Lummis, "As I Remember."

As his knowledge of the Pueblo people, customs, and language increased, Lummis was no longer treated as a stranger but rather as a helpful member of the community. He knew everyone, chiefs and basketmakers, witches and magicians. He began to see and learn things that were concealed from the outsider. The *estufa*, the sacred medicine house where the ceremonial magic was performed, was just behind the adobe in which he lived. Already familiar with the legerdemain of famous magicians, he was amazed at the skill of the Indian medicine men who performed in a round room of solid adobe with only one trap door—the single outlet through the roof. They worked without trick apparatus or hidden mechanical equipment. Some were naked but for a breechcloth. None wore flowing garments or full sleeves. Yet in this bare setting their performances were beyond anything seen on much more elaborate stages.

All performances were done in reverence, none for show. To the True Believer even the lighting of a cigarette was a ceremony. From the sacred *estufa* Lummis learned how linked to "Those Above" is every act of a Pueblo's life. Irrigation and other phases of farming, the foretelling of the year, and the curing of sickness were as much a part of the Pueblo religion as giving thanks to the Trues. In *Mesa, Cañon and Pueblo*, Lummis describes the "making" of a thunderstorm by Pueblo medicine men, how lightning flashed and thunder rolled inside the *estufa*, although outside the stars were shining.

He tells of the terribly realistic ritual of the witch killing, in which "blood" falls from the "bodies" transfixed by the medicine arrows. Only a few years later

. . . my wise old friend, Remigio Abeita (whom I brought over with 50 other Isleteños in 1895 to the Fiesta de Los Angeles) was executed officially in his pueblo by the Alguaciles as a witch. They called him to his door at midnight and as he stepped out, one on each side drove an agate-tipped ceremonial arrow through him from side to side.

In *Some Strange Corners of Our Country* there is a minute description of the *T'u-a-fú-ar* ("Mad Dance"), a scalp dance in celebration of a victory. This Lummis witnessed in 1891. There were but few after that. In the same book he devotes ten pages to *Tu-shee-wim* ("Spring Medicine Making"), with translations of the ceremonial songs and his eye-witness account of the ceremony, the shamans shaking ears of the sacred corn and showering the assembly with a quantity of grain far out of proportion to the number of ears involved.

Also described is the startling fire dance of the nine-day medicine dance of *Dsil-yíd-je Quacal*. This was also seen by Dr. Washington Matthews, another authority on Pueblo culture, who said of it, "I have seen many fire scenes on the stage, many acts of fire eating and fire handling by civilized jugglers, but nothing comparable to this."[3]

Lummis saw and described many other things. Others he never got around to committing to paper, and some secrets, told in confidence, he never revealed.

What he garnered in this peaceful pueblo bore fruit in many of the achievements of his life. The whole time of his paralysis was one of his richest experiences, for in it misfortune "gave his inborn pugnacity a worthy foe and a beneficial struggle."

On the lower right side of his jaw Lummis had a dimple that he affectionately called "my Valentine." It was the hole made by a bullet the time that he was "assassinated."

When I went to New Mexico to recover from paralysis, the Territory was undergoing one of its most important revolutions. The system of peonage and boss rule was making its last stand.

Under this system the head of the clan would loan one of his needy workers 40 or 50 dollars to be "worked out" in labor. As current wages were $2.50 a month, the great clans came to boss not only whole families but whole townships. This was how they were able to run Territorial politics to suit themselves.[4]

By 1888 public opinion had already turned. Courageous editors and younger blood had declared open war against the barons. Before Lummis had been a guest at the Chaveses for long, he sided with them publicly against the peonage system. It was a dangerous step for any man, more so for an outsider.

Lummis found himself in the thick of an ugly situation. Family was arrayed against family, brother against brother. In two years there had been five murders, all directly traceable to this one cause and to the door of one man—the son of the Gran Amo ("big boss") of Valencia County.

A few strong clans such as the Chaveses, the Bacas, and the Lunas, had controlled Valencia County for years. Much later Lummis referred to the Gran Amo as Don Adán A. Coran. Perhaps in his old age Lummis had friends on both sides and did not wish to offend. Those who care to know the real name may proceed to the Los Angeles Public Library, secure the microfilm of the *Los Angeles Times* for 1888, and spin it to the issue of December 2. On the front page is his original story; he was not afraid of offending in those days. The name, like Chaves, has been famous in the history of New Mexico, and like Chaves it appears on the state map. In later years however, Lummis chose to present the story in this way.

Don Adán was a man of intelligence and courage. He had been a famous Indian fighter. He owned 50,000 sheep and belonged to one of the finest families of New Mexico. But he was a man without scruples. Though the Order of the Penitentes was dying out elsewhere, it suited his purpose to keep it alive among his own peons.

Finally his high-handed methods, together with the five brutal and cold-blooded assassinations, led to open revolt. It was not a matter of party politics but of sheer self preservation. All the victims had been murdered simply because they stood in the Gran Amo's way. Who might be next?

In such a period the outcome of every election was

[3] Lummis, *Mesa, Cañon and Pueblo*, 324.

[4] Lummis, "As I Remember."

vital. Valencia county was normally Republican by a thousand majority. When rebellion broke out, every white man in the county voted against the alleged Republican ticket—in reality a Coran ticket—and the fight was on.

Never before had the Coran rule been disputed. Don Adán's son entered the fray. Tiburcio Coran was a young blade in his twenties whose eastern education was said to have cost $36,000. On the 17th of October in order to win over a few votes, he joined the Brotherhood of the Penitentes, receiving their seal—six gashes with a flint knife over each kidney. He put a barrel of whiskey on tap in the morada ["lodging"] and then he made a speech in Spanish against the leader of the opposition, against the newspaper which had ridiculed the Order—and against the one-armed Gringo who had dared to photograph the rites.

The night before the election the bosses held a conference in San Mateo. A woman in the adjoining room overheard them plotting. If the vote went against Coran, the judges of election in all the important precincts were to be killed and the books were to be seized.

The judges were the best citizens of San Mateo. When election day came, every one of them was armed with a six-shooter and a Winchester; besides this there was a strong armed guard. Voting at sunrise, the 46 independent voters set themselves to wait for the remaining 40 votes of the town. In a short time Don Adán himself rode into the hamlet, accompanied by a heavily armed bodyguard of 60 men. Forty of these were the legal votes, the remaining twenty were imported. Don Adán was told that he could not vote the illegal twenty. He threatened war. But the independents, Winchesters in hand, had filed in behind him and his crowd and two of them followed his every move. He voted the legitimate forty.

The bosses were at the same time being beaten in San Rafael. They determined to carry out the emergency plan. By nightfall rumors of danger had reached San Rafael. The room where the ballots were being counted was cleared of all but a few of the picked men of the village. Among the latter was Dumas Provencher, a kindly and respected pioneer. About one o'clock that night seven 50-calibre Government rifles were pushed through the narrow un-

curtained window, a trigger was pulled, Provencher fell dead. Six more bullets were ready for the remaining five men in the room, but Marshall Martín Gallegos shot out the lamp and saved their lives.

The Provencher killing was now the sixth murder in the Coran series. The fifth had been that of a fine old Scotsman named Sam Barrett. Everyone knew that Tiburcio Coran had been responsible but no one dared speak openly. Witnesses were simply not to be had.

There was at this time in the Territory what New Mexicans considered a novelty—an honest United States District Attorney, Clifford S. Jackson. The Barrett case was an offense to his integrity. One day he said to me, "I'm pretty much disgusted. I can't get a shred of evidence and there isn't a man in the Territory who isn't afraid to help me."

"Hold on!" I said. "There's one man who isn't. I know where the evidence is to be gotten and I'll get it. But you know what they'll do to you if you push the case."

"You get me the evidence," said Jackson. "I'll take care of the rest."

I got the evidence. But on Sept. 25 I found on the station platform at Grants a letter in Spanish from old Don Adán beginning "Idolatrado Hijo (Idolized Son): Don't worry. U.S. Grand Jury is 'fixed.' Cousin Ciriaco has got on county grand jury" which [jury] was trying to indict Tiburcio for selling liquor to Indians....

The letter was prophetic. Nothing was ever done to the idolotrado hijo; the juries laughed Attorney Jackson out of court. The technical murderers of Provencher also went scot free. A bill was actually passed through the legislature to compel the prisoners' removal from the secure jail where Jackson had ordered them to be held. The day after they were returned to the flimsy Valencia county jail, they escaped and were never heard from again.

The Bosses tried to get Jackson's job, although strangely enough, not his life. For me, however, there was another story.[5]

Lummis' friends were frightened all over again. He had defied the bosses by photographing the forbidden rites of the Penitentes. He had openly taken

[5] *Ibid.*

54

sides against them. Not only had he gone so far as to write about the murderers, he had given real names and incriminating details and had deliberately helped to find evidence for the prosecution of Tiburcio Coran.

For some time there had been rumors that the Gran Amo was out for Charles Lummis' blood. He simply laughed at them. In spite of all that had passed, it was sheer dime novel to think that anything could happen to *him*.

On September 4, 1888, word was brought to Lummis that Tiburcio Coran had offered a one-hundred-dollar reward for the death of the obnoxious Lummis. One hundred dollars was a good deal of money in those days. It was flattering that the boss of a political empire should consider it worth that much to get rid of a man with only one good arm. "But youth is incredulous of the traditional adversary. I might talk about the danger of death but I was care-less of it."

Tiburcio's peons made several attempts to earn the tempting reward. But it was no light matter to kill a man who chopped holes through the ice to take a bath when the thermometer stood below zero! Clear-ly he was in league with the devil. Each time they shot at him the bullet went astray—not from ner-vousness, but from a diabolical spell on them!

Finally Tiburcio imported a pelon[6] from old Mex-ico unhampered by such superstitions. For some days he lay around Isleta getting a line on me. He soon learned that every night about midnight I always stepped outside my bachelor's quarters to take the fresh air and open up my lungs.

The midnight of St. Valentine's Day, 1889, was dazzling moonlight, extremely cold. Sitting by the hot stove I had taken off my vest with its shoulder holster and my precious six-shooter and hung it on a chair. Stepping out, I put on my coat only. Lucky I donned that. The rude board door swung to behind me as I stood in moonlight and swung and stretched high my right arm. From the adobe pig pen 20 yards from my door rises a black silhouette against the sky —that of an extremely tall man with unforgettable

sloping shoulders—and fires both barrels of a long shotgun loaded with buckshot.

Luckily it was an old burned-out muzzle loader and scattered fearfully. While the door behind me was riddled with buckshot, only about eight hit me. One burned the tip of my little finger some six inches higher than my head. Two cut small furrows in my scalp. One that would have struck my heart went through my fat pocketbook and stopped in a little "Birch Bark Poems" I carried. The only serious one hit my right cheek. Only the fact that I was yawning prevented it from shattering my lower jaw. As it was it went through without touching a tooth, traversed my throat and lodged far back in my neck. There it is to this day [1927] unless it has "traveled" as bullets are reputed to do by gravity.

The bullet knocked me down. . . . Blood spouted profusely. Feeling sure that I was killed, I scrambled to my feet in a surge of blind rage and rushed into the room for a gun. As already my eyes were getting dim I did not dare to trust the six-shooter but ran on farther to the loaded single-barrel shotgun. As I came back past my trunk the blood from the wound was heavy enough to splash up from the adobe floor and spatter some newspapers[7] in blotches half an inch across. By the time I got out the assassin had, of course, disappeared. As long as I could run I fol-lowed him, scouring the blind alleys and indetermi-nate streets. (Next day the Indians traced me by the blood on that deep sand.) Then I knew that my time was about to come and I made for the house of Archibald Rea.

Every night they made ice by setting a dish of water outside the window. With a cake of this I soon staunched the blood. And after a little rest on the couch I got Rea to help me back to my own adobe a couple of blocks or so away. I pulled my mattress up to the open door and lay there the rest of the night with the shotgun cocked beside me hoping my Friend would return. I would know him in Australia. Those shoulders were unmistakable. But I never saw him again.[8]

[6] In Spain a *pelon* is a poor, indigent man; in Mexico, also a soldier of the line.

[7] Lummis saved everything. The bloody shirt was around for many years, and some of the bloody newspapers are on file in the Southwest Museum in a red leather scrapbook.

[8] Lummis, "As I Remember."

This latest episode stirred up intense indignation. Wrote the *Albuquerque Democrat,*

This thing must stop and at once.... In November it was Provencher, in February it is Lummis. Who is next is the question asked by people who live in the vicinity of these crimes and are terrorized to such an extent that even the telegraph operator dared not send the particulars which were obtained by a special messenger sent out by the Democrat.... *The world has not enough such men as Charlie Lummis that he can court the death that we fear is coming all too soon. Lummis is a martyr to his convictions and obstinate to a fault. His work in New Mexico has been magnificent from a journalistic standpoint and grand from hoped-for results. But Lummis lying wounded and mayhap dying (in the Rea home) . . . is stronger than the man who sought his life. The time is come for every man who has hopes for the future of the territory to swear to avenge the deaths of Kusz, of Provencher, of half a score of brave men and true, who, loving country better than life, offered it up in upholding a principle.*[9]

Archibald Rea's great-hearted wife, Alice, was the only person he would trust to take care of him. Poor Al! Two days after the shooting, her patient got up and managed to make his way to his own adobe one hundred yards away. An hour later, Mr. Rea found him there walking up and down in delirium. Shortly afterward he fainted and lay too ill to speak. Again it was Dr. Dorothea's turn to be sent for.

The most alarming and conflicting rumors went out. Some of the newspapers began issuing bulletins. One dispatch actually stated that Lummis was being "tenderly cared for" in the home of the very man who had ordered his murder. Nine days after the shooting, on February 23, the *Chillicothe Leader* published an

[9] It is interesting to compare this article with one appearing in the same newspaper some five years earlier after Lummis had impugned in print the sobriety of the editor: "He is a big brawny bronzed fellow . . . and when he got too drunk to waddle I ground out editorials for him. . . ." The *Albuquerque Democrat* retaliated: "A young newspaper tramp named C. F. Loomis who came through this city about two months ago . . . has turned up in Los Angeles, California, and has written a long letter to one of the papers there in which he abuses and satirizes this city just as any scrub kid would be likely to do who thought he was saying something smart. . . . He is a shallow, flippant and selfish little Yankee who would tell a lie for 50¢ at any time and while he has lots of the spirit of vagrant adventure in him he ought not be allowed to write for a newspaper."

obituary: "Mr. Lummis was one cast in an heroic mould. He had the intelligence to properly estimate danger, privation and suffering and yet he unhesitatingly confronted them all when the accomplishment of an object sought brought them before his face and never turned back because of their threat.... God be with him if it be true that he is dead."

As soon as Lummis could hold a pen, he demanded paper and ink and insisted on going to work. Eleven days after he was shot he got up and went out hunting. Locally he became known by the cognomen of El Cabezudo, "The Headstrong."

Twelve days after the shooting I was on my way to Albuquerque. When I climbed up the steps of the train I came face to face with Tiburcio Coran and his father. You never saw faces turn so many colors ending in a deathly pallor. Curious how the old conventions are usually with us. They said, "We were so shocked and sorry to hear of your accident."

I said, "No doubt! Next time send a better marksman. Or come yourself."

It came near being a finish right there. It would have been in any other region. But in those times and in that territory the boss and his son could have walked up behind me in broad daylight on the streets of Albuquerque and shot me in the back—and have been acquitted by a Mexican jury of their peers on the grounds of self-defense. Whereas if I shot them in the plainest case of aggravated attack and self protection I could not possibly have escaped conviction.

I had my fun, though, holding them there on the open platform of the train during the half hour ride to Albuquerque. They dared neither to get their hands in their pockets nor to retreat into the coach. When the train slowed down at the Albuquerque yards half a mile south of the station, they both tumbled off and kept out of sight during my stay.[10]

Back in Isleta it was reported that Don Adán had sent word that Lummis would never dare to return to the stronghold of the Coran family, San Mateo. Lummis immediately got a horse and rode to San Mateo. There he called at every house in the village, remarking to each householder that he had come "to participate in any shooting that was to be done hereafter and henceforward."

[10] Lummis, "As I Remember."

For two days running he repeated this "gentle admonishment." It worked very well, and he never was shot at again. As a matter of fact the townsfolk liked the hotheaded El Cabezudo. Only Don Adán and his *idolatrado hijo* held a grudge against him.

The Gran Amo's seventh hired murder was "the only one that didn't take," but the scar did, and El Cabezudo wore it as though it were an order of merit.

He was not the only man or the bravest who had risked his life to bring the truth into the open. But it was fitting that he who held New Mexico so dear should have played a part in its development. His pen was one of the influences that helped break the strength of the boss rule, and certainly the public opinion aroused by his near assassination contributed to the freeing of the territory.

14

Explorations

In the 1880's the Southwest took its marvels for granted. Elsewhere they were completely unknown. In three years the crippled man travelled thousands of miles by rail, on horseback, and on foot. Lummis had come to know and love the land, and he was the first to popularize its strange corners, secret rituals, people, and history. There were hardships and adventures. Once he and an Indian companion were attacked by Navajos; their pack mule fell into a canyon and was killed, but they managed to escape unharmed.

As Lummis lived close to the people of the pueblos, he gathered legends that had been ancient even in 1540 when Coronado had passed through. To each of these he gave thoughtful consideration, firmly believing them racial memories needing only proper interpretation. It was from Martín Valle, the "noble and wise old Pueblo statesman, seven times governor of his little cliff built republic" of Acoma, that he learned the tale of Katzímo, the Enchanted Mesa, a sheer-sided island of rock in the desert.

In the old days the Hano Oshatch dwelt on the summit of Katzímo as many as here today in Acoma, about 600. They were safe and happy. Their fields were in the valley, good with corn and beans. There was much game of deer and antelope and wild turkeys and rabbits and quail; and the people made round hunts, hemming in much country and killed great store of game with arrows and the rabbit stick; and jerked the meat in the sun; and the storerooms were abundant with corn and parched meat and piñon nuts and frijoles . . . there were tame eagles and tame wild turkeys for the feathers, which are good medicine. . . .

Martín Valle, seven times the governor of the Acoma Pueblo.

58

Their houses were like our houses in Acoma now and three rooms high; and the estufa was like ours in a room upon the rock; and all the top was solid rock, bare, without grass or trees. But they sang and danced just as we do in the same times of the year . . . and they made tinajas and ollas just as we do now but better. These tepulcates ["shards"?] that we find everywhere are from them and some are glassy as no one knows how to make now.

There was only one way to come to the top of Katzímo. On the side toward Acoma, a very great piece of the cliff had fallen so that it leaned from the valley up to a very high cleft that ran from the top of the mesa half way down . . . and up there they were happy, longer than anyone can tell. . . .

One summer in the time of the harvest all came down from the rock to gather their corn and beans, men, women and children, with buckskin bags to bring the harvest home. All but three women who stayed behind because one was sick. And while they were all away at their fields, down in the Long Valley, *there came such storms as no one ever saw; and the rains did not stop; and floods ran down the cliffs of the Valley of Acoma and the waters ran against the foot of Katzímo and ate away the sands and rocks that grew there and burrowed under the great rock that was their ladder. And it fell out into the plain shaking the earth. When the storm ended the people crawled out from under the ledges where they had taken refuge and came home. But their ladder rock was gone and from the top of the sand hill to the cleft was higher than a tall pine. So they could never get up there any more. Neither could the three women on top come down. And there they died after a long time —except one who threw herself off the cliff. And then the people came to this Acoma that is today and built it, a town like the one they lost."*[1]

Charlie Lummis was fascinated by the old Indian's tale, and he rode many times around the foot of the four hundred-foot cliffs without finding a route to the summit. He published the story, it caught the imagination, and received international attention.

In time one William Libbey, a professor at Princeton, felt called upon to debunk this Indian "fairy story." Borrowing a cannon and wagon loads of equipment from the U.S. Life Saving Service, he set up at the foot of Katzímo. After four days of "hardest work," Libbey got a line over the mesa and was hauled to the top. A storm was coming in, the professor glanced around hastily, saw no buildings, retreated to the valley and telegraphed to the waiting world that "the Enchanted Mesa was Disenchanted; Professor Libbey had surmounted that inaccessible cliff and was convinced that no human foot had ever pressed that lofty summit before."

Lummis was unconvinced, and the dispute raged on. Libbey wrote "A Disenchanted Mesa" in *Harpers Weekly* in 1897, telling how the "capacity of the native for spinning yarns has always been noted" and how the "medicine man of the future will now have to publish a new and revised edition of the story for . . . an inquisitive scientist by the name of Libbey has been up there and found that the summit had never been inhabited."

One month later Fredrick Webb Hodge of the Bureau of American Ethnology got together a small

Lummis' photograph of David Starr Jordan's party atop Katzimo in 1898.

[1] Lummis, *Mesa, Cañon and Pueblo*, 214–19.

A fiesta at Laguna, New Mexico Territory, September, 1901. Photograph by Charles Lummis.

party, including A. C. Vroman, the great photographer of Indian life. Using ropes and short extension ladders, they reached the top of the mesa in three hours. They found arrow heads, stone axes, fragments of cooking pots, and shell beads caught in the angles of the rough bedrock in such a way that they had not been washed off the cliff by the centuries of violent desert storms. There was no doubt that the mesa had been inhabited. Lummis demolished Libbey with his most belittling epithet. He called him a "tenderfoot."

It was vaguely known that at El Morro (Inscription Rock) there were signatures and writing. Lummis sought out the rock and there photographed the actual handwriting on stone of a score of the heroes who had explored and colonized in the New World when the English barely had a foothold.

Typical of the dramatic records is "Pasó por aquí el adelantado don Juan de Oñate al descubrimento de la mar del sur a 16 de Abril ao 1605" ("Passed by here the provincial governor Don Juan de Oñate from the discovery of the southern sea on the 16th of April 1605"). There are many others.

This magnificent monument to pioneers who were marching to unknown lands and fates had already suffered vandalism. Lummis set out to make the entire country conscious of the need to save "this most precious cliff . . . and, I am ashamed to say, the most neglected." He finally had the satisfaction of seeing

The Dance of San Esteban at the Acoma Pueblo, New Mexico Territory.

Inscription Rock made a national monument, carefully protected.

One of Lummis' favorite sayings was, "Cuando menos le espera, salta la liebre" ("When least you expect it, up jumps the rabbit").

One day of August, 1888, in the teeth of a particular New Mexico sandstorm that whipped pebbles the size of a bean straight into your face, a ruddy, bronzed, middle-aged man, dusty but unweary with his sixty mile tramp from Zuñi, walked in to my solitary camp at Los Alamitos, New Mexico. Within the afternoon I knew that here was the most extraordinary mind that I had met. There and then began the uncommon friendship which . . . will be one of my dearest memories. . . . He was Adolph Bandelier, the great Americanist.[2]

[2] The 1918 edition of Adolph Bandelier's *The Delight Makers* contains this in the introduction, "In Memory," written by Charles Lummis.

In later years Lummis wrote pages of praise of "this extraordinary genius—the judicial poise, the marvellous insight, the intellectual chastity. I have known many scholars and some heroes, but they seldom come in the same original package."

The two became fast friends and trudged many thousands of miles together.

There was not one decent road. We had no endowment, no vehicles. Bandelier was once loaned a horse; and after riding two miles, led it the rest of the thirty. So we always went by foot; my big camera and glass plates in the knapsack on my back, the heavy tripod under my arm; his aneroid, surveying instruments, and satchel of almost microscopic notes which he kept fully and precisely every night by the fire (even when I had to crouch over him and the precious paper with my water-proof focusing cloth) somehow bestowed about him. Up and down pathless cliffs, through tangled cañons, fording icy streams

Adolph Bandelier, the great Americanist, in 1878.

unknown "Somewheres." He has always reminded me of John Muir, the only other man I have known intimately who was as insatiate a climber and inspiring a talker. But Bandelier had one advantage. He could find common ground with anyone. I have seen him with Presidents, diplomats, Irish sectionhands, Mexican peons, Indians, authors, scientists and "society." Within an hour or so he was easily the Center. Not unconscious of his power, he had an extraordinary and sensitive modesty, which handicapped him through life among those who had the "gift of push." He never put himself forward either in person or in his writing. But something about him fascinated all these far-apart classes of people, when he spoke. His command of English, French, Spanish, and German might have been expected; but his facility in acquiring the "dialects" of railroad men and cowboys, or the language of an Indian tribe, was almost uncanny. When he first visited me, in Isleta, he knew just three words of Tigua. In ten days he could make himself understood by the hour with the Principales in their own unwritten tongue. Of course, this was one secret of his extraordinary success in learning the inner heart of the Indian.[3]

The partnership recognized neither poverty nor

and ankle-deep sands we travailed; no blankets, overcoats, or other shelter; and the only commissary a few cakes of sweet chocolate and a small sack of parched popcorn meal. Our "lodging was the cold ground." When we could find a cave, a tree, or anything to temper the wind or keep off part of the rain, all right. If not, the Open. So I came to love him as well as revere. I had known numerous "scientists" and what happened when they really got Outdoors. He was in no way an athlete—nor even muscular. I was both. . . . But I never had to "slow down" for him. Sometimes it was necessary to use laughing force to detain him at dark where we had water and a leaning cliff, instead of stumbling on through the trackless night to an

[3] *Ibid.* The woman's view is always illuminating. Many years later, Lummis' second wife, Eve, recalled Bandelier. "Just before 1892 he went to Peru on an archaeological expedition for the great financier of New York and chief owner of the *New York Evening Post* and the *Nation*, Henry Villard. It was then, while we were in New Mexico, that I came to know Mr. and Mrs. Bandelier and they were frequent guests in our home. Mr. Bandelier was one of the most brilliant men I ever met; at times he was very cheerful and gay, at other times in the depths of despair. At one time, when things looked black, he threatened suicide and friends had to come to his rescue. But frequently he loved to jest and I can still hear him pretending to make love to the Pueblo Indian girl who in those days used to bring water to the house from the Rio Grande in a jar balanced on her head.

" 'Oh, Juana,' Bandelier would say, '*Como te amo!* How I love you! I love with all my heart, with all my soul, with all my body. . . .' At this point the love making threatened to become slightly warm and we would have to break it off. Fortunately Juana did not take him seriously and merely giggled.

"Bandelier was exceedingly learned and to hear him talk of the Indians of America was an intellectual treat. His wife was the domestic type, an excellent housekeeper. Dinner at their home in Santa Fe was something to remember. However, Bandelier longed for more intellectual companionship and was easily dazzled by brilliant women. Friends said this marriage was not a very happy one because it had been made by parents in Switzerland. . . . In Peru the first Mrs. Bandelier died and Bandelier married a beautiful and cultured young woman of Lima. . . . The new wife translated the story of the Spanish explorer, Cabeza de Vaca."

discouragement. Bandelier's absolute scientific maturity was a perfect balance for Lummis' enthusiasm. Joined by a common devotion to truth, they made a study of ancient Spanish documents that gave light on hitherto unknown points of Southwestern history. They pored over the autographs of El Morro. Together they solved one of its most puzzling inscriptions, that of the Lujan expedition, garbled by previous translators. They examined and cross-questioned Henry, the young Carlisle Indian, on many phases of Pueblo lore. They explored some of the least known and most hidden ruins of the territory.

We had come pretty deep into the suspicious confidence with which he was testing me before Bandelier said to me one day, "I think we will go and look up the Tyuonyi. My 'brother' Jose Hilario Montoya of Cochití, where I lived for two years, says he will take me there—to the home of his forefathers, the cradle of the Cochití."

This thrilled me. The Tyuonyi (better known by the Spanish name of Rito de los Frijoles) is the most historic of the tremendous cañons which cut the Jemez plateau into wedges or "potreros." The Jemez itself teems with clues to early Southwestern man. Among them are the first homesteads settled by pre-Columbian man after he had left his Plains brethren and migrated west to form another branch of Indian civilization.

I spent all my spare money on 5 x 8 photographic plates and carefully prepared my waterproof sheepskin-lined knapsack for the big camera.

We went in an old army ambulance as far as the Cañada, where we took to Shank's Mare—Bandelier with his heavy portfolio of notes and ground plans, his transit and other surveying materials and I with my camera outfit.

The Jemez plateau is one of the most romantic corners of our new world. More than seven thousand feet above the prairie, it is slit . . . with cañons pillared by strange columnar cliffs from 1000 to 2500 feet high. Pines and cedars frame vistas of violent drops and sudden changes. Dotted over certain of its cliffs are the homes of the cave dwellers.

Our first stop was at the Cueva Pintada (Painted Cave), a big natural hollow in the tufa cliff. It was a shrine of deep importance to these aboriginals and of

long antiquity. Here as well as in the ruins adjacent, Bandelier and I surveyed and measured and photographed and made ground plans.

At the Potrero de las Vacas we found the ruins not only of a great pueblo on its summit but infinitely more important, the Mountain Lions of Cochití—two of the only four Zoomorphs in North America above Mexico. Around them was their almost unique enclosure of tufa slabs—about the only Stonehenge we have.

It was hot, our loads were heavy and the climbing heavier yet as we made our way up 1000 foot cliffs, trudging across mesas, descended into wild cañons, across and up other cliffs. But we were happy as schoolboys. The dry wine of the high air filled us down to our diaphragms and everywhere the eye rejoiced with noble beauty.

On the last (or next to last) Potrero it was as though we had struck a miniature valley of the rocs—the whole mesa-top was several inches deep with calcite crystals which glittered in the sun like diamonds. Except for the agate and jasper chips of the Petrified Forest of Arizona, I have never trodden a page so remindful of Revelations.

The Tyuonyi had been familiar to the Indian, of course, for untold ages. But it was unknown to the white man until that day of October 1890, when it was "discovered" to literature and to science by Bandelier and myself.

The blue peaks of the Jemez Range loomed to the left. At our right now and then a glimpse of the Dark Gorge of the Rio Grande. And suddenly we stood on a rim rock and looked full into Tyuonyi!

I have seen many marvels and in this case there was the Balboa thrill besides, but I am sure I never saw a more beautiful picture in all my life. It was well down the afternoon and the light was perfection. At our very feet to the right were the deep shadowy Bocas [Jaws] of the Tyuonyi where its little stream leaps down to the wild gorge of the Rio Grande. At our feet in front and far to the left were virgin pine forests on a steep slope, so that we looked over their heads to see the whole belly of the valley and its northern verge. The north wall surely has no rival in America, if in the world.[4]

4 Lummis, "As I Remember."

The photograph Lummis made of it, probably the first ever taken of the Tyuonyi,[5] shows the mighty cliffs converging to the narrow Bocas, with the far wall perhaps five miles away. In the second picture he caught the amphitheatre of creamy cliffs, the pine-clad mesas, and, though they are two miles or so away, the tiny rabbit warrens of the first Americans of milleniums ago are clearly shown.

That same afternoon we found what Bandelier termed "The Cacique's House," a beautiful domed roof in an angle of the cliff with a tiny "door" at each side. Here we slept that night; blanketless of course but the cave was warm and clean and the tufa rock was plenty soft enough for our accustomed bones.

[5] Tyuonyi is the aboriginal name of the canyon now known as the Rito de los Frijoles, the site of the Bandelier National Monument.

I have always felt that the remains of our greatest Americanist should be brought back from Madrid where he died in March 1914 [Bandelier died in Seville] and made a part of the New Mexico that he really made known to the world.[6] And that his bones should be put, not in the fine Plaza in Santa Fe but in this very House of the Cacique which he gave to Science; and which is now very properly the Bandelier National Monument. I would have him sealed up there with a bronze tablet outside and the date of the first night he slept in that Magic Valley later immortalized in his Delight Makers.[7]

[6] In 1969 the author inquired at the Catholic cemetery in Seville, but no record of Bandelier could be found. Later, the distinguished scholar Ernest J. Burrus, S.J., editor of Bandelier's *History of the Southwest*, which he had discovered in the Vatican's collection of manuscripts, endeavored to locate Bandelier's remains with no greater success.

[7] Lummis, "As I Remember."

15

Exit Dorothea

DR. DOROTHEA, still doing her best to speed her husband's recovery, was writing now with all the cheerfulness that she could muster, sending him his beloved "cheroots" and other little luxuries that he could not afford, sharing the humorous episodes of her practice, and keeping him in touch with the *Times*. "Bates [the telegraph operator] absolutely wails over the state of things. 'The reporters mean well but they sit around and watch for a scoop or a big sensation and when Lummis was here they were out getting it.'"

However, the time finally came when she felt she could no longer go on with a marriage which had brought her so much suffering, and she so informed him. Apparently the emotional shock brought on another attack of his peculiar malady.

Lummis was taken to the Catholic hospital in Santa Fe. He was bedridden for many days, unable even to speak and in the most serious condition he had been in since the original attack in Los Angeles.

Once again Dorothea, with her infinite patience, gave up her practice and came to New Mexico to take care of him. Presently he recovered to the extent that she could move him to an adobe house. He dragged himself around, fighting his weakness and slowly recovering.

The one consolation during this period was that he was able to write. In one month he produced three short stories, twelve poems, and scores of humorous paragraphs. Afterwards he was able to capitalize on his suffering by writing a book, *My Friend Will*, which was widely used to encourage persons afflicted with similar ailments. One of the many persons who was helped by the book was Edward Marshall, a war correspondent whose spine was paralyzed by a bullet at Las Guasimas. According to Lummis,

While he was obeying the doctors and dying as they advised, someone gave him My Friend Will, *"just meantime." But then he said, "Lord, if that duffer out there in New Mexico could do it—so can I." And he did. He wrote to me later: "That story saved my life." But that is a generous mistake. Marshall saved it. Anyone else could not do it for him.*[1]

This latest illness wiped from his mind all the Spanish songs that he had taken such pains to collect. But as he rode out into the air of Santa Fe, Lummis often found the melodies coming back to him. One day, months after he had lost the power of speech, he was riding up the north fork of the Santa Fe Canyon humming "Me es preciso el despedirme." Suddenly he heard himself singing the words.

As soon as Lummis was well enough to take care of himself, Dorothea went back to her disrupted practice. He went back to Isleta. They realized that their marriage could no longer be patched up and that this was really the end. Neither was happy about it.

He dramatized his adversities:

I have to ask no courtesies of Fate
    Nor plead for quarter at her reeking hands
The only fate am I; and soon or late
    It is and must be but myself that stands.[2]

He had come to a crucial decision—to give up city life and newspaper work. He took his thin savings to Albuquerque, bought a little keg-shaped heater stove and some kitchenware, toted them home in gunny-

---

[1] Lummis, *My Friend Will*, foreword.
[2] *Ibid.*, 37.

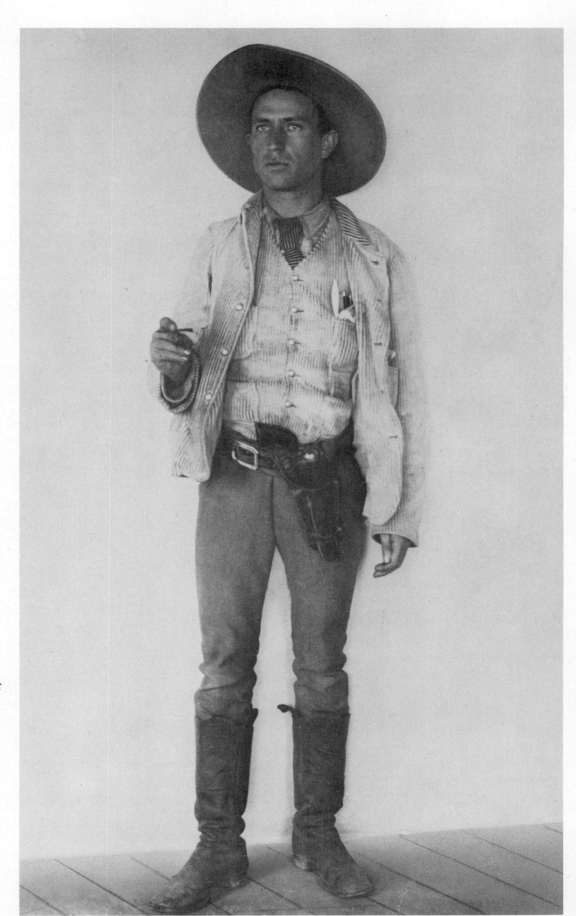

The Southwesterner
—Lummis in 1889.

sacks to Isleta, and settled down in the fall of 1889 to keep house permanently at the pueblo.

His left side was still crippled, Dorothea and he were permanently parted,[3] and he had had to give up his dream of Susana Carmen. Yet he could still say that period of his life was a Good Time.

For at last I had Found Myself. And while there wasn't very much left of me when I first made this finding, it was worthwhile—because it was Mine and it had no collar.

I have never worn a collar since.[4]

He was wearing no man's collar as he wandered on foot and on horseback across the arid face of old New Mexico in search of the legend that had not yet perished. The Old Man of the Sea on his back added zest to the fight, gave odds to the enemy. Whatever came, El Cabezudo would meet and take on with one good hand.

In a photograph of the *pistolero* lighting a cigarette just rolled with that one good hand, a notebook can be seen poking out of the left-hand pocket. This worn notebook is intimate witness to the range of interest of the scribbler. Here are memos on lost mines, outlaws, murders, and jail breaks; detailed instructions for finding forgotten pueblos; indications of the evidence against the Gran Amo, and notes on the history of Indian lands.

There are long lists of colloquialisms: Not enough there to water a hatful of bluebottles, You kin see thet brand afore you kin see the animal, Little by little like the hog et the clothes line. Here are collected Indian words together with Spanish sayings and idioms: Hasta la semana de tres miercoles. Cara de beata y uñas de gata. Por la plata baile el perro, y el gato sirve de guitarrero. Se halla entre la espada y la pared.

Hundreds of witticisms appear in various stages of development. "The river makes its own bed but doesn't have to lie in it" changed to "River takes up its bed and runs" and so brought a dollar from *Puck*. After chewing over "Lot and salt" for a time, Lummis

came up with "The first corner Lot was he who kept his wife in such a pickle that she turned to pure salt," which also went to *Puck*, while "The first salt shake was when Lot left his wife" was awarded to *Life*. We shall never know which publication was benefited by the "Moon never goes out until it's spent its last quarter."

Of course, song is always there and poem. Songs in Spanish garnered from sheep camp and fair lady, verses in Spanish and English, some of which later were published and some of which were fleeting notions that never materialized.

> *Al salir de esta casa*
> *Yo tengo que sentir*
> *La riqueza del acordarme*
> *La tristeza del partir.*
>
> (Camulos, Aug. 24)
>
> *Yo me llevo los recuerdos*
> *Del corazon tan fiel*
> *De los ojos tan divinos*
> *De los labios de miel.*

In the same notebook another scrawl apparently unpublished and clearly unpolished, points up a problem that was frequent with him—to acquire the new without losing the old.

> *Tis seldom to my pillow's swoon*
> *From days whose walks with spectres teem*
> *The dreamland watchers come to croon*
> *And rouse my soul enough to dream.*
>
> *But when they do, I see above*
> *One only vision fair as fire*
> *The sweetest flower that ever love*
> *Forsook to chase a new desire.*
>
> *And when awake I dare to think,*
> *Then desperation dogs my feet*
> *Who spilled for one untasted drink*
> *The truest heart that ever beat.*

Clippings are also pasted in this bug-eaten notebook that was rescued from the leaky attic of "El Alisal" long after El Cabezudo was reduced to ashes. One clipping from the *Albuquerque Citizen*, while clearly not of his pen, was apparently of special interest:

A GRAND RABBIT HUNT—Sunday was a gala day among the Indians of the pueblo of Isleta. At an early hour the stalwart bucks of this tribe began to

---

[3] In 1896, Dr. Dorothea Lummis married Dr. Ernest Carroll Moore, whom she met at Hull House in Chicago. He was later professor of education and director of the University of California at Los Angeles. They had one adopted child. Dorothea died on March 4, 1942.

[4] Lummis, "As I Remember."

gather en masse and in troupes of a dozen or more, proceeded to the mesa lands west of the village, some on horseback, others on burros, while many were on foot, each man and boy armed with from three to five or more short clubs, the only weapon to be used in the grand rabbit hunt, to be inaugurated under the command of the "El Capitan" [sic] of the pueblos, who with face painted in rich carmine hue, was mounted on his fleet broncho charger. . . . Before proceeding to give a detailed account of this grand hunt, THE CITIZEN *must record the great honor conferred upon a young American lady, Miss Eva Doug-las, who was honored by being the Queen of the day's festivities—bright, intelligent and beautiful, as only one developed upon the broad prairies of our western lands, with eyes in whose liquid depths is seen mirrored the purity of a maiden's life. By unanimous consent this fair flower was honored by the half-civilized red men of New Mexico as "Queen of the Day." Not upon a throne, in royal robes arrayed, was there ever a more bewitching or graceful queen than this fair lady, who with the utmost ease and grace, guided her steed over beds of cactus, and the treacherous burrows of prairie dogs or rabbits. . . .*

16

Enter Eve

ALL OF THE DOUGLAS girls were remarkable, each in her own way. Their father had been a locomotive engineer in New England, and he was unable to carry on after his wife died in 1875. Alice, the eldest girl of the nine children, had promised her mother to hold the family together, and this she did, sewing, struggling, and getting some help from the older brothers. Finally her pioneering spirit took her to New Mexico where she married Archibald Rea, the well-educated younger son of an English family, who was then an Indian trader in Isleta.

Eva, or Eve, as her friends called her, was left in Lime Rock, Connecticut, where relatives owned a hotel and the twelve-year-old girl could earn her board by getting up before daybreak to wait tables and make beds all day long. When Alice became established in Isleta, she brought out the two younger sisters, Eve, then sixteen, and Flossie, fifteen.

Eve's schooling was slight, but she was intelligent, ambitious, and studious. At nineteen she spoke Spanish and the Tigua dialect. When the local padre saw inroads being made into his flock by a Protestant mission school, he decided to revive the Catholic school that had functioned in Isleta off and on since 1709. He hired Eve, an Episcopalian, as teacher.

Eve and Flossie had helped to nurse Lummis after the midnight attempt on his life. He went riding and rabbit shooting with both of them. Flossie's sharp and sometimes caustic wit amused him; Eve was beautiful but she was engaged to the Indian agent at Isleta.

I have often suspected that if it hadn't been for a certain game of croquet I should never have made the alliance which gave me my four beautiful children. I had admiration but no sentimental interest whatever in the Indian Agent's lovely young fiancee. But when one day they tolled me into a game in the rough adobe patio and he mocked my one-armed plight, I Saw Clear—and shot a game that would have beaten an expert. He so thoroughly lost his temper that his lady broke with him at once. Then for the first time it occurred to me that I was Missing Something. I felt I might venture to speak.[1]

It took Eve Douglas aback to be wooed by the venerable Mr. Lummis. Why, he was thirty-one! Besides, he was very poor, and though he was handsome, "famous," and had a remarkable mind and an almost legendary glamour, he was still married. Yet he did offer an escape from the tiny Indian village into a new and exciting literary world.

True to their compact Lummis told Dr. Dorothea of his new hope. Again she agreed to a divorce, again she counselled and encouraged him when he was downhearted. She even invited Eve to visit her.

Charlie Lummis and Eva Frances Douglas were married in March, 1891. Their honeymoon was a horseback trip of many hundreds of miles. In forgotten pueblos where centuries ago brown men and women had faced new lives together, among ancient ruins that he and Bandelier had explored, they shared the thrill of discovery in this world so unlike her native Connecticut. In his poems of the period one can trace the joys of their campfire meals, of the nights they slept out on the ground under the New Mexico stars.[2]

When they came to the Chaves home, Don

[1] Lummis, "As I Remember."
[2] Lummis, "A Frontier Bridal," A Bronco Pegasus, 71.

Eve Douglas, aged eighteen, at Isleta, New Mexico Territory.

Amado, in the manner of the grandee, ordered an-other roundup of wild horses and offered the bride her choice. Lummis picked a three year old and broke it for Eve "with much difficulty for it was a striker, striking with its forefeet in a way that would have disembowelled a bear. But he was a beautiful creature and very bright." Lummis named him Adán, Spanish for Adam, Eve's beast.[3]

In his diary for March 31, 1891, Lummis wrote, "Estoy enteramente feliz por la primera vez" ("I am entirely happy for the first time").

It was during the honeymoon that "the great thing happened." On July 5, 1891, they were in Bernalillo visiting Dr. and Mrs. Lund, lifelong friends. Eve was

kneeling beside him, and he was stroking her hair when she saw him change color. He was stroking her hair with the left arm that for three years and seven months had been paralyzed. He suddenly realized that he was able to use his arm again.

In two adobe rooms of Juan Rey Abeita, they took up housekeeping in Isleta. Often they had not enough to make tomorrow's meal. But what had that to do with happiness?

We never felt "abused." We knew perfectly well that many people in many places had comforts we hadn't, but we had comfort inside ourselves, intrinsic, unlacking, inalienable as long as we depended on it. The less Eve and I had, the more we valued—the better our sense of proportion. Above all we had (unknowing) our superiority to outer needs.[4]

[3] Alas, poor Adán! He finally became addicted to loco weed, and it was necessary to give him the only known cure—a bullet in the head.

[4] Lummis, "As I Remember."

Eve with her pupils at the Pueblo Indian Church and Mission School, Isleta, New Mexico Territory, 1889.

Probably no woman he ever loved could have lived a lifetime with his restless spirit. But his marriage to Eva Douglas was the nearest he was ever to come to happiness in his home life.

In his diary for 1892, at the top of the page for June 9, he has written in blue pencil and capital letters the word *BABY*. Below, in Spanish, "At 7:30 Eva delivers a woman of 8½ pounds who shall bear the blessed name of Dorothea."

The whole pueblo rejoiced. The Indians loved Eva as well as "Por Todos." She had come close to them all when she taught their children in the church school. Over sixty years later they breathed her name in a way that showed how she stood in their thoughts, "*Ahhh, Ee-va!*"

When her baby was born, the Isleteños took their dimes and quarters and dollars to Jose Martín the silversmith to pound into rings and bracelets and cups and necklaces for the *mujercita*.

Perhaps the most outstanding woman in Isleta was Doña Marcelina Abeita. She asked to be the new baby's godmother. This meant giving up all temporal matters, including the running of her busy store. She

had to fast for four days, even from water. On the morning of the fifth day, in the blue light before the yellow light of the sun, she was "shown" her godchild's name—Tur-be-sé, Rainbow of the Sun.

In the years that followed, Lummis made that child his close companion. He took her with him for thousands of miles of travel, took her where no white child had ever been. In his New England way he tried to give her the best of all that he was.

In 1891 the Bandeliers were living in Santa Fe. Lummis had frequent conferences on science and Indian lore with the historian and copied old Spanish manuscripts for him. Unexpectedly one day Bandelier said, "We will go to Peru. . . . We will find the money. . . . I have proved you, you will do."

I have always felt that it was the highest tribute ever paid me by civilized man when he chose me for his lieutenant and companion. . . . I felt very humble. Still I felt very clear. I didn't want to be made a scientist. . . . I felt it wasn't my best service to science. I said to him:

"What you need, what the science of man needs

71

A gathering at Isleta. From left to right: Archibald Rea; Frederick O. Douglas; Bonnie Kemmerle Douglas; Flossie Douglas holding Louis Douglas; M. C. Williams, an Indian agent; Charles Lummis, just in from a sheep camp; Alice Douglas Rea; a Mexican friend; an unidentified child; Eve Douglas; Benito Jojola; and his wife, Maria.

now, is not so much more students, nor more scientific societies run by Latin professors nor even more devoted souls toiling and starving to investigate—but an audience. What I should like as my part is to say to the world: 'Look, don't be scared! All these Greek words are harmless. All these Ologies are only the story of man—of you and me—carried back five or ten thousand years. And it's fun.' "

It was my thought then (a hundredfold proved now) that if we could give back to that perennial story the humanness that belongs to it, a million Americans would understand where one understands now, and the epoch-making research now buried in sacrosanct reports for a few Bostonians would become not merely history but part of the consciousness of America.[5]

Bandelier accepted the idea with enthusiasm, rising to embrace Lummis. They immediately began to work on plans for financing the expedition, which developed into one of the most memorable of their lives.

This was also the beginning of a campaign that lasted almost forty years as Lummis carried on his crusade to simplify and popularize archaeology,

[5] Ibid.

Eve and Turbesé Lummis.

Turbesé Lummis, 1898.

ethnology, and related "ologies." In his writing and through work with libraries, museums, and scientific societies, he attacked intellectual pomposity, sometimes with the ferocity of De Bergerac slashing at "bloated and pompous Silliness."

At a meeting of the second Pan American Scientific Congress, held in Washington, D.C., December 27, 1915 to January 8, 1916, Lummis delivered an address of some three thousand words entitled "Humanizing the Sciences of Man." Gently tugging at the scholarly beards of his distinguished colleagues, he reproved them for their traditional concealment of knowledge from those to whom Greek was not the natural language.

. . . Human nature is natural. The study of it is natural. When it is done naturally there is no living person who cannot be made interested in it. . . .

The old fakir spirit of the ancient medicine man who had to impose on his followers by using some empiric knowledge to make his living has, of course, disappeared from all really scientific circles. But his mystery, his obfuscation of mere humans by cabalistic words and phrases, and by due solemnity—that has not disappeared. The words that science uses are enough to scare a child and freeze the interest of the average intelligent, God-fearing grownup.

At a field meeting of one of the foremost anthropological activities in America, a ribald member of the managing committee, after some days' sessions, sang at the campfire:

Our mental range is the whole exchange;
We're the craniological IT!
'Twould drive Hrdlicka[6] to Wilson's Whiskey
For a nomenclature to fit.
The scare words fly both fast and high,
We're the polysyllabical crew;
For we're megalocephalous,
Hydro-acephalous,
And dolichocephalous, too.

[6] Ales Hrdlicka, curator, Division of Physical Anthropology, Smithsonian Institution, Washington, D.C., from 1910 to 1942.

Science means knowing. Knowing what? Incantations, formulas, abracadabras, Greek words, mystery, condescension? Not on your life. Science is knowing how to live. . . . Greek is like swearing. It has its place and the place of either is not in the kindergarten.

Unfortunately the music to the song was not included in the published report, but there is little doubt as to the identity of the "ribald member."

17

Peru

ONLY a visionary such as Adolph Bandelier would have dreamed of an expedition to South America when penniless, without backers or prospects. Early in January, 1892, Lummis and Bandelier went to New York to seek financial support. Often Bandelier did not have the money to pay his hotel bill or buy a meal. Lummis, who at that particular time happened to have some money, shared his. He fed Bandelier, encouraged him, and bought him an overcoat.

Bandelier had neither the front nor the gall to be a promoter. He spent weeks of heartbreaking labor before that day when he came back with the almost unbelievable news that he had won a promise of $7,500 a year from Henry Villard, builder of the Northern Pacific Railroad. Bandelier and I had a hugging match that day![1]

But a strange thing had happened to Lummis, the incorrigible wanderer. He could not bring himself to leave his young wife even to go to South America. Finally Bandelier consented to let her go along. Then at the last moment he sent word that there would not be enough money. Moreover he considered the trip unsafe for a woman and child.

It was a hard choice. On the one hand to leave my wife and baby for three years with visits of but two months each year. On the other hand the chance of a lifetime—at least of mine. . . . I sweat blood, thinking it out. My family was very dear to me. But Eve was of the blood of the Black Douglas. She was brave and sure that I must go. And so in the autumn of 1892 when the baby was four months old, I installed my little family in modest quarters on Hill Street in Los Angeles and set out on the expedition.[2]

The Villard Expedition departed in October, 1892, on the little steamship *San Jose*, arriving in Lima, Peru, on November 21. Lummis' diary mirrors his enjoyment of the trip, the beauty of the sea and shore, the excitement of storms, and the charm of the road steads where they went ashore to wander through the markets and listen to Spanish songs.

Soon they were ready to explore the ruins of Surco, Chorríllos, and Pachacamac. Arriving at the inn, called *tambo* in Peru, they found the natives asleep. It was a long time before they could get a meal of wine, four chunks of bread, and a little cheese.

The tambo is an L-shaped "building" of bamboos stuck into the ground and thatched, about as open as chicken wire. But it gives a shade from the sun. In my "room" which is about 20 by 40, there are many hundreds of skulls, about 20 hens and all the fleas in the world. These never bite me but actually make a procession of me, promenading up one leg and down the other until I am literally black and have a crawly feeling that makes sleep impossible. . . .

The tambo is about a half mile from the foot of the hill of the ruins which cover several hundred acres, its huge adobe walls still standing unbreached in this rainless climate. In the big valley at the center of the ruins is a big cemetery of probably millions. At any rate the interments are four tiers deep, the lowest being about 35 feet below the surface. It is in those that we work. We sink a shaft down past the other

[1] Lummis, "As I Remember."

[2] *Ibid.*

The Tambo de los Huesos, an inn for weary travelers, 1893. Photograph by Charles Lummis. (*Courtesy Southwest Museum*)

three tiers of graves, then "drift" just as in mining.[3]

In his *Gold Fish of Gran Chimú*, Lummis describes the operation, even to the dust.

It is an awful thing, that dust of the mummy-miners . . . dust the like of which is nowhere else in the world. One might say that it has been drying out since Time Began. . . . through milleniums of drouth and tropic sun the Peruvian sands have been steadily baking; and in the ruins . . . is a dust drier yet—the dust to which we return . . . literally humanity turned to powder. . . . Because of this extraordinary dryness . . . articles under these ruins are so marvelously preserved that one can wear today a bit of lace that was buried beside a Yunca mummy before the time of Alfred the Great. . . . The square leagues of ruins had

broken out with something like an eruption of dust geysers. Look whichever way one would, little clouds were puffing up so thickly that at fifty feet above the earth they united in a great canopy which quite hid the sun and turned the landscape from its ashen grey to a curious smoky yellow. . . . The dust puffs flew up and now and then a spade flashed above the surface; but in that strange soil there was no sound of digging. Only now and then a faint voice seemed to exhale from the underground or there was a husky cough.[4]

Every few moments the young *cientifico* would leap down from an adobe parapet and bend over a hole that was belching its dust cloud. "Give me."

Then a grimy hand would come up from below, holding a pottery vase or a metal mace-head . . . which

[3] *Ibid.*

[4] Charles F. Lummis, *Gold Fish of Gran Chimú*, 58, 38, 41.

Pachacamac, Peru, December, 1892. The Castillo, with graves in the foreground. Photograph by Charles Lummis. (*Courtesy Southwest Museum*)

he would stow in the big pockets of his horsehide coat or in the red alforja *over his shoulders. . . . Now he clambers down into the stifling dust of a shaft to make a diagram of the position of some mummy—or the construction of a peculiar burial chamber . . . or to make a "flashlight" of an unusual find before it should be disturbed in the bed where it had slumbered for ages.[5]*

The Gold Fish or legendary *Pez Grande* was the priceless ransom of Atahualpa for which many other *huaqueros* ("mummy miners") were searching. For certain this was where it was buried! Had not a *Pez Chico* worth nearly three hundred thousand dollars been found here in the 1500's, making its owner the richest man in Peru? So it was that the explorers had

to contend with the venal politics and the changing laws of Latin America, the mummy dust, and the danger of collapse of untimbered tunnels, but also with other *huaqueros*, who threatened them with covert or open violence.

Since it was not for buried hordes of gold that the Villard Expedition was searching, but for an understanding of the life of an ancient civilization, uncovering the burials provided the most exciting moments. The laborers would lift from a pit a shape like a big carboy, enclosed in a wickerwork of woven rushes. The jacket was split and husked off. Beneath would be fifty yards of white wrappings, woven more than five hundred years before Columbus set foot in the Americas. Under the wrappings were brilliant fabrics of rich design and a strange carved wooden face with reddish hair, the identification mask by

[5] *Ibid.*, 42.

A burial niche at Pachacamac, Peru, December, 1892. Photograph by Charles Lummis. (*Courtesy Southwest Museum*)

which the departed was to be recognized on his arrival in the other world. The mummy was laid out according to Indian beliefs, in the posture of the unborn fetus: knees drawn up to the chin, bony hands clasped about the knees, head bowed as if in thought. The long hair, stained red by the nitre in the soil, might be surmounted by a tall plume of thin gold and a headdress of parrot feathers, and an ironwood comb might be found in the lap. Clearly by the quality of the inner wrappings, by some intangible dignity and power that still surrounded the mummy, this would have been some chieftan of Peru—one who perhaps helped to mould her history. Each time that the thousand-year-old ceremonial wrappings were removed from a mummy there was the same special excitement.

Many finds were made near the Temple of the Sun in Tiahuanaco. From this temple Pizarro had long since removed the golden image of the sun and had

shod his horses with silver because there was no iron. The explorers acquired a unique drinking cup of horn carved with the figure of the alligator deity holding up by its headdress the decapitated head of an old man.[6] There were thirty arrow points from Tiahuanaco and one from Pachacamac, proving that the Incas did use the bow and arrow. Again at Pachacamac they found the ironwood beam of a prehistoric balance, the first to be identified in Inca culture. Then there were bronzes that established the Inca knowledge of casting, soldered hollow silver fetishes, and many other treasures of archaeology.

Despite some harassment from professional mummy miners and politicians, Lummis was able to say of the people:

Everybody nice, including the [native] girls at the

[6] This item is now at the Southwest Museum and is still controversial. See Hasse von Winning, "A Carved Bone from Tiahuanaco," *Masterkey* (October–December, 1972), 24–36.

Archaeological finds at Pachacamac, Peru: a mummy, its envelope, a jar, and a mask. Photograph by Charles Lummis. (*Courtesy Southwest Museum*)

Tambo, whose only dolls, society, accomplishment and amusement is to wander up to the diggings, pick over the discarded skulls, select some of women with especially fine hair and then spend about a week combing out the abundant silken tresses. . . .

The key that will unlock Spanish America is not Yankee inventiveness, not Yankee Drive, gifted machines nor the ability to boss. It is not even Yankee money. It is the Human Touch. In all my years I have known of no tangle so knotty, no request so far-reaching, that a favorable answer could not be reached by the exercise of courtesy, the Spanish language and a real warmth of human feeling. As a mild example, the amiable captain of the port at Puno got me through the custom house with bare lifting of the lid of one of my many trunks. This sort of thing happened to me not once but many times while other passengers stood about chewing cigars, cursing in-

audibly or attempting to get through with bulldozery or a bribe.

It is so obvious and easy a lesson I have never gotten over my amazement at the blindness of us of the north who send to represent us in the southern republics men who know neither the language nor the literature and do not even have the grace of simpatía. No wonder we hold such crude ideas of Latin America and that we have such diplomatic problems. . . .

In spite of Bandelier's genius for making friends and my Latin sympathies, it was not all plain sailing for the pure and remote cause of Science. The whole of Peru was pimpled with a revolution under the surface. One of the most characteristic sounds of the day was the rattle of shots and the famous cry, "Cierra puertas!" (Close your doors!) as certain revolutionistas were hunted down and potted by whatever faction was then in power.

The bones of Pizarro, photographed by Lummis at Lima, Peru, in 1893. (*Courtesy Southwest Museum*)

It was constantly necessary for Bandelier and myself to steer our way through underground politics, to exercise the most delicate diplomacy in a country whose social condition was as touchy as a boil.

I wanted Bandelier to let me walk over the Andes to Cuzco, with a pack mule for my camera and belongings. It was about 300 miles of nearly impossible country but he had seen me in the Bad Lands before and it was not the physical danger and hardship which balked him. His hesitation was for political and diplomatic reasons. He set me to packing for the New York Museum of Natural History the finds he had made at Pachacamac.[7]

Not being able to hike over the Andes, Lummis carried his five-by-eight-inch view camera everywhere

that there was the possibility of a picture. He was particularly pleased when he was permitted to take the first pictures ever allowed of the mummy of Francisco Pizarro, conqueror of Peru. Previously no one had even been permitted to sketch the case in which Pizarro lies.

One evening in Arequipa he experienced his first South American earthquake.

In about two seconds there were a thousand people in the narrow street between the one-story buildings. There was no screaming or crying, even from the children, though some had been grabbed by the hair or the feet and dragged out of their homes. Everybody was kneeling in the center of the street praying and quietly telling their beads. The shock went on rocking, not for seconds, but for several minutes.

[7] Lummis, "As I Remember."

And when it was safely over, the street suddenly cleared as a fog in the Grand Cañon.[8]

For the sake of his wife and baby, Lummis was determined to get everything possible out of his salary. "In order to save a sol a day," he refused to move to a better room in the Hotel Maury. "Also I am not going to drink wine." But there were three things he could not give up even for them—cigars, archaeological trophies, and bullfights!

An impassioned aficionado of this duel between skill and death, the Yanqui fan went to every *corrida de toros* for which his conscience would let him squeeze out the price of admission. He followed the outstanding *toreros* of the day, became acquainted with some, and after some thought, turned down an offer to take up the hazardous profession. Anxious as he was to get together enough money for a home for his family, that did not seem a practical approach.

His scientific conscience forced him to turn down another offer. The *Century Magazine* had contracted with him for a series of articles on discoveries made in South America. They were to pay him four hundred dollars an article, more money than he usually made in a year. But when he found that "instead of the scientific truths Bandelier and I were discovering and proving, *Century* wanted sensational 'Lost Races' and 'Buried Cities' and 'Lands of Dwarfs' and all that sort of yellow trash, I promptly cancelled the contract."[9]

There was also time for a trip over the Andes on the new railroad, the Peruvian Central, completed on January 11, 1883. Nothing like it in the world existed at that time. The road rose 15,600 feet and went through fifty-six tunnels. Lummis had a special genius with railroad men, from section hands to presidents, and soon he was in a private car, setting out at daybreak to get pictures of the Verrugas Bridge, then the highest in the world. His interest in the bridge, however, was tempered by the common belief that the waters of the Verrugas River caused goiter.

Very noble structure—from New Jersey. Red hot day and I wanted a drink of the sparkling Agua de Verrugas. Indeed, not to be scared by old women's stories

8 *Ibid.*
9 *Ibid.*

The Verrugas Bridge, along which the Peruvian Central Railroad ran. Photograph by Charles Lummis. (*Courtesy Southwest Museum*)

that the waters of this crystal icy brooklet caused goiters I had vowed to do so.

I clambered down the 500 foot precipitous cañon wall to the shallow, brawling Rimac. But just as I set down the camera to stoop for a drink an Indian came toiling up from below and I started—for he seemed to have two heads on his shoulders. The other head was a goiter nearly as large as his real head, growing out of his neck back of the ear and resting on his shoulder. He had a sort of a saucer shaped pad for it, so that it wouldn't roll and tug at the ligament. I greeted him with Indian courtesy and asked him about the brook, and the stories he told me about its effect and about the mortality among the laborers who built the bridge were fearful. As a matter of fact there is a whole cemetery in Lima for the victims of the Verrugas Bridge and its innocent looking brooklet. Later I visited the little Indian hamlet on the Rimac above where the poisoned water comes in, and there I found that about half the adult inhabitants had goiters all the way from walnut to coconut size or even larger.[10]

Lummis' fascination of the expedition was almost overshadowed by his loneliness. He realized that he had changed to the point that he would rather be at home than in Peru alone, despite all the interest and possible fame. The thousand or so words a day that he wrote to Eve describing in detail every scene and event were interspersed with passionate outbursts of love and loneliness.[11] He considered every possibility, but at last he threw himself on Bandelier's understanding. Bandelier had lost his own wife a few months before and generously consented to let Lummis bring his family to Lima. It was agreed that he should wait until fall when the climate would be less dangerous. But two nights later, as he wrote in his diary: "Unable to stand it any longer I call B. at 11:30 and tell him that I have to go to Eve now. He is very kind and very just and promises to arrange everything for me. I pack until 2:30 in the morning."

When Charlie Lummis had married Eve Douglas, he had supposed that they would always be "hand to mouth paupers" without a home of their own. With the Peruvian expedition and its salary of fifteen hundred dollars a year, he dared to believe for the first time that he might give his family something better than rooms in a lodging house.

[10] *Ibid.*
[11] At the same time he was writing Eve, Lummis was also writing frequently and affectionately to Dorothea. In a letter begun January 4, 1893, and ending January 9, Lummis wrote about four thousand words to her, mainly justifying his trip to Peru and asking advice. "I couldn't go on forever filling the public with New Mexico and Arizona: I could feel that my rope there was about at an end. With my sharply limited capacity—a gift of the magic lantern, the power to make others see what I see but utterly without the imagination and the creative—my pen is very little good without my legs. I must run and see or I've got nothing to write about.... And above all, please tell me what I ought to do next. You are the only one who can advise me, whose advice I value."

Back again in the bright warmth of family life, Lummis soon realized that he could not after all expose his wife and baby to the dangers of the tropics. He would again have to steel himself to leave them behind. But at least he told himself, they would have a home. It took courage to make the down payment of $298, almost all the money they had. It was necessary to sell many of their cherished curios.

Fifteen Forester Avenue was a stiff clapboard cottage of the nineties, with gewgaws a later generation found comical. Lummis saw it with the eyes of a man who had waited over thirty years for a home of his own. He recorded each step of the cleaning and painting, the selling of the treasures to buy needed furnishings, the unpacking and arranging, and of the crowning day when he and his family went in the front door and began living in "our house."

The Forester Avenue cottage had an aroma of its own. In the cellar was the fragrance of Indian blue corn bread, of preserved and brandied fruits, and the pungent ingredients of Spanish-American cookery. Upstairs the house smelled of photographer's chemicals and of the mothballs in which he jealously preserved his Indian blankets and vicuña skins.

Lummis spent almost as much time making room for his curios as for his family. Inca fabrics (woven long before Leif Ericson went forth on his voyages), obsidian knives, petrified wood, mysterious fetishes —he gave each one its considered place. He knew when one had been meddled with, too!

Two months after his return to Los Angeles, the baby took her first steps to his knee. The day after, he had to go back to Peru. On June 24, 1893, Lummis wrote in his diary: "We leave the house at 7:15. Eve companions me to the depot ... Que triste adios, y si nunca volviera ["How sad a farewell and if I never return"].

Yet with all the loneliness and exasperation, he could not leave the Villard Expedition, one of the most glowing experiences of his life. Never again would he have the opportunity to roam among the marvels of Peru and Bolivia where "every day and every hour brings me some new wonder, some new beauty."

Bandelier, genius and scholar that he was, did not always function on the practical plane. Once when Lummis returned to Lima low in funds and wholly dependent on the check that Bandelier had promised to leave for him, he was assured that no money at all had been left. After a panicky search the check was found, one thousand soles (then five hundred dollars) lying around in an unaddressed envelope.

Just before setting out for some explorations in Bolivia, Lummis learned that Bandelier had been taken prisoner in Cajamarca on suspicion, strangely enough, of being a Pieroist spy, the Pieroists being the political "outs" at that moment. That a man so innocent of political entanglements and so valuable to science should have his important researches stopped by "the stupid burros of that city" was galling. But there was nothing Lummis could do.

Early in September, 1893, Lummis took the first leg of his journey to Mollendo, Peru,

. . . the worst port in the world serving a great interior. No steamer ever comes nearer than three miles from the "wharf" (we were five) and the wharf itself was a thing of less area than a good-sized colonial house. It was a mild day when we landed, but the swell was such that our thirty-foot launch was at first 25 feet below the wharf, and then swooped up level with it, when we had to jump like wildcats to land before the boat went down again. Imagine landing baggage! Also Women! More serious, they cannot land oil and while the railroad from Lima to Cerro de Pasco had the first oil burning locomotives in the new world, the Peruvian Southern still has to burn moss and llama dung.[12]

From Mollendo it was a seven-hour ride to Arequipa at the foot of the nineteen-thousand-foot living volcano, the Misti. Here Lummis took lodging in the Grand Hotel Central, an old monastery. The architectural influence of this building and of a flying staircase he discovered tramping through the city are evident in the home he later built in Los Angeles and in the design of the Southwest Museum. He had other experiences, too.

In Arequipa I became acquainted with a certain neighborly local custom. My door gave on the narrow street. . . . Every evening for some nights until I got a bad reputation as unsociable, there would come a gentle knock at the door. There stood a nice young

Lummis on his Peruvian travels.

lady in a rebozo ["shawl"] who would relate in gentle voice and well chosen words some tale of woe. For observe you, Senor, her mother was consumingly ill, they had no money to buy her medicine and "if your Grace could minister to our needs, it is I who will know how to reciprocate." Truly a more delicate way of putting it than I have known some of us of the north to employ.[13]

From Arequipa to Puno among the lofty peaks,

---

[12] Lummis, "As I Remember."

[13] *Ibid.*

Lummis went across Lake Titicaca to the Desaguadero where the lake discharges and where

I secured two mules and an arriero, the lovable, stupid, loyal Andresito de Lanza.[14] He cinched my steamer 'trunks, big camera, tripod and plate box on one mule. I stepped up on the other, and with Andres trotting along behind the cargo, I rode at will the thirty miles to mystic Tiahuanaco. That was the first home and perhaps the birthplace of the Incas. The name itself is a corruption of Tiari Huanaco, meaning "sit thee down, Huanaco."

Here at Tiahuanaco I was fortunate enough to see the wonderful dance of the cannibal Chunchos, with their 6-foot headdress of reed with crane plumes worn like a dancer's skirt inverted, stuffed foxes hanging over their backs. The dance, in honor of the Exaltation, is held in the churchyard of the Catholic temple built of the heathen carved stone of the Incas. I took many photographs of the ruins with their monoliths of from 60 to 200 tons each. Another photograph was of the old woman of the Tambo, a mass of wrinkles, and withered dugs that hung below her belt. . . .

There was much measuring and exploring to do in addition to the photographing. The trip to Laja, 7½ leagues in as many hours, was hard but handsome; the whole valley, highly cultivated and the wonderful Snowy Range ever present. . . .

We met hundreds of Indians driving their flocks of burros and llamas. Playing their flutes and Pan's pipes, they were strumming their little mandolins of armadillo shells. The women, walking along too, spinning as they went, would give their spinning sticks a twist, let them drop to the bottom of their short skirts, then deftly catch them up again for a new twist. And here where the white man had hardly breath to live, much less to talk, both sexes kept up a constant chorus of their mournful Yaravies. The whole family or group trudged sometimes all day thus singing, spinning, and tending the herd.

Planning to climb the 26,000 foot Illimani, the highest of the new world's peaks, I called upon and held conference with the U.S. Minister Grant who courteously advised me in my arrangements for the ascent. Got ropes for that terrific climb, Bolivian, ex-quisitely braided, light and of great strength. Engaged my Indians and made all arrangements. Characteristically enough the Indians came too late on the first day, and when I appointed another day they came but disappeared. When they turned up it was again too late to start. So as it fell out, I did not get my trip to Illimani, for word came from Bandelier recalling me from Bolivia.[15]

According to his diary, that September Lummis covered 1330 miles, made seventy-four photographs, sent off sixty-five letters totalling over fifty thousand words, and despatched thirty-two packages.

Bandelier had not explained his reason for recalling me, nor did I find any explanation when I reached Arequipa. When word came at last it was to tell me that Henry Villard was "busted." This meant our contract with him was void. We would lose almost two years of exploration. What little money Bandelier had would last less than ten weeks. The work could not go on. No more hunting for the treasure of the ages, no voyages such as we had planned down the mysterious Amazon, no more of the scientific discoveries and conquests we had dreamed. We would have to give up all that, knowing that such opportunity would probably never come again.[16]

In Arequipa days passed without further word from Bandelier, who was still at Cajamarca, more or less under duress. Time after time Lummis went hopefully to the post office or to meet the steamer in Callao. His money ran out; he had to borrow and even pawn his personal effects. Writing stories of South America and reading Spanish-American literature kept him occupied.

Lummis was able to make one last climb, up the nineteen-thousand-foot Misti and down into the crater carrying his view camera. And he had one last fling at trading. For their weight in Peruvian silver soles, then worth fifty cents on the dollar in gold, he bought the massive silver spoons of old Inca carving which later figured in many a Lummis banquet. He bought the last two-volume set of the 1723 edition of Garcilaso de la Vega for fifteen soles. Of this he wrote to Eve on September 4, 1893:

---

[14] See Charles F. Lummis, *The Enchanted Burro.*

[15] Lummis, "As I Remember."
[16] *Ibid.*

In 1893, at the end of his stay in Peru, Lummis, carrying his forty pounds of camera equipment, climbed the nineteen-thousand-foot Misti to photograph this crater. (*Courtesy Southwest Museum*)

. . . got the two ancient volumes of Garcilaso de la Vega for $15 (soles). They were written before 1600 but this edition (the 12th) is of 1723. Garcilaso was a Peruvian Indian, well educated, who wrote his Comentarios Reales ostensibly as a purely literary and historical work, but really to make out a claim that he was a descendant of the Incas & therefore induce the Spanish Crown to "do something for him." As you can see that makes him a very partisan, & often false, witness; & his annals of the Incas are not much as history, nor for science. Of course, for instance, a special pleader on his position did not wish a Catholic King to believe that the Incas (his alleged ancestors) were the brutal idolaters they were; & he tried to make out that they believed in the Supreme God, in the cross, &c&c., & that the reports of their gross idolatry and fetichism were slanders.

It is to this precious source that Squier & others owe most of their idiotic credulity in the purity of the Inca religion, the spirituality & unity of their Supreme Essence &c. But when one understands how to take the book, how to put aside its palpable false-hoods & allow for the mercenary aim of the writer it is valuable to any student; & particularly to me, because it has much quaint tradition, tho' confused enough.

But he capped the climax in the deal that

. . . separated that remarkable Jewish dealer, pawn-broker, capitalist and connoisseur of Lima, Jacoby, from the priceless musket of Juan de Soto, six times great grandson of the discoverer of the Mississippi. It was made in 1793 and is a masterpiece of gold wrought on steel by the artificers of Eibar, Spain. I

had to give Jacoby my best-beloved Colt six-gun, my $15 cartridge belt, my $50 camera, and a few other things for it, but even so I got a museum piece worth thousands.[17]

Bandelier was released at last. One November day the two had a reunion. Despite his past silences and periods of forgetfulness, the great Americanist was now all tenderness and understanding. He gave Lummis what was due him, and the next day Lummis was on the way home.

Through all of the years thereafter that experience lay in the storehouse of Lummis' mind like one of Peru's own Inca fabrics, priceless and time defying.

[17] *Ibid.* The musket is now in the possession of the Southwest Museum in Los Angeles.

At a word or even an odor its recollections would rush to his mind: Indians of the Bolivian uplands winding along the brick-red trail playing their Pan's pipes and flutes as they drove their flocks of burros and llamas before them, the carvings of ancient *palacios*, the sandaled natives, the windswept crudity of Peruvian *tambos* where he had sought shelter at night, the awful glory of the cordilleras. Perhaps there was never a time when he could not still feel the Andean gusts in his face and remember the pound in breast and ears as his lungs tried to find their fill in the gasping rarity of skydrawn heights. Even when Lummis became what men call old and would never see equatorial nights again, just by closing his eyes he would feel once more the triumph of wresting the secrets from Inca dust.

18

To the Rescue of the Missions

IN THE far loneliness of Peru it had been a joy to Lummis that his wife and child were in a home of their own. He wrote to Eve:

It comforts me the last thing before I am asleep and first when I awaken. Before it used to be just your faces but now it is your faces set with the dear and beloved little home that is ours. I don't think you have ever dreamed what a desperate hunger I had for a home of our own . . . and it seemed so absolutely hopeless.

The abrupt end of the expedition made prospects of meeting the payment on 15 Forrester Avenue look dim. But he had made a vow: "My wife and baby shall be no vagabonds but people." Everything had to be turned into money—articles, photographs, even cherished curios. So Lummis dickered away with Wilbur Campbell of the Curio Store (then a landmark down on lower Spring Street) or with Mrs. T. S. C. Lowe, wife of the noted Civil War balloonist and scientist who had invented the Mount Lowe railway.

It must have made quite a picture, the slight Lummis and the weighty Mrs. Lowe laying siege to one another! Her shape suggested her husband's fondness for balloons, although she was said to have been a former circus equestrienne. Collecting was a passion with her, and she put into her trading the same grace and verve that must have distinguished her appearance in the ring.

Eve was frail then and undernourished, but her husband set her to printing hundreds of photographs to sell to tourists curious about the bronco-busting explorer, his scenes of the Southwest, and his collec-

tions. Many friends and friends of friends came to the cottage to see the man and his treasures.

Lummis had a remarkable knack of giving life to specimens that had been mouldering for a thousand years and relating them to the human values of all times. The humor of an ancient race was demonstrated by a monkey figurine from Pachacamac that whistled mischievously when water was poured from its spout, and the love of music and beauty was evidenced by the delicately decorated musical instruments. Lummis would show a woven grass basket from Chimbote, Peru, which had been placed by loving hands in the cold lap of a brown mother that she might take up her familiar duties in the next world or, even more poignant, the mummy of a pet parrot buried with its small Incan owner so that she would still have her playmate in the other life. The visitors would depart with a new feeling of kinship for the members of a long-departed race.

Lummis was not long at home, however, before he was called to a new crusade. Shortly after his return from Peru, Miss Tessa L. Kelso, the librarian of the Los Angeles Public Library, turned his attention to the desperate condition of the unoccupied Franciscan missions of southern California. The only ones kept in repair were those still used as churches—San Gabriel, San Buenaventura, and Santa Barbara. San Diego, the "mother mission," San Luis Rey, the Asistencia of Pala, San Juan Capistrano, and San Fernando Rey "were falling to ruin with frightful rapidity, their roofs being breached or gone, the adobe walls melting away under the winter rains."

Miss Kelso had gathered together a number of women who had raised money to continue repairs begun by the body of priests at San Luis Rey. She

Lummis, Turbesé, and the sacristan at San Juan Capistrano, 1899.

urged Lummis to head this work. When in 1894 he was at last able to do so, he found that there were few who felt as he did—that these missions meant more to California, even in cold cash, than all her fabulous gold mines.

It seems incredible now what uphill work it was to arouse any interest whatever in this cause. In the first place a tidal wave of the thrice-damned APA[1] (precursor of the Ku Klux Klan) had swept over even California and religious bigotry (on one side) was intense. Absurd as it seems, it is a literal fact that thousands of otherwise sane business men and citizens in Los Angeles firmly believed that the Catho-lics were drilling every night in the basement of the Cathedral to rise and massacre the Protestants. The fact that the cathedral had no basement cut no figure at all. Thousands of less credulous persons joined in saying, "The Catholic church owns those old Missions, don't it? Let the Catholic church take care of them!"[2]

To this kind of thinking Lummis answered: "Those mighty piles belong not to the Catholic church but to you and to me, and to our children and the world. They are monuments and beacons of Heroism and Faith and Zeal and Art. Let us save them—not for the Church but for Humanity."[3]

[1] American Protective Association.

[2] Lummis, "As I Remember."
[3] *Ibid.*

To carry out this dream Lummis organized a club and invented a name for it; it was the first of the many Landmarks Clubs in the United States. He undertook the project with a characteristic explosion of energy, sparing neither himself nor his family. If at times the larder at 15 Forrester Avenue ran low, it was because he felt that what he was doing was in fact for his children—far more important than earning a fat living.

With the backing of some of the broadest minds in Los Angeles, the club began by saving that "jewel of the Missions," San Juan Capistrano, the original church of Junipero Serra.

The motto of the Landmarks Club was to save for our children and our childrens' children, the Missions and other historic monuments of California.

I went to that fine old Spaniard, Bishop Mora, then head of the diocese of Los Angeles and Monterey and told him I felt that it would make it easier for us to carry out this patriotic work if he would give the Landmarks Club a ten-year lease at one dollar a year on San Juan Capistrano . . . whose transept and great dome over the altar are among the noblest pieces of cement work in North America. Our possession would a little disarm the APA fanatics. He promptly did so and we promptly went to work.

We were fortunate enough to have resident on the ground that rare old Irish type, Judge Richard Egan. He was not a Catholic; but he was a big-hearted man and he loved the gray old ruin. Incidentally he was also a director of the Santa Fe RR. With my own strong friendly connections with the heads of that great system, we were able to get help in the way of bridge timbers, freight rates on materials, and other necessary repair materials.

Sumner P. Hunt and Arthur B. Benton, whom I had chosen as our architects on account of their particular understanding and sympathy with the Mission architecture, gave their time liberally and the best of their talent. The Club paid no salaries, merely the expense of postage and stationery. We reroofed the great cloisters on the two sides of the patio which was all then left. We repaired the breached and weakened adobe walls, put on strong roof structures of Oregon pine, and replaced the original tiles; and before another rainy season we were protected against

The interior of the San Fernando Mission in 1896, prior to its restoration. Photograph by Charles Lummis. (*Courtesy Southwest Museum*)

it. *We also took out 600 cartloads of debris from the ruins of the great stone church.*

Some years later we had to campaign to save the dome. C. J. Kubach, later builder of the Southwest Museum, loaned me Henry Newton, the little Yankee giant. The handsome pilasters at either side of the Capistrano dome, of a pretty but fragile country rock, were fast crumbling under the weight. Newton shored up the dome, took down the pilasters stone by stone, marked each stone, put in the back a mighty steel core; and then replaced the original stones to the very digit, so that no one would know that they had been tampered with at all, and the great dome is secure for centuries to come.

Big as the Capistrano job was for a struggling club supported by voluntary subscriptions, mostly $1 a year memberships (some life at $25) that at San Fernando Rey was far greater. Its monastery is 246 feet long by 60 feet wide. Its tile roof was broken in 100 places; and in its back walls were breaches into which a 2-story cottage could have been pushed. San Fernando was the largest of the Missions; and though its "mile of buildings" is now nothing but low ridges of adobe, it is still one of the largest adobe buildings in California.

We lifted off the tiles, removed the crazy rafters of sycamore and other incompetent poles, built up solidly the broken walls, put on a massive pine structure, good for centuries; and then replaced the tile on this—having had to ransack the countryside for miles around to retrieve thousands that had been "borrowed" by ranchers to roof their pigpens. It took 40,000 tiles to reroof that monastery.

The 130-ft. long adobe church had lost its roof altogether. We put on a shake roof, all that we could afford. A "twister" wind lifted this off in a few months and we had to replace it. In 1897, the centennial of the founding of this Mission, we had a celebration. San Fernando is now in a park donated to the City of Los Angeles by a public-spirited citizen.

At San Diego we were able to save what little was left of the buildings of the Mother Mission. San Luis Rey was no further care to us, having been continuously in occupancy as a church and sometimes also as a seminary.

Pala is an Asistencia (branch chapel) of the Royal Mission of San Luis Rey, a score of miles from it, and in one of the most beautiful valleys of Southern California. Its Campanario, standing by itself out in the churchyard, is unique and beautiful.

This Mission had been lost by the Church under our astonishing "Bartlett Act" of Congress in the early Fifties, which in effect required everyone in California to come to court and prove that he hadn't stolen the house he lived in. Many poor Californians and Indians lost their homes this way; and even the

Church lost one or two important properties—though the title was indisputable and no one else had or made any claim.

A squatter named Veall "jumped" the Pala Mission and homesteaded most of the valley. His wife, a Kanaka, was a good Catholic, but Veall a rabid APA. Somehow, however, he had liked me in the old days when I went down there hunting and photographing. In about '95 or '96, having learned that he had violently refused all overtures from the Church to sell it back its property, I suggested to him one day that maybe he would sell it to me.

After some argument (and drinks) he agreed. So in a few weeks I was the happy possessor of the Pala Mission. What a beautiful thing if the Landmarks Club could have a Mission of its very own, a public park, with all its value as a monument of tradition and romance and achievement, but without any other "string" whatever. But at the next meeting of my associates when I wanted to expatiate on this dream, my tongue went flat, and almost to my own surprise I said, "Damn it, Boys! Pala wasn't built for a landmark or a park, but for a temple! I think we would be fences with stolen goods to keep it!"

To my delight there wasn't a hem nor a haw. Not one of us was a Catholic, but we all felt this certain fitness and reverence—as no one could help feeling who had worked so long in the presence of the work done by those great Apostles.

We had paid $300 to Veall. I went to Bishop Montgomery—the blessed Irishman who had succeeded the venerable Spaniard, Mora—and made the suggestion to him that if the Church would like to have Pala, we would surrender it for the $300 we had paid, only asking him to give us a 10-year lease that we might repair it. He was more than delighted; and Pala went back to its original destiny.

We had a beautiful time there. Mrs. Phoebe Hearst sent $500 to apply on the repairs, about 1/3 or 1/4 enough. I wrote Frank Salmons (who had a little Indian trading store in Pala) to call a meeting on Saturday night at his store. We had our meeting of about 20 men in the crowded dingy adobe store with 2 candles and a smoky lamp.

Two or three were "Americans," the rest Spanish Californians and Indians. The Americans talked Spanish also, so my sermon was in Spanish. I told them about the lovely rich lady 600 miles north who had sent us $500 to help us mend this beautiful chapel. "We are very grateful to her," I said, "and will send our thanks. But this is OUR chapel and OUR graveyard, and we're not going to let her nor anyone else do it all. For it takes work and shovels and teams and strong backs as well as money to do this work, and that is just as good as her cash."

Old John Giddings said, "I'll give 20 days work with my team." And so they went along the line, till I was able to say, "Boys, we've raised twice as much here tonight in teams and stout backs and lumber and adobe bricks, as she sent us in cash!"

And they all made good! In a few months the Mission was as good as new.

The influence of the Landmarks Club was felt in many less obvious ways. Not often do we see, in other parts of the land, a home or building done in the old New England style. But for each one such, there are a thousand of the "Mission architecture" today. It is quite common in California to see a Methodist or Baptist church calmly adopting the identical lines of the old Franciscan Missions—which of course makes them better architecture than their denominational brethren.

The world do move! The Mission architecture is as Catholic as the Pope himself. Yet when the Landmarks Club began its crusade, it is safe to say that not a Protestant church extant would have "stooped to Romish architecture."[4]

In Lummis' opinion perhaps the most extraordinary thing he ever did in Los Angeles was at the first public meeting of the Landmarks Club when he induced Catholic Bishop Montgomery and Protestant Bishop Johnson to sit on the same platform and speak for the same cause.

It is hard to realize today what that meant then. The audience (nearly all Protestants) actually gasped when Bishop Johnson walked into the room and up to the stage, shook hands with Bishop Montgomery, and took the seat I proffered him at Montgomery's side. That one evening and the far reverberations it made in society did more to break down the brutal fences of intolerance than any other single thing could have done.[5]

A new cause presented itself to Lummis when in 1903 the Los Angeles City Council decided to take over the historic Spanish plaza of Los Angeles and make it into a public market. The eight hundred members of the Landmarks Club rallied

and raised a mighty protest. In the first place the Plaza founded in 1781 was the historic center of Los Angeles; in the second place its "rubber" trees were the largest and finest in the United States or anywhere north of Southern Mexico; in the third place this little park was a civic necessity for the people dwelling in its vicinity. We killed off the measure.

While we were in the saddle it seemed a good time to look after the historic names of the city. A commission of three of us appointed by the Mayor put in 5 or 6 months and found 280 odd duplicate street names—thanks to real estate men who had named their streets and subdivisions after their children and pets. We restored a good many of the historic names and added several other historic ones that should have been applied.

Unfortunately after our time the real estate vandals succeeded in changing Buena Vista to North Broadway, and Downey Avenue (named after old John G. Downey, Governor of California, and the man who gave East Los Angeles to the city) to North Main Street. Before our commission the equally egregious blunder had been made of changing Fort Street (named for the fortification thrown up on the hill in the first American occupation of Los Angeles) to Broadway, and that was impregnable in the big-minded administration.

The most humorous episode of our hard-working months was when we decided that Georgia Bell Street was rather a juvenile name for a thoroughfare in a Metropolis (of course metropolis, in 1903!). Thereupon into our council chamber stalked Major Horace Bell, one of Walker's pirates in Nicaragua in the '50's and looking the part. He was straight as an arrow, about six feet two, with huge grizzled mustache and a great shock of iron-gray hair, broad shoulders, as gallant a figure of a man as you could

---

[4] Ibid.

[5] Ibid.

find. He made his living by publishing the Porcupine, a weekly whose nature might be guessed by its name.

Well, Major Horace marched in. "Gentlemen," he said, "I understand you think of laying sacrilegious hands on the name of Georgia Bell Street. I want you to understand, gentlemen, that that street is named after the most beautiful and the purest woman that ever lived, my wife. And I want you to understand, gentlemen, that I will kill the first man that lays profane hands on that sacred name."

We looked at one another and at the Major. I said, as chairman: "Major Bell, we sympathize with you strongly in your reverence for that noble woman, your wife. It was a generous thought of you to name that street in her honor. But Major, in the judgment of this commission, which has no object on earth except the greater glory of this city, the entire name sounds rather juvenile for a metropolitan population and we have decided to shorten it. If there is any killing to be done you might as well begin now, because the name is going to be changed. You may have it Georgia or Bell Street, just as you prefer. Personally I think it would be rather more distinguished to call it Georgia Street. That would honor your wife and the gallant state from which she came, and would be sonorous and handsome on the map of the city."

The Major snorted that he would never consent to such vandalism. But he didn't pull either of the big guns under his long coat. And it is Georgia Street today.[6]

[6] *Ibid.*

19

A Glimpse of the Man

DURING his life of travelling and recording, Lummis used uncounted thousands of glass plates in his heavy view-camera. A quick glance at the lighting was sufficient to determine the exposure, and the shutter speed was controlled by the bulb in his hand. Failures were rare, and many of his pictures reflect a fine feeling for mood and composition.

While making the contemporaneous photographic record of ways of life even then disappearing, Lummis also left the world an impressive collection of pictures of himself. After the frightened little boy whose big ears stand out over a stiff and proper suit, there is a college lad of arrogant expression and sensuous mouth with a great wave of hair at the back of his neck, the complete dandy with wide lapels, gold chain, and flowing tie. Next, a young editor swaggering across the country under a western hat, Indian blanket over the shoulder, and pistol carried on the left hip for the "California draw." After the stint with General Crook, Lummis posed with his face stained, wearing an Apache outfit that might have deceived any but a member of the tribe. A one-armed cowboy (during his paralysis) is followed by a character in a Navajo blanket. At last we come to the familiar figure dressed in the corduroy into which he finally settled. One wonders at these varying roles. Was it vanity? showmanship? developing personality? seeking identity? Perhaps a bit of each, but the final effect was impressive.

Small though he was, Lummis' appearance was striking. He had a burning, ruddy complexion that suggested great vitality, an imperious nose, and an unruly shock of hair. Voice and movement projected the vigor of his restless personality, and he always seemed to be travelling under a full head of steam.

Lummis in his corduroys and wearing a medal conferred by the King of Spain.

There was a subtle co-ordination between his nature, his dress, and his writing style.

. . . for 40 years my easy and invariable corduroys & sombrero have reflected independence without re-

bellion & the conclusion that the clothes & English were made for me and not I for either. I know Academic English & several other Dead Languages—& respect them all too deeply to be their parrot & reverently enough to insist that all my liberties with their crystallization shall be true to type & not pyrites instead of gold.[1]

His wardrobe was actually modest. In prosperous years Lummis had two corduroy suits. The earliest were of sand-colored domestic cloth. Later a Spanish admirer sent him bolts of lustrous Spanish corduroy, one rich brown, the other dark green. He loved their softness and warm color. The browns were for business, the greens to meet such folk as bishops, prima donnas, presidents, and men of art or science.

Lummis' tailor bill was also modest. He wore a suit until even he admitted that it was worn out, then went to Nicholl, his favorite tailor. No doubt Nicholl turned the suit out in the usual way. It seems hardly likely that a tailor could bring himself to omit creases, but no one ever saw Lummis' sleeves in any stage other than one of comfortable roundness. Creases were for dudes and store dummies. Yet the dandy he was in his youth was still evident. He was fond of a certain shade of rich red, the red of the Pueblo belt which was both useful and handsome. This he boldly wore wound several times around the waist, Indian fashion. In Isleta he had admired the drawnwork shirts and had some made for himself.

Since derbies and straw hats looked ridiculous and served only to enrich the haberdasher, Lummis chose to wear the kind of hat that had proved itself suited to the climate and condition of the Southwest, a Stetson sombrero. As he preferred faces on which were etched their owner's history to those which were blanks of prettiness, he liked his Stetsons best when they had the richness of age, sweat, and service.

Lummis' pockets bulged with treasures—flint and steel (few tenderfeet matches for him!), blue and red bandanas, a hunting fetish picked up on New Mexican mesas, Bull Durham tobacco in a gourd tobacco pouch, brown cigarette paper, notebooks, writing material, photographs, pamphlets, a present

[1] Lummis, "As I Remember."

for a friend or two, arrowheads, a Roman coin, a bit of snakeskin, and a flask of the *chuchupate*.[2]

When he was entertaining at one of his famous "noises" of later years, Lummis wore his "charro" suit, the riding costume of soft suede worn by the caballeros of Jalisco, Mexico, with a short jacket and skin-tight trousers with bell cuffs. They clung so snugly that his children did not know how he got out of them. One young Lummis who had dressed in the finery without permission was barely able to shed it in time to escape parental wrath.

Lummis wore exactly what he pleased, and his children wore exactly what pleased Lummis. Turbesé's head was adorned with a peaked Peruvian cap with ear flaps which she was sure set her apart as a freak. She had to endure the further handicap of having hair cropped as short as a boy's, while a son spent years battling young tormenters who made fun of his bare feet and long dutch bob.

In Lummis' days many felt personally insulted by the unconventional. Thus, inevitably Lummis came under attack for his unique dress. The *Graphic*, a local weekly long since defunct, made the most vicious slash on February 24, 1904. Referring to his talk before the Friday Morning Club, it sneered: "Never before was a body of refined ladies so insulted [by his appearance] with his cowboy hat and dirty corduroy suit . . . with the unspeakable odor of perspiration. . . . Perhaps Lummis is so filled with Indian lore that he is acquiring their antipathy for water." Yet within the year the same *Graphic* carried a long and flattering article, including: "His cowboy hat and corduroys simply reflect his individuality which is more pronounced even in his clothes than that of

[2] Lummis "Journal," August 31, 1927, Santa Fe, New Mexico. On the subject of *chuchupate* Lummis has this to say: "By bull luck a Mexican boy was purchasing 15¢ of osha and had not the money. Now that heavenly aromatic root, chuchupate, which Dr. Lund taught me to use for various purposes, including the mitigation of whiskey, but also as one of the greatest stomachics in existence is frequently called osha by the Mexicans though quite another root. I plunged in the dark and bought the package, getting it home, tasted it, and found it really was the long-lost chuchupate." According to L. S. M. Curtin, "The herb is a member of the parsley family *Lingusticum Porteri*; also called *Angelica Pinnata Wats* or *Umbelliferae* locally known as *chuchupate* or *osha* and was used by the natives as a cure-all. It was smoked, made into tea, taken orally as a powder, made into a salve." See Curtin, *Healing Herbs of the Upper Rió Grande* (Sante Fe, Laboratory of Anthropology, 1947).

his fellows. . . . The Lion, which is his *nom de plume* in his magazine . . . is a wiry person, a bunch of nerves and can whip his weight in wildcats either with pen or paw."

The *New York Evening Post*, on December 24, 1904, without mentioning a name, referred to "a California editor and author . . . an apparition simply seeking publicity and trading on an outworn tradition. . . ." The *Washington Post*, on February 14, 1905, was milder:

. . . [he] is famed not only as a scholar, traveler and writer but as a wearer of clothes so picturesque as to astonish folks . . . last night his raiment was toned down a bit, yet it could be distinctly heard as far as Baltimore. . . . Mr. Lummis' peculiar dress is his own affair and does not mitigate against his reception in the most cultured homes in the nation. . . . [he has] one of the most beautiful homes in the nation . . . fine command of language . . . profound information . . . regarded by competent critics as without a peer.

The fact that these clippings are all mounted in the family scrapbook indicate how little distress they caused.

The *Los Angeles Times*, always gentle with the idiosyncrasies of its first city editor, on August 23, 1905, carried a witty, illustrated half-page story on the rumor that he was contemplating a change of costume due to the unavailability of corduroy. Lummis did, at this time, have a conventional suit made, posed for a few pictures, and wore it a little while. The beloved corduroy was soon back on the market, and that conventional suit was perhaps the only Lummis suit that was discarded before it was completely worn out.

Still another impression was that of H. Clay Needham, at one time a candidate for president from the Prohibition party. Coming west in 1889, Needham bought two opposite sections of the Pullman to insure against undesirable encounters. At Albuquerque, however, the conductor came to him and said, "I see you have a vacant berth. I have a party I would like very much to accommodate but I haven't a vacancy and thought maybe you would allow him to have your unused seat."

Needham replied, "Do you know the man and could you guarantee that he would be a pleasant party with whom to travel?"

"I know him well and can assure you that you will not only find him entertaining but he is the best-informed man on the Southwest to be found in the United States."

Years later Needham recalled the meeting in a letter to Turbesé.

After a few moments the porter came in with a rather small man whose left arm was dangling at his side and whose left foot was slid along the floor with difficulty. He was clad in a faded suit of corduroy, wore a typical cowboy hat and underneath the dangling arm hung the accompaniment of almost every Western man of that period, the .44 revolver.

Myself and wife exchanged glances which expressed the thought that we had been handed a lemon by the conductor. In thanking me for the accommodation, he asked my name and told me that his was Lummis.

"Not C. F. Lummis, the author of Quito's Nugget?" remarked my wife with an inflection that plainly said, "I know you are not the party." He modestly replied, "Yes, I wrote that tale."

During the remainder of that journey was laid the foundation of a friendship which was to grow stronger through forty years.

Mr. Lummis was somewhat eccentric in his habits and dress and had an utter disregard for the formal rules of etiquette as assumed by the shallow intellects of some of the elite, whose only claim for recognition was wealth. His measure of men and women was their intelligence and their aspirations for a higher and better standard of living.

I was proud to join him as a charter member of the old Landmarks Club; and later in the formation of the local branch of the Archaeological Society which afterwards grew into the Southwest Museum . . . all children of his fertile brain and vision.

While he was intensely interested in scientific pursuits and the writing of numerous books and articles for magazines, yet he was one of the most approachable of men and possessed one of the most lovable of personalities.

I shall ever cherish the hours spent with him in that rambling home built by his own hands in the

Arroyo Seco, all the while being regaled by the legends he could tell of each individual specimen in the great collection he had gathered from every nook and corner of the great Southwest he loved so well.

El Alisal, an etching by Orpha Klinker.

20

El Alisal

THE DESIRE that Lummis had for a home of his own was at first satisfied with the place on Forrester Avenue. Then on November 15, 1894, his first son was born and named Amado Bandelier after his father's two best friends. Amado translated from Spanish is "beloved." There are many references in Lummis' diary to the gentle little boy with blond hair. A new line of Lummis had been founded and with it came the need for a great family home that would last forever. It became an obsession.

Poor all his life, Lummis had never longed to make money. But, "now I do and wish I could strike a windfall some way or other to make sure for the dear lives that depend on me." He began to keep careful account of every penny, hammering away about economy ("If you could just save one dollar a month on the groceries"), until Eve cried when she had to bring the bill to him. Still, however, he felt he had to keep open house and feed all comers in the style of Old California.

After long search Lummis found two and a half acres of wild land "way out in the country" six miles from the center of town by the Arroyo Seco. This he liked, with its sycamores and elderberries, quail and cottontail, and its view of the Sierra Madre, the mother mountain. He decided to build around a certain giant sycamore, *alisal* in the local Spanish,[1] and from this tree the home drew its name—El Alisal.

Lummis at work on El Alisal, 1904.

[1] According to Harris Newmark, "Jean Louis Vignes came to Los Angeles in 1829 and set out the Aliso Vineyard of 104 acres which derived its name as did the street from a previous and incorrect application of the Castillian *aliso*, meaning alder, to the sycamore tree, a big specimen of which stood on the place . . . The northern boundary of the property was on Aliso Street." See Newmark, *Sixty Years in Southern California*, 197.

It was a large project for a couple with such limited finances, but drawing on their last hundred dollars to hold the property, Lummis went to work. Although he had never done any but rough carpentry, he felt

El Alisal, showing the staggered windows.

that the only way for a man to make his home his own was to build it himself.

It was three years before Lummis could move his family from Forrester Avenue into a four-room shack he had built as a first shelter on the property. Having done this, he began the permanent building, using the cobblestones that lay on the land.

Indian boys brought yearly from Isleta did rough labor. Sometimes a famous visitor would lend a hand hoisting a beam. There were transitory carpenters, roofers, masons, and electricians. Turbesé and even tiny Amado brought rocks and tamped mortar with their bare feet.

Naturally he first must build a great hall, the *Museo* ("museum"), in which he could safeguard and display antiquities. Completing this, with its concrete floor, Pueblo fireplace, unique hand-framed windows, and ceiling of huge beams, Lummis turned his hand to making a room for his wife and children.

During these years the patio was his reception room. Here he stood at his workbench near the old sycamore in his working costume of white jeans, sawing, planing, rabbeting, carving. Visitors came from all over the world, and he would continue to work as he talked with them. To sit down would have been to lose time. An awestruck woman once

98

The Museo at El Alisal, containing Lummis' collections.

breathed over a shaving curling from his block plane, "Mr. Lummis! Did you make this? May I have it?"

Other guests came to learn, to give their advice, even to lend a hand. Professor William H. Holmes of the Smithsonian Institute, dean of American archaeologists and ethnologists, came to pay a formal call and discovered the founder of the Southwest Society high on a wall pouring concrete. "Pick up a hodful and come on up," said Lummis. Professor Holmes picked up a hodful and went up, ever thereafter to boast of his career as a "hod carrier for Lummis."

For over twenty years the house continued to grow and inevitably it reflected the builder, his character, and his travels. Each window was designed to recall some building in Peru or New Mexico; some were located to permit a view of a favorite garden spot. Every door was handmade and unique. Eve noticed a beautiful door in the background of the Velasquez painting *The Maids of Honor*, and the replica still hangs at El Alisal. The hinges on the main entrance were forged in the shape of the sacred serpent of the Inca ruins of Tiahuanaco.

In 1899 there was another addition—the red morocco House Book. As the house grew, the book filled, and its four hundred pages of names, comments, and illustrations are a record of the many happenings and thousands of visitors.

The Boks and the Doubledays of publishing fame signed it in 1903. In a privately printed story of experiences *On the Santa Fe Trail*, the "Hayseeds from the East" wrote of their visit.

This Recording Angel's lips need to be touched with a live coal if she is to tell of Charles F. Lummis —PERHAPS THE BEST KNOWN MAN IN CALIFORNIA—and filled with the spirit of the just (though the tenderfeet are not unanimous on that point): Certainly a good deal of a crank and more or less of a genius. We found him dressed in white cotton overalls and jacket, his flannel shirt open at the throat, hatless, an aureole of bushy, grayish hair around his keen but pleasant face; with trowel in hand—for he was laying a wall—but he quickly dropped his tools to welcome the Sequoya Leaguers. Some time if he lives to be two hundred or so he will finish the house which he has built thus far with the help of only an Indian boy . . . we enter upon rooms that every museum in the land must envy. . . . Artistic, historic and prehistoric treasures galore . . . with such alone is his house adorned. Surely a tangible exponent of the theory that a home should contain only that which is useful or what is believed to be beautiful. . . . (The Hayseeds—Mr. and Mrs. F. Colt Johnson, Mr. and Mrs. Edward Bok, Mr. and Mrs. Frank W. Doubleday, and Dorothy Doubleday.)

Some were not impressed with the house itself. In a letter written by David G. Hogarth, a Fellow of the Royal Geographic Society of the British Academy and a distinguished archaeologist, to H. R. Fairclough of Stanford these remarks appear.

Salt Lake City, Nov. 9, 1907
I found Mr. Lummis strangely interesting and attractive. He has the real temperament of the artist and superabundant energy and natural ability, expressing itself in all sorts of strange ways. I have not seen his like, nor indeed anyone in the same class, so far in America. I was prepared for a poseur but found too much reality behind the pose to care whether it were there or no. . . . I found a man of real taste and power. . . . The house is a casual higglypiggeldy place, more uncomfortable than a tent in the wilderness but full of interesting things. They gave me a Spanish

The blond-haired Amado, a pencil sketch by Maynard Dixon.

dinner with guitars and Carmencitas and I enjoyed it hugely. In the end I abode three days with them and was sorry to quit.[2]

Perpetuating the family name was vital to Lummis, and his hopes were centered on his gentle-faced first son, Amado. When in 1900 a second son was born, Lummis was delighted. The Indians chose for this blond boy the name of Quimu, Little White Lion, but his parents named him after an admired friend.

Jan. 19 [1900], 12:30 a.m. Man child is born. Write to David Starr Jordan that we had for months intended to name the Promised one for him if it chanced to be that kind of a cat and that it was and that we were taking that liberty in the christening. . . . Few days later, letter from him, congratulations and

[2] Quoted by permission from *Warming Both Hands*, 613–14, the autobiography of H. R. Fairclough of Stanford University.

pride on his godfatherhood and "he must have been born about my own birthday which is the 19th." We had no idea of this but it is a gentle coincidence.[3]

While Lummis' dream of making the home a center of such family life as had warmed his heart in the Spanish haciendas was not to meet with great success, he was one of those who knew how to keep a good Christmas. He made each a memorable celebration with whiskers, pillow in trousers, sleigh bells, and a tree of California pepper, the best available in that warm lowland so far from pine and fir.

One Christmas brought great suffering. Lummis wrote in his diary:

Dec. 20, 1900. Amado and Jordan [11 months old] both sick with pneumonia, former critical, and I am up all night

Dec. 22. Amado worse. Eve exhausted. Get my Christmas tree from Morgans and 11 lb. turkey in town. . . . Jennie Hagan and trained nurse come evening and spend night. I make lunch for them at 11 and send them to bed and care for babies till 2:30.

Dec. 23. Tuyo [Indian boy] running house alone, kitchen and all. Eve resting from grueling strain. Feli [Indian girl] caring for baby Jordan. . . .

Dec. 24. 14-year-old Tuyo makes the Christmas dinner including turk. At noon Dr. Buell finds Amado much relieved and Jordan in less danger. Morgan brings my selected pepper tree and I set it up and dress it with great labor. Many bring gifts. . . . Serious difficulties about it but I feel the way to do it is to go ahead and to give ours whatever of the Xmas joy we can and trust to God for our sick ones.

Christmas Day. My lovely boy Amado dies at 8:30 P.M. and we lay him out. One thankfulness—his wonderful golden hair is unspoiled. Now I take off the beautiful curls to save.[4]

Lummis did not believe in coffins or funerals nor any of those settings of death which "we have made ghastly with tiptoe hirelings and rented plumes and the rattle of clods. . . ." Chiseling "a precious board of tulip wood . . . made it ready like the burial board of a Pueblo Indian for my boy." He who had known Pueblo love and reverence and hope of a life beyond was well content to follow in the footsteps of the True Believers.

Dec. 27. Rev. John Gowan, Father's pupil 35 years ago at Tilton, N. H. read short services. . . . My golden haired son swathed like a little Indian and in a white Moqui blanket with buckskin thongs and turquoise. . . . And I take it in my arms in the hack with Dr. Wills and with my hands deliver it up to the rosy mouth of that Final Chamber . . . and home at last to the lonely house and consolation.[5]

In January, with the death of his first son heavy upon him, the grieving father wrote in the Lion's Den, the editorial section of the *Land of Sunshine*, "The Little Boy that Was."

The Den is dim this month. It is at best but a room for the Lion's passing thought; and today his thought paces up and down a narrow bound. He has just closed the eyes of one he hoped should one day do that office for him. He has just surrendered to the incorporating flames the fair husk of what had been his tawny-maned cub . . . the lad who was a Man at six and an old-fashioned gentle fearless little knight whose first thought was always for others; whose last words in the agony for breath were "Yes, please" . . . one noted that his undefiant eye never fell before any eye . . . that he never lied nor dodged nor shirked his fault nor sulked from its consequences. Love we are born into but to win respect is victory for a lifetime, long or short. It is well with the boy. But the Lion had not cubs to spare. . . .

However, four years later, in 1904, Lummis was able to say in a letter to Mrs. Phoebe Apperson Hearst:

. . . I want to send you now word of our good news, the arrival of a little son, August 20th. He is robust and healthy, sleeps about 23 hours out of the 24— thus making a sort of Jack-Sprat-and-wife balance

[3] Lummis, "Diary."
[4] Ibid.
[5] Ibid.

with the Old Man. The New Comer has been named Keith Lummis....[6]

At the same time he sent the news to his friend,

William Keith, the artist, informing him of the birth of his namesake and continuing: "Now let the next great poet [sic!] who gets a son call him for John Muir ... Keith and Muir! California ought to be the proudest state in the Union for having within her borders two such pillars of artistic strength."

[6] Courtesy John Barr Tompkins, Bancroft Library, University of California, Berkeley, California.

Color plates from the House Book

A note and watercolor by Edward Borein.

Dear Lummis

Here's to your friends and mine.
The people who took their color
from the parrots wing.

Edward Borein,
1923.

A watercolor and poem by Charles M. Russell.

To My Friend
Charles F Lummis
A Scout that back tracks
Dim trails.

If wishes were hosses I'd Combe the range
And corrill a bunch to day
I'd put a top hoss under you
one with wind that'ed Stay.

You'r ridden a hoss called romance
And he damned near throwed you too
So a steady strong hoss named health
Is the one I'd put under you.

C M Russell

May 7th
1922

The cliffs along the Green River of Colorado, a watercolor by Thomas Moran.

A Sketch of
Green River cliffs
Moran.
1923

409

21

"I Have Not the Art to Say Things Softly"

IT WOULD BE difficult to designate a period of Lummis' life as the one most active. The years following his return to Los Angeles in 1893 until about 1910 were the most productive. The Landmarks Club and its work with the missions was but one of many causes he took up. There was his concern for the Indian which motivated the Sequoya League, the determination that the city should have a museum and hence the Southwest Society, an eagerness to improve the city library and its personnel which inspired the Bibliosmiles, nine books in nine years, and in every spare moment more cobblestones and mortar carried up the rugged walls of the new home.

At the same time Lummis was editor of a magazine and its principal contributor. Although he was able to juggle these matters more or less concurrently, keeping them sorted out in the many compartments under his sombrero, they must be considered separately to avoid confusion.

Late in 1893 the secretary of the Los Angeles Chamber of Commerce, Charles Dwight Willard, urged Lummis to take over the editorship of the *Land of Sunshine*, a small twenty-four page folio advertising and promoting southern California. Although completely disinterested in advertising, Lummis accepted when promised absolute editorial control and the privilege of working when and where he pleased. He was seldom at the desk; his office remained under that same sombrero.

The first step was to get the *Land of Sunshine* out of the tourist advertising class. Lummis secured a striking cover design and began building the little pamphlet toward magazine fitness. By January, 1894, his first issue was ready—Volume II, No. 1. It gave promise of what it was to become. The lead article was "The Seal of Spain—the Spanish American Face." Although copy in the nature of a real estate boost was "shut severely back among the ads, only letting it in under protest and after a battle with the business office," his enthusiasm for his adopted land was contagious. In his first article Lummis admitted that he never expected to reach the jumping-off place of interest in southern California, and, intentionally or not, his barrage of books and articles on the many charming aspects of the Southwest and the motto he coined, "See America First," contributed to the ever-increasing westward immigration. The Los Angeles Chamber of Commerce had no complaint.

In June, 1895 (the beginning of Volume III), the magazine was greatly improved—a large eight octavo with the California lion couchant against the full-rayed setting sun, its legend, "A Magazine of California and the Southwest." (When the *Overland Monthly* put the same words on its cover, Lummis referred to their publication as the "Warmed Overland.") The motto held special significance coming from a transplanted New Englander—Los Paises del Sol Delatan el Alma—"The Lands of the Sun Expand the Soul."

The tint block which formed the background of the new cover was a direct reproduction of a piece of cactus "lace"—the structure of a lobe of the prickly pear. The editor remarked, "The *Land of Sunshine* is the only magazine in the world whose cover was ever embellished with drawings by the Almighty."

It was deemed quixotic to try to make, away out here at the Jumping-Off-Place, a real magazine. New York and Boston were the only cities in the Union where such a periodical had ever managed to live—

[but] in a little city in the Wild West—preposterous!

But there was a faith that the West was different—of enough higher average education than the East (that it is higher every reader of the census knows); that the West has a larger proportion of readers; that it is more independent, more American, less timid, fonder of fair play and free speech—so that it be cultured speech—and that it would support a Western magazine if truly Western.[1]

In the beginning it was difficult to find enough material which met Lummis' standards. It was necessary for him to do most of the writing himself.[2] He studied and edited the manuscripts submitted, giving a great deal of time to his contributors. All their letters were answered by hand, manuscripts of any worth criticised, writers of promise encouraged.

The editor's broad acquaintance in the world of western letters soon enabled him to cajole many established writers, artists, and scientists to contribute.

This was easy when their generous spirits found in the magazine something solid as well as something provocative. Early in the magazine's history I formed the Land of Sunshine League, an astonishing rally of writers and artists mostly in the far West. Among the outstanding personalities who thus pledged their interest and support were such men and women as David Starr Jordan, Benjamin Ide Wheeler, Ina Coolbrith, Theodore H. Hittell, Edwin Markham, (then a school teacher in Oakland) Charles Warren Stoddard, Charles A. Keeler, Charles Howard Shinn, Emerson Hough, Paul Norton, Elizabeth Benton Frémont, Hugh Gibson (later ambassador to Belgium) Ella Wentworth Higginson, Mary Hallock Foote, John Muir, T. S. Van Dyke, Henry Wallace Phillips, George Hamilton Fitch, Arthur Guiterman, Charles Frederick Holder, Joaquin Miller, D. P. Barrows, (later President of the University of California) John Vance Cheney, Grace Ellery Channing, Charlotte Perkins Stetson. Among

artists, William Keith, Charles Walter Stetson, Alexander Harmer, Thomas Moran and others.[3]

There were many "competent undiscovered" to whose early efforts Lummis gave a hearing. Among them were Mary Austin (to whom he gave her first chance in print), Maynard Dixon, Sharlot Hall, Frances Douglas (Eve Lummis), Eugene Manlove Rhodes, Ed Borein, and Jack London.

History, both local and Southwestern, soon became an important feature. I printed here my own critical translations of unpublished Spanish sources of the highest historical value—like the diary of Fray Junipero Serra, himself, on his first journey from Mexico to San Diego in 1769.[4] This original, preserved in the famous Ramirez collection, was loaned to me by the late Edward Everett Ayer, the great book lover and friend of scholarship. Many other "sources" responsible to the history of the Southwest were printed in this little far-off magazine. For instance, never before published in English: the "Relation" of Fray Geronimo de Zarate Salmerón, covering the history of New Mexico from 1538 to his time of writing in 1626, about 26,000 words. The letter of Fray Silvestre Valez de Escalante on the Pueblo Rebellion of 1680. Some 8,500 words.[5]

There were many more historical items of this nature. Lummis also sought and published personal narratives of the men who had survived the horrors of Death Valley or of the men who had been swept along with the gold rush. These fresh glimpses gave his readers a new understanding of history. Subscribers soon realized that the *Land of Sunshine* proposed to deal with public affairs, literature, civilization, and life.

The literary department was called "That Which Is Written." Here Lummis reviewed a good number of books "according to what was in them" and also according to his personal philosophy. When his good friend Brander Matthews wrote in praise of New York, Lummis replied:

[1] Lummis, "As I Remember."
[2] Any articles signed C. R. Lohs or C. Arloz in the early editions were written by Lummis, playing on his local nickname, Don Carlos. They were so signed to avoid the appearance that most of an edition was written by himself.

[3] Lummis, "As I Remember."
[4] Translated from the original difficult old Spanish by Eve Lummis.
[5] Lummis, "As I Remember."

Ina Coolbrith, one of many writers whom Lummis encouraged to contribute to the *Land of Sunshine*. Photograph by Charles Lummis.

In so comfortable a book one can almost forgive the author's local heresy that New York is really a "university." Men can learn something anywhere. Many of us will get a liberal education Hereafter; and the natural retort to the statement that New York is very educative, is "So is the Other Place" . . . the real University of life is anywhere that man is made to do for himself. . . . If New York taught any broad education, there soon would be no one left in it.[6]

He approved of John Muir.

A man who writes only because he has something to say on subjects it is worthwhile to say something about and who says it in a medium as unanilined [uncolored] as the Word, is nowadays one of the rarest bipeds without feathers. It would be a little of an impertinence to "review" John Muir's "Our National Parks." It doesn't need it. There are only a few people alive competent (by equal parts of knowledge of the theme and an equivalent literary gift) to appraise it. But all that have the Breath of Life in them are competent to read it and grow by it; nor will any of them find it hard reading. . . . And it is one of the books everyone should read who cares for beauty either in nature or in letters.[7]

Lummis felt that "the privilege to criticize severely or even savagely carried with it the obligation to praise as heartily when it was called for." Having allowed his quota of praise he turned to the attack.

In a day when words are about as precise as bean bags . . . Mr. [Cyrus Townsend] Brady is not solitary in his concept of the functions of the historian— that one needs to take a few short-order meals of pre-digested food and atone with adjectives for the rest. Of the historical digestion he is innocent as a babe.[8]

A certain novel was described as one that "runs at times after the fashion of New Orleans molasses through a bung—by alternate hesitations and blobs." Under the subtitle, "The West as a Tenderfoot Guesses It," Lummis disposed of a hopeful author in few words, "Joseph Allsheler seems to like to write

about the West—perhaps on the principle that those who know nothing fear nothing."[9]

As far as the literary world was concerned, the Southwest that he had "stumbled upon," christened, explored, and fought for was his private domain. Any new writer who ventured into this territory did so at his own peril. Generally if they came to Lummis, he counseled and supported them, but even then he could not endure a careless, unscholarly, or pretentious approach.

Mary Austin was one who admittedly sought him out as the route to literary success, and both he and Eve gave her help. Yet of her he wrote:

. . . She has the most oracular impudence of any-one that ever wrote about the Southwest. Even Gee-whillikens James was modest beside her. . . . A brilliant lady but without conscience and without sense of humor; above all, she has the misfortune of Doubling for the Almighty. She never would study any-thing for it all comes to her by divine revelation but she, naturally, with her oracular way and her incalculable nerve, imposes on a lot of people to believe her a wonder of wisdom.

The above-mentioned George Wharton James, a clergyman turned western authority, described as concisely as his own style permitted Lummis' dominion over western writing. He used great discretion for the Lion was still on the loose.

. . . Mr. Lummis took upon himself the task of being the censor of everything dealing with the Southwest. When it came to matters dealing with this subject, his virile pen became an instrument of torture to all those who were dealing in an incompetent and incapable manner with subjects connected with this region. It became the standard question, not only in California and the Southwest but even in the libraries and magazines in the East, "Who will Lummis pillory next?" Many a man who deemed himself almost above criticism found himself stripped naked, as it were, shot through with arrows and even scalped because he had presumed carelessly to handle subjects that were within the domain of Mr. Lummis' interests.

[6] Charles F. Lummis, *Land of Sunshine*, Vol. X. No. 1 (January, 1899), 121.
[7] Charles F. Lummis, *Out West*, Vol. XVI. No. 3 (March, 1902), 313.
[8] *Ibid.*

[9] Charles F. Lummis, *Land of Sunshine*, Vol. X, No. 4 (April, 1899), 151.

John Muir, as photographed by Lummis in 1905. Lummis held Muir in great esteem as a writer, a naturalist, and a friend.

I could mention a dozen such cases but perhaps the three most notable are those in which he attacked Dr. Stephen Peet, editor of the Century Dictionary. *I, myself, was the third victim of these onslaughts. Dr. Peet had written a book on the* Cliff Dwellers of the Southwest. *Lummis clearly showed that Peet knew nothing of the subject and that the book was a pretentious fraud—which censure, as anyone who knows the subject, will agree was not too strong.*

In the second case Dr. Smith certainly regarded himself so far above Lummis' criticism that he treated him at first with a haughty supercilliousness which we, who knew Lummis, were assured would speedily bring its own just results. We were not disappointed. Dr. Smith was pilloried, laughed at, scorned and treated as if he were an overgrown schoolboy who had pretended to the knowledge of a professor. Those articles make good reading—of a sort—even to this day. In my own case, perhaps the least said the better, but Mr. Lummis took an article of mine, which the editor had mutilated and altered without my knowledge or permission, and proved that I was writing upon a subject of which I knew nothing.[10]

Lummis was always ready to give a hearing to causes unpopular at the moment. The Theosophical Society that maintained a school on Point Loma near San Diego was under considerable criticism at the time. Lummis visited it, took pictures, and published a highly favorable article. In order that Mormonism be better understood, he printed a long descriptive article by Lorenzo Snow, the president of the Church of Latter Day Saints, with the footnote, "Always interested to hear the other side of the story."[11]

But it was in the editorial department, the "Lion's Den," that Lummis came into his own. The motto there was "To love what is True; to hate Sham, to Fear Nothing Without; to Think a little." Many causes were heard there.

One was conservation in its various phases. Those who were trying to lumber the Calaveras Grove were

. . . vandals, whose only god is their belly, moving to cut down the Calaveras Grove of Big Trees. If we permit them, we are as base as they. Savages, of course, are never such brutes. They take what wood they need to keep warm and no more. It takes the camp followers of civilization—the men who have grown up within reach of schools, churches and art— even to conceive of such a barbarity as turning this grove of the noblest trees in the world into boards to be peddled at $17.50 per M.

The Lion believes in law. And he is sure that there are enough laws in the United States to suppress crime. But if there are not, let us find out; and meanwhile advise these public enemies who are infinitely more dangerous than a public murderer, that if they go to chopping there before we can get a law, some of the Calaveras redwoods will dangle a new kind of cone.[12]

On the slaughter of fish and game Lummis wrote:

. . . They do it not even for "sport"; for the titter-witted wantons have no more conception of Sport than a pig has of Predestination. . . . Day after day tons of fish are caught by half-baked anglers, are brought into Avalon to be shown off, to be photographed with their proud captors, then dumped into the ocean. . . . No savage tribe on earth . . . no cannibals on the Amazon ever do such things.[13]

At that early date there was already a realization that the great cities had become a threat to the integrity of the individual.

. . . Only in December President Roosevelt expressed to me personally his deep concern over this abnormal depletion of the American soil of its best crop—the people. . . . The adult pays for acute civilization. For our modern conveniences we, in the long run though likely in installments, have to pay with our inborn self-dependence. For the fullness of civilization, the price comes out of our human nature. . . . The city is more or less a disease. It is more or less an intoxication. Speaking in terms of evolution, man can endure on this planet only when

[10] George Wharton James, *Overland Monthly* (May 10, 1923), 10.

[11] Charles F. Lummis, *Land of Sunshine*, Vol. XV, Nos. 2–3 (September 1901), 158.

[12] Charles F. Lummis, *Land of Sunshine*, Vol. XII, No. 4 (March, 1900), 252.

[13] Charles F. Lummis, *Out West*, Vol. XIV, No. 2 (August, 1903), 215.

The Lion's Den. From this room in El Alisal Lummis directed the publication of and wrote for the *Land of Sunshine* and its successor *Out West*.

he has his roots in the earth.... Like Anteus of old, our strength comes from our touch with the Brown Mother. We may forget her ... but we shall surely pay for our thoughtlessness.[14]

The Lion took on a different tone in discussing the proposal to unify the territories of New Mexico and Arizona and to admit to the Union one state burdened with the name of "Montezuma." He hooted this idea down, but again became deadly serious in rebutting the contention that statehood should not be granted because of the illiteracy of the populations.

As a matter of fact, the very people in whom this inability to read and write so horrifies the Tender-

foot, *are Educated enough to live happy, decent, honorable and self reliant lives—which is at least as much as any of their critics do.... They are Educated enough to be human to strangers ... they understand their environment and their relations to the world and their obligations to it, far better than does the average Eastern community....*

With regard to the disputed admission of Negro representatives to a convention of the National Association of Women's Clubs, he had a great deal to say.

Probably no other matter will be touched by the convention which the historian would take up for an instant; but this is a matter of permanent value and so will be the Federation's attitude on it.... We have been asked ... "to give women a show...." We have given it. Now we would like to see how they use it. If

[14] Charles F. Lummis, *Out West*, Vol. XX, No. 5 (May, 1905), 354-56.

the white woman who twenty years ago dared not speak in a public meeting and who only ten years ago never dreamed of such a function as the Biennial will be, is going to use her new privilege to choke the woman next under her, she will delight the stupid brute who has opposed her progress, but she will grieve the man who has made it possible for her to "have a chance." And . . . she will write herself among the failures of history. If she has demanded justice for herself and not for all women—and all creatures—if she has sought equality only that she may make someone else unequal—she is not ready for the Emancipation Proclamation.[15]

Railing against those who physically abused the Negro, he wrote: "Americans! Bah! They are not even dogs. Neither in morals or brains. For what they think they do to the Negro individual, they are doing in fact to themselves and to their own children and their children's children."[16]

The Lion bitterly opposed what he considered American imperialism in its relations with the Latin American countries, particularly Cuba, the Phillipines, and Panama.

Our Spanish War was needless. It has been proved that Spain made every concession we asked . . . that President McKinley did not inform Congress or the country of this vital fact . . . that Congress declared war on Spain for not doing what Spain had already done.

But . . . the Newspapers which could sell copies, the Promoters who could get franchises, the contractors who could poison American soldiers with Alger-Egan beef, the Congressmen who could play to the Gallery . . . these had to have a war. . . .

. . . The Panama mistake, for it is a mistake if there is a god in Israel or anywhere else . . . if no one else on earth cares to protest against the forgetting of fair play . . . the Lion is content to.[17]

The atrocities that flared up in the fury of the Phillippine War have now been replaced in the pub-

lic mind by later similar crimes, but the aging files of the "Lion's Den" still carry one man's cry for justice. Lummis' protests brought out scattered cries of treason and some subscribers cancelled. To the Lion attack was always the best defense. Speaking of a pamphleteer who had been suppressed, Lummis wrote:

The Administration mumbles terrible but indefinite threats (which it dare not carry out) of its intention to punish other "treasonable" Americans if they dare print facts. If the Administration could change all minds as easily as it changes its own, this would not be a Democracy but a sheepfold.

A flaxseed poultice is useful on a boil, but a poor substitute for brains. It seems, however, to satisfy the needs of the people just now engaged in yelping "Treason" at every American who stops to think. As everyone knows whose head is lined with anything sounder than mush and milk, the Constitution of the United States precisely defines what treason is. It isn't free thought or free speech and in this republic it never will be.

. . . This is the first time in our history that the nation has ever waged war upon a country against which Congress has not declared war. . . . There are men in the United States who would fight if they were in the Filipino's shoes. . . . Oh Liberty! how many Benevolent Assimilations are committed in thy name! . . . "Destiny" is the excuse of cowards; brave men make their destiny.[18]

The Lion supported Theodore Roosevelt on some things and criticized him bitterly on others. He looked dimly on the Panama Canal project, offering to pull out all of his teeth on the nearest doorknob if the project was completed in twenty years. He never had to—time took care of them for him. In spite of all this, however, their mutually valuable friendship remained unimpaired.

In January, 1902, Lummis had changed the name of the magazine to *Out West* with the motto, "The Nation Back of us, the World in Front."

The geographical limitations of the West?

Well, there is not a dead black line on the map that can define it. Out West is anywhere that is far

[15] Charles F. Lummis, *Out West*, Vol. XVI, No. 4 (April, 1902), 416–17.

[16] Charles F. Lummis, *Out West*, Vol. XIX, No. 2 (August, 1903), 216.

[17] Charles F. Lummis, *Out West*, Vol. XIX, No. 1 (July, 1903), 676–79.

[18] Charles F. Lummis, *Land of Sunshine*, Vol. XI, No. 3 (August, 1899), 116.

enough from the East to be Out from Under. It begins whenever man can find elbow room and Freedom; wherever he can escape from crowds and the obsessions of their strange superstitions; wherever he has space to stand erect and must stand because he will and not because he is so wedged in that he could not fall down if he tried. . . . It makes him a larger individual by giving him range to see his relationship to his kind. . . .[19]

Westerners, as he saw them, "are the people who have moved because they could Do Better . . . for the typical Westerner is an Easterner graduated . . . he has made his choice as an intelligent being."[20]

The first issue of *Out West* was noteworthy. It opened with a poem entitled "Out West" by a ranch girl named Sharlot Hall, who later became poet laureate of Arizona. For the frontispiece Maynard Dixon drew an allegory of the Genius of the West. David Starr Jordan and other great westerners made contributions. Wendell Phillips Garrison of the *Nation* had already spoken of the magazine's lively independence and its genuine learning as "a steady evenness of worth and interest." President Theodore Roosevelt, despite the magazine's severe criticism of some of his policies, said publicly, "I always read it —I am tremendously in sympathy with many of the things for which it works." Moreover, he allowed the publisher to carry that quotation on the masthead. Francis Fisher Browne, the great editor of the *Dial*, called the publication "the most valuable magazine of locality every published anywhere."

[19] Charles F. Lummis, *Out West*, Vol. XV, No. 1 (January, 1902), 60.
[20] *Ibid.*

Nevertheless, "we were poor all the time and sometimes had pretty serious tangles with the printers before they would trust us for another issue."[21] Lummis' salary as editor was fifty dollars a month. There were never enough hours in the day; he never went to bed before midnight. Despite the warning of the stroke, month after month he drained all there was in his mind and body. After a day's work of ten to twelve hours carpentering, planting, editing, preserving fruit, photographing, weeding, battling for the missions or similar causes, lecturing, trading in curios, and doing whatever he could to augment the family bread and butter, his strength would falter without something to spur it. Awakening in the morning to find that his "brains for the day had not arrived yet," he would take a drink to rouse them, a few more during the day to keep the show on the road, and at night he would have a glass to quiet his galloping mind.

There are frequent notations in his diary: Dejo de tomar aguardiente ("I give up taking whisky"). But that jinn slides out of the bottle more easily than it goes back in. Bastante juisque ("plenty whisky") also appears many times. He had, however, a remarkable capacity for absorbing vast quantities of liquor without its becoming apparent.

In fighting to achieve the perfections he desired, Lummis was as reckless in the demands he made on his health as he was in the demands he made on the family he loved. In this he was wooing eventual disaster.

[21] Lummis, "As I Remember."

22

A Champion for the Oppressed

If the American People could see some things that go on under their national nose, there would be directly no such things to see.

A national convention of Indian educators and managers in 1899 stirred Lummis to write a series of articles in the *Land of Sunshine* on United States Indian policy. He called the series "My Brother's Keeper."[1] "Our Indian policy is not just something which concerns a few thousand dark-skinned individuals," he declared. "It is actually vital to our own white existence."

The Indian, poor devil, will presently die off. His obliteration somewhat gruffly begun by the border ruffian, is now much more spiritedly (though less courageously and frankly) carried on by those who make their living by philanthropy. But we shall remain and our children's children will have to live by the record we make.

It is entirely true that our long-infamous Indian service is grown cleaner. But its task has only just begun. . . . The First Americans, upon whose stolen lands we live, have been taken out of the hands of the ward-heelers and given into those of theorists and ignorant system-makers.

Their system aimed, wrote Lummis,

. . . to take the Indian from home as young as possible, "educate" him and turn him loose on the population . . . as many thousand miles from home as possible, and never let him go home again. The confessed theory is that he has no right to have a father and mother and they no right to him; that their affec-

tion is not worth as much to him as the chance to be a servant to some Pennsylvania farmer or blacksmith, and generally at half wages.

The head of the Carlisle Indian School, Major Richard H. Pratt, "a monumental organizer, a just and a manly man" had for almost two decades been responsible for Indian education. Yet, according to Lummis, he had never "learned that the Indian has a soul; that he loves his parents and his children, and even the birthplace that we have stolen from him." This educator defined Indian family devotion as "the instinctive and superstitious regard for the mere tie of blood."

"All humanity rests on the family and nothing can compensate for the wreck of it," said Lummis. He laid down certain basic truths "as scientific as they are decent."

A mother is a good thing;

A mother without a child is void.

Likewise a child without a mother.

Education is meant to be an enabling for the life of the person educated; not . . . designed simply as the easiest way for the teacher to make a living.

No country is bettered by having children who have forgotten their fathers and mothers.

If we must "educate" the Indian, we should adapt our curriculum to his capacities and our demands to his humanity. . . .

. . . Every one of these truths (as well as a number of others) our Indian service is today violating. . . .

Well, then, what should we give the Indians? My answer is very simple—common sense, justice, and mercy.

[1] Charles F. Lummis, *Land of Sunshine*, Vols. XI–XII (August, 1899–February, 1900).

*Employ no one professionally ignorant of Indians....
... remember that education must reckon with the pupil as well as with teacher and public.*

Sensible education strikes a balance between what the ideal man should have and the actual man can assimilate....

It is well that he learn to read and write and get what comprehension he can of this nation's laws and genius and acquire our language ... chiefly as some protection against being robbed by our rascals. But most of his education should be in better methods of life ... sensible farming, fertilizing and rotation of crops and grafting, and grading up his stock ... the rudiments of sanitation ... a little carpentering, a little wagon-making, a little of many other homely, useful things.

[With all this] he should be allowed to believe that our government is not a liar when it makes him a promise ... and that it is not every American who hankers to rob him of his lands or his children.[2]

Lummis had known many excellent professionals who made their living by educating the Indian, but as an extreme example of the "brains employed in the service" he cited the lady teacher "who acquired an ancient gray gelding ... found a colt running with it in the fall and soberly claimed the colt was hers, " 'the offspring of my gelding.' "[3]

The good gentleman responsible for the methods at Carlisle saw nothing odd in his admission that "Unquestionably there results [from the school's teaching] a certain modification of that blind loyalty to family and clan which in the Indians amounts to a religion."

"I simply wish to ask any American that has children," said Lummis, "whether he is looking after some 'higher education' to lessen the religion of filial loyalty?"

A humane and experienced teacher in the Indian schools, Bertha S. Wilkins, added her testimony in an article in the *Land of Sunshine* entitled, "The Pity of It."

To one who has lived and worked in an Indian boarding school with heart and eyes open, the life of the children appears as it really is, lonely and forlorn. . . . Tribes which have yielded to civilization and have given their children to the school are dying out, while tribes like Navajos, who have strenuously opposed our overtures, have increased in number since 1868 from 12,000 to 22,000.[4]

She cited the statements made by a government physician as he watched almost a hundred coughing boys (some as young as six years) retire on a cold night.

"These places are death-traps. It's impossible to protect the healthy from tubercular contamination ... and the windows must be open for ventilation and there is no mother or father to see that the covers are not kicked off."[5]

"Ah, friends," wrote a pupil in one of these schools, commenting on the advantages given the Indian inmates,

We have been happy without these things in our Indian homes where love was; in school we have them and are not happy because love is not there.

Among us Indians, only the wiser teach the children; among the Whites it seems as if those who couldn't make a living at anything else get a job to teach Indians....

Many of these [white] teachers mean well. But I think that when a contract is let to put up a school building, the contractor isn't paid for meaning to put up a building. He doesn't get his money until he puts it up—nor then unless he puts it up right. . . . The teacher is paid for attempts, the contractor only for results. If half as much care ... were given to the pupils as to the buildings, the Indian might have some chance to be really educated.[6]

However, the theorists of the Indian Bureau did not, according to Lummis, "remotely dream of any such commonsense and justice as trying to uplift the Indian father and mother, at least enough to enable them to understand and sympathize with their

[2] Charles F. Lummis, *Land of Sunshine*, Vol. XI, No. 5 (October, 1899), 263–64.
[3] Charles F. Lummis, *Land of Sunshine*, Vol. XII, No. 6 (November, 1899), 334–35.
[4] Charles F. Lummis, *Land of Sunshine*, Vol. XII, No. 4 (March, 1900), 244.
[5] *Ibid.*
[6] "Lame Dancing Master," *Land of Sunshine*, Vol. XII, No. 6 (May, 1900), 357.

'educated' child. . . . The soundest way in education and the only merciful way in humanity to educate an 'inferior race' is to educate it at home and all together...."

There were some who were angered by "My Brother's Keeper" and thought it was absurd to think of treating "a conquered and inferior race" with justice and brotherhood.

However, the articles aroused fifty representative citizens of Los Angeles to hold a meeting. Lummis called on "every man and woman who cares . . . that we do justice, and who believes that any system is accurst whose cornerstone is the breaking-up of the family" to form a national organization to aid and protect the Indian.

Fortunately Theodore Roosevelt had been reading Lummis' writings on the Southwest and the Indian problem and was himself writing *The Winning of the West*. Soon Roosevelt was asking Lummis for information about the Spanish influence in the West and words used by cowboys.

I was able to answer his questions to his full satisfaction. But when he wanted to know the derivation of "hoss-wrangler," I was stumped. I think this one etymology did more to pull us together than any volume of ordinary words; for piqued by the problem I trailed the word back to the Spanish caballerango, in Mexico the vaquero who tends the herd of spare riding ponies. Every Texas cowboy knows that caballo means horse. And not knowing what the termination meant, they adapted it to a familiar English word—and there you were, "hoss-wrangler." Roosevelt wrote me a delighted letter saying, "I wish I had the kind of head that would pop into!" From that time on he seemed to follow my writings more closely and to rely on my judgment.[7]

Shortly after Roosevelt was catapulted into the presidency, he telegraphed Lummis that he wanted to consult with him in Washington prior to the first message to Congress. On December 5, 1901, Lummis arrived in Washington and was informed that lunch was waiting at the White House. It was a remarkable concession for him and an indication of the high regard he held for his former schoolmate that he telephoned the White House for assurance that his

travel-dusty corduroys would do. The luncheon party included a number of political and business figures.

To each of these Roosevelt presented me formally . . . and then said in that characteristic way of his—which newspaper men would call "boxed," "Lummis runs the Land of Sunshine *out in Los Angeles. I want you to know that I always read the* Land of Sunshine *though it is the only magazine I have time to read now. I read even its Anti-Imperialist editorials. And I am tremendously with so many of the things it is working for." Later he quoted my book on Mexico* [The Awakening of a Nation] *with that astounding accuracy which characterized him. I have seen him reading; he seemed to take a page at a bite. . . . On the second day after lunch again, he asked me to write out certain information for him in set form. These were questions he had to deal with in his message. I dictated them later to a public stenographer and they became, without noticeable change, paragraphs in Roosevelt's First Message to the Congress.*

During our talks I told the President that the Bureau of Indian Affairs quite naturally looked on outside suggestion or advice as "from the enemy," and that any attempt to reform or change had no earthly show to get very far before the red tape of the Indian Bureau had strangled it.

"Mr. President, it is hopeless to attempt any of these things unless there is someone in the White House in sympathy. This has been burning in me for more than a dozen years, but I knew it was wasted effort to start anything. But you understand the West. We would not bother you with trivialities nor with old wives' complaints; but if the ideas I have outlined appeal to you as right, I will start the ball rolling—if I could be sure that at a pinch you would stand behind us."

"To the last gun!" he half shouted, clicking his teeth and bringing his fist down on the table. That he meant it was proved several times in the next few years—sometimes dramatically. It was on this assurance that I founded the Sequoya League.[8]

In December, 1901, at the home of C. Hart Merriam in Washington, D.C., Merriam, F. W. Hodge, Professor J. McGee, Professor W. H. Holmes, Dr.

[7] Lummis, "As I Remember."

[8] *Ibid.*

Lummis and Theodore Roosevelt, Harvard classmates and two men who admired each other greatly.

Gilbert, and Charles Lummis agreed to create a league to help the Indians. Early in 1902, Lummis formally organized and christened the Sequoya League after the American Cadmus who was the only American Indian to invent a written language. The league set out "To make better Indians by treating them better." As founder, Lummis was made chairman of the executive committee.[9]

Almost concurrent with Lummis' command trip to the White House, there was for the first time in the history of the United States the official announcement of an Indian policy of "real mercy, justice, and

[9] The Sequoya League was headed by such citizens as Mrs. Phoebe A. Hearst, founder of the Department of Anthropology of the University of California; Major J. W. Powell, explorer of the Grand Canyon and head of the Bureau of American Ethnology; Miss Alice C. Fletcher, Fellow of the Peabody Museum, member of the Council of the Department of Anthropology, University of California ("and the most successful intermediary with the Indians the Government has ever had"); F. W. Hodge of the Smithsonian Institution (successor to Dr. Elliott Coues); Washington Matthews; David Starr Jordan; C. Hart Merriam, head of the United States Biological Survey; and many others equally distinguished.

common sense." The annual report of the Honorable W. A. Jones, the commissioner of Indian affairs, came to precisely the same conclusions as were reached by "My Brother's Keeper" and by many persons whose competent reports were published in the *Land of Sunshine* and *Out West*.

The first purpose of the Sequoya League was not so much "to arouse sympathy but to inform with patience and wisdom the widespread sympathy which already exists." Undoubtedly some of Lummis' own involvement had originated in Helen Hunt Jackson's *A Century of Dishonor*, a book which had first roused him in the 1890's.

Lummis now learned that the Mission Indians of California were in a distressing condition.

. . . due not to the fact that they are Indians and improvident but to the fact that our government has not fulfilled its obligations to them and has suffered them—in its distant ignorance of the facts—to be crowded into the deserts where a horned toad might scratch a living if single, but must inevitably starve if led into matrimony. It will be a function of the league to remedy some of these shocking facts. Its creed is based on the faith that the government's intentions are honorable—and that the present administration is peculiarly "horse sense."[10]

In San Diego County, not far from the great telescope on Palomar Mountain, there lies a beautiful tract called Warner's Ranch. For hundreds of years these golden meadows, rolling hills, and acres of bottom land dotted with oaks had belonged to the Mission Indians. All that was dear to them was there —religious memories, bones of their ancestors, their children's graves. But now the white man claimed the land was his, and in 1902

. . . in ignorance of the fact that under Spanish law (from which every land title in Southern California derives), there is no procedure whatever under which an Indian can be evicted from the land on which he was born, [the United States Supreme Court] evicted the 300 Warner's Ranch Indians from their memorial home.[11]

When these "stolid" Indians received the eviction order, they were struck down with grief. The young were bewildered and sullen, the old weeping and clinging to the only home they had ever known, not knowing where to turn. The Indian Bureau and the Department of the Interior would have let them scatter and starve on the desert as other wards of our government had done. But the Sequoya League went to work. They

. . . forced the Bureau to move to provide these Indians with a place to live. The Bureau sent out a veteran inspector, a stranger to California, who looked at a few properties in February when the wild flowers were knee high, and recommended the Monserrat Ranch at $75,000. We proved that this ranch hadn't even enough water to drink for 300 Indians and that the records showed it had been sold three times within a decade for $30,000. But—the Bureau pushed on with the purchase.

This looked like the authorized "crisis" in which we might bother Roosevelt.

Roosevelt responded by immediately creating the Warner's Ranch Commission.[12]

Serving without a salary, with $1000 for expenses, we spent several months by wagon and saddle, making thorough examination of 107 ranches and an elaborate report in two volumes. The commission was not like most commissions. There was no graft, there were no prerequisites. No contractor got his little dib, supplies were not bought at inflated prices, members gave up valuable time without pay. This might be considered a minor landmark in civic history.[13]

At Pala, California, this commission was satisfied that they had found land five times more arable and with over one hundred times more water and at half the price of the choice of the Indian Bureau. More pressure was needed from President Roosevelt, but Pala was finally accepted.

Lummis had many powwows with the Indians to convince them that it was necessary for them to move. They made impressive and emotional pleas for

[10] Charles F. Lummis, *Out West*, Vol. XVI, No. 2 (February, 1902), 179.
[11] Lummis, "As I Remember."

[12] The Warner's Ranch Commission was made up of Charles L. Partridge, Russel C. Allen, and Charles F. Lummis, chairman. Judge Richard Egan joined it as the land and water expert and William Collier as land title expert.
[13] Lummis, "As I Remember."

their right to live in the land of their ancestors. Even after he had won the majority into agreeing to move there were still a few stubborn holdouts. And in the end they blamed their eviction not on the Supreme Court or the government policy but on Lummis.

Nevertheless, as he pointed out, while "it has been our whole history that the Indian has had to move, the Warner's Ranch case is said to be the only one in which he was moved to a better home than he was deprived of. For all of which, they have to thank T. R."[14]

It was in May, 1903, that the actual move was made and in the same month Roosevelt came west. Consistent with his earlier theories of compulsory presidential education, Lummis wrote urging him to visit Acoma, Isleta, and, of course, the Grand Canyon. The schedule did not allow visits to the Indian villages, but the president requested Lummis to meet him at the Grand Canyon. This Lummis did, bearing a gift of a tiny pistol which actually fired blanks. The president was pleased with the revolver, but he was delighted when Lummis, using his famous power over railroad personnel, casually slipped him into the cab of the big oil-burning engine that was pulling the official train. By prearrangement with the engineer the train immediately pulled out with Teddy at the throttle. The distressed Secret Service operatives were forced to swing aboard following cars and were not able to catch up with their charge until he had piloted the train through the Cajon Pass.

Conscious of the support of the White House and motivated by the desire to help less fortunate fellow men, the Sequoya League was able to aid some six hundred Mission Indians, including the Campo Indians of San Diego County. These had been pushed off their own fertile lands onto bleak desert reservations. They were literally starving. The league found a market for their basketry and weaving after re-establishing these dying folk arts. In its comparatively few years of service, it is estimated that the Sequoya League did more for the relief of the Cali-

Lummis and President Roosevelt about to board a Santa Fe engine during the president's trip west in 1903.

fornia Indians than all former activities of government and philanthropy put together.

Pleased as Lummis was with the Warner Ranch victory, he was almost equally delighted with a small personal victory over the behemoth of government red tape. He handed in his expense account listing exactly the items purchased, including cigars, whisky, and wine. He was requested to disguise these items as "laundry, stationery and incidentals," but he refused.

Some time I am going to have specially bound my correspondence with the Secretary of the Treasury on this matter. My final letter proposed that he send his most trusted man and I would give up my time for another six weeks to take the gentleman over the same route . . . and if he himself didn't need as much whiskey and wine as the commission consumed I would pay his expenses from Washington and back. That did it.[15]

14 *Ibid.*

15 *Ibid.*

23

Brawls and Books

THE Sequoya League and the Landmarks Club, El Alisal, *Out West*—these and other products of Lummis' prolific mind were all extant at the same time, and it is indicative of his tremendous energy that he was able to keep them all moving. The building of El Alisal, aside from fulfilling his dream of a home for himself and his descendants, satisfied his need for physical activity and his wish to keep his body in good condition. Probably, however, the long hours of overtime and the hard work that he put into moving the huge beams and building walls burned up what was left of his youth. His diary notes that one day he hoisted three tons of boulders to the top of the wall he was building.

One organization, the child of his fertile imagination, gave him considerable satisfaction and no effort. He, alone, retained the privilege of nominating members to the Society of Self-Made SonsofBitches—an example of the caustic wit that made him relentless enemies. Admittedly he loved a fight and sometimes went out of his way to start one. The extremes of his character were such that he made friends loyal unto death—and enemies still bitter after his cremation. Nor were all of his battles with words only. Fist fights were not uncommon at the turn of the century, and one whole section of "As I Remember" is devoted to boasting about those he was involved in.

Perhaps the last whole-souled rough and tumble fight I ever had was a good many years ago coming across New Mexico on the old A & P. It was about the time when the infamous, unAmerican and thrice damned APA wave was at its height.

This was the same American Protective Association which preached that His Holiness was conspir-ing through the minions of the papacy to annex these United States to the holdings of Vatican City. Charlie was in the smoker making notes when the conductor began pouring out this "incomprehensible, incredible and insane blather—but the very thing that masses believe under emotion and that we have seen the whole country swallow when excited." Lummis tried to shut him up, but when the conductor began a vile tirade against the Sisters of Charity who had given the paralytic such gentle care in Albuquerque, the fight was on. It must have delighted the occupants of the smoking car. The brakeman had to do the honors at the next station. Lummis' only worry was that his precious pass would be revoked, but he heard no more from the incident.

His attitude toward women had not helped him in an earlier encounter, however. Going home early one morning from the *Times* office, having "put the paper to bed," he answered a woman's scream to find one Billy Manning, then a champion wrestler and prize fighter and owner of a small tavern, brutally beating his huge wife, herself a heavyweight female pugilist from England. By virtue of his prestige as a newspaper man Lummis was finally able to break up the family fight. But because they were nasty about it, he put a story in the *Times* calling the attention of the authorities to the Palm Garden, the disorderly place run by Billy and his wife.

The next morning as I came down Spring Street past the corner of second, the huge British Frigate came diagonally across the street at me under full sail— Mrs. Billy with her 5 foot 11, the build of Juno and 185 pounds. She caught me by the throat. "I'll teach you to scandalize my husband! The best husband

*ever a woman had!" And so on, emphasizing her re-
marks with drives of her right to my nose, which
promptly laid over on its side—and that is some lay
me down for my nose was never inconspicuous until
then. I was enough of a boxer to have laid her out
with one blow but I have never emerged from the
ancient superstition as to petticoats. I suppose I
wouldn't wish to hit a woman now when there are
none. Petticoats. Some Women. So I simply grabbed
her wrists and tried to hold them but as they were
fully as large as my knees, I couldn't get my short
fingers half way around them and as she had 60
more pounds weight than I to drive those wrists I
found in a moment that it was useless. So I simply
folded my arms and stood there. Perhaps this is the
best thing I could have done for she gave me only
three or four more stunning welts and a final warning and sailed majestically back across the street to
the Palm Garden, triumphant virtue in every stride.
I lost no time getting to the Times office, washing
the blood from my face and sending out for a new
shirt but it took me a long time to jack up that pros-
trate nose and get it to stand by itself. And while my
nose is still a proud promontory, the handiwork of
Mrs. Billy is ever obvious on the bridge.*[1]

There was another set-to with Billy that afternoon
which was broken up by the police. Eventually, however, they all became friends. "Billy in particular was
a very staunch friend for many years, willing to go
almost any lengths for me. He became rather famous
as a physical trainer and taught Leonard Wood and
other noted men some of his really valuable secrets of
training."[2] And so our hero took a pummeling—the
price of chivalry.

Be that as it may, Charles F. Lummis' chief claim
to fame and some degree of immortality was not due
to his penchant for street brawling. The earnings that
paid for his corduroys and fed his family and secretaries resulted from the popularity of a number of
books he wrote. They generally received kindly treatment from the reviewers, but, inevitably, there was a
share of unfavorable comment. Fortunately, however, the criticism was never as vitriolic as that which
was sometimes poured on him because of his eccentric garb.

[1] Lummis, "As I Remember."
[2] Ibid.

That his own works were authentic and sincerely
written was attested to by Edgar L. Hewett, director
of American Research for the Archaeological Institute of America, Museum of New Mexico, who
stated: "a new book on the Southwest by him is an
event of high importance. . . . That fascinating region
has been well explored from the time of Coronado
and scientific and historical reports concerning it
make sizeable libraries. But in literary description of
it, Lummis took the lead and has never been over-
taken. It is safe to say that he never will be."

Lummis' first book was *A New Mexico David,*
published in 1891. "When America's younger writers
include Richard Harding Davis and also the author
of *A New Mexico David* . . . it behooves the dismal
prophets to cease their wails and tune up for the
coming paean of victory," said Tudor Jenks in the
Book Buyer. Jenks added a gentle word of caution
(other critics were not always so gentle): "Perhaps
he [Lummis] would do even better if he did not
always travel under a full head of steam. But gratitude rather than fault finding is due from the reader
of such stories. . . ."

Edward W. Bok, soon to become editor in chief of
the *Ladies' Home Journal,* had this to say about the
new western writer and *A New Mexico David.* Lummis' work lay "with the unusual, the virile, the active,
the dramatic: In these respects, at least, I know of no
writer so worthy of [being honored by comparison
with the] young genius Kipling as . . . Charles F.
Lummis. [He has] the trained observation of a lifelong student, the vivid fancy of a born poet, a close-
ness of sympathy with nature matched by few in our
generation and a queer tang of the aboriginal and
gypsyish."

Lummis followed these "true pictures of the wonderful and almost unknown Southwest" by a book
that we owe partly to the influence of a writer he
admired. Charles Dudley Warner had enjoyed the
newspaper accounts of Lum's long walk across the
country. He advised Lummis to revise the slangy
phrasing and make the stories into a book. It was
largely due to Warner that Lummis dropped the
flippant journalese of the *Scioto Gazette* and began
to develop a style of his own. He called the resultant
book *A Tramp Across the Continent,* the story of
"joy on legs"—"the diary of a man who got outside

the fences of civilization and was glad of it." There were conflicting opinions about the book. The *Philadelphia Evening Telegraph* wrote, "He tells us that it was done for pleasure . . . but . . . a more dolorous outing cannot be conceived," while, on the other hand, the *Saturday Review of London* found *A Tramp Across the Continent* a story with "such heart in it, such simplicity and strength, [that] it is as good to read as any story of adventure may be." To the *Toronto Week* Lummis' book was "indeed a graphic and spirited narrative of unique travel . . . by a young man of superb physique and indomitable will and pluck . . . an honest manliness of tone and kindliness of disposition which makes us overlook much that would otherwise seem conceited and exaggerated . . . one of the most interesting and instructive books of its class that we have met with."

That same year Lummis published *Some Strange Corners of Our Country*, a book written, like the first, for his "young countrymen." In it he introduced the deeper message he was to preach the rest of his life: Americans must learn to be proud of America and ashamed not to know it.

Other civilized nations take pride in knowing their points of natural and historic interest but when we have pointed to our marvelous growth in population and wealth, we are very largely done and hasten abroad in quest of sights not a tenth part so wonderful as a thousand wonders we have at home and never dream of. . . . There is a part of America—even of the United States—of which Americans know as little as they do of inner Africa.[3]

Said the *New York World* of *Some Strange Corners of our Country*: ". . . there is not a line in this beautiful volume beyond the comprehension of any intelligent child, there is not a single page . . . that can fail to interest, aye, fascinate the oldest and wisest reader. Such a book is worth more than 10,000 of the silly stories cooked up for young minds. . . . To read this volume is to make one religiously resolve to some day make that trip—never mind about Europe."

The Land of Poco Tiempo, published in 1893, pleased a reviewer of the *Baltimore Sun*. "The en-

chantment of the scene has entered into the soul of the author and he speaks as a lover under a spell to whom no words can be too endearing, no description too heightened." "Uniformly and surpassingly brilliant," the *Boston Traveler* called the book. "We shall not know how many lives have been affected by its opening paragraph: "Sun, silence, and adobe—that is New Mexico in three words. . . . Here is the land of . . . Pretty Soon. Why hurry with the hurrying world. . . . The opiate sun soothes to rest, the adobe is made to lean against . . . the hush of daylong noon would not be broken. . . . Let us not hasten—mañana will do. Better still, pasada mañana."

In curious contrast, the *Milwaukee Sentinel* concluded that the New Mexico Lummis described "seems to be a God-forsaken country, hot, rocky and barren, picturesque only in its desolation." Although the critic found "much that is interesting in the book . . . at times the style is pedantic and unpleasantly aggressive . . . and it is too often suggestive of the arid wastes which it spreads before the readers."

In a long article the *London Spectator*, in spite of an evident interest in the book itself, sternly cited the author's use of "a language which is not our own, though it is said to be the best kind of English . . . familiarity has not endeared it to our minds. It is, we regret to say, the language of Mr. Lummis. Sometimes it is picturesque and forgiveness is easy; more often it is the reverse . . . 'gritty Belle Davis'—is that an epithet to be applied to a heroine?" The *Spectator* was further annoyed by the author's misuse of familiar words or his use of words unknown to the ordinary dictionary. "What, for instance, is 'the *roily* pulse of the river?' And what kind of an ass is a 'devoluted donkey'?"

Lummis believed that "Every other young Saxon-American loves fair play and admires heroism as much as I do." For them he wrote *The Spanish Pioneers*. In this book he challenged for the first time in popular literature the leyenda negra—the "black legend" that Spain showed cruelty in exploring and colonizing the New World.

In this country of free and brave men, race prejudice, the most ignorant of all human ignorances, must die out. We must respect manhood more than nationality and admire it for its own sake wherever

[3] Charles F. Lummis, *Some Strange Corners of Our Country*, 1–2.

found—and it is found everywhere. The deeds that hold the world up are not of any one blood. We may be born anywhere—that is a mere accident, but to be heroes we must grow by means which are not accidents nor provincialisms, but the birthright and glory of humanity.[4]

The Spanish Pioneers spotlighted the heroism of tiny bands of Spaniards pushing their way across the harsh, unknown lands. It flatly denied the old teaching of Spain's inhumanity. "The legislation of Spain in behalf of Indians everywhere was incomparably more extensive, more comprehensive, more systematic and more humane than that of Great Britain, the Colonies and the present United States, all combined."[5]

The book went through sixteen editions and earned for the author La Reál Ordén de Isabella la Católica, the Order of Isabella, presented by King Alphonso of Spain.

Other books Lummis completed during this productive period were *The Man Who Married the Moon*, a collection of Pueblo Indian folk tales; *The Gold Fish of Gran Chimu*, inspired by the Peruvian adventures; *The King of the Broncos*, stories of the Southwest; and *The Enchanted Burro*, which took its name from an Indian legend. (One may imagine the author's reaction when the jacket came out with the caption: "The Enchanted Burro Charles F. Lummis.")

[4] Charles F. Lummis, *The Spanish Pioneers*, 11–12.
[5] *Ibid.*, 24.

From Boston came this poetic review of *The Enchanted Burro*.

A reader may pass a space of time with enchanted thoughts that will cause him to leave the book with a sigh and with also a wonderment as to the origin of the spell that Mr. Lummis has cast upon him. We have all read many stories of New Mexico and South America . . . but none . . . written from the same clear consciousness which . . . has absorbed into itself so much of the fascinating fragrance, mystery and beauty. . . . few can so color [travels and researches] and so rythmically intone their lingering cadences as to make this little volume . . . a genuine mosaic impossible to duplicate."

After Lummis returned from Peru, he travelled through old Mexico to get material for *Harper's Magazine*. As a result *The Awakening of a Nation* was written. He said that it was written "not as a description of Mexico but as a fingerboard along the path to comprehension."

"If he had done nothing more than write his latest book on Mexico," observed George Hamlin Fitch in the *San Francisco Chronicle*, "he would deserve the thanks of those who are looking for the coming of the day when our national prejudice against one of Spanish birth shall be wiped out."

The Awakening of a Nation was the last of the books that Lummis produced during this busy period, perhaps because he became deeply involved in a number of other matters.

24

"The Most Beautiful Museum in the World"

EARLY IN THE 1890's, Lummis, the incorrigible collector, had prompted the amusement of even his ardent supporters when he began to preach the necessity of a museum for Los Angeles, then considered a frontier town with its population of less than twenty thousand people. He continued to press the idea that this city with its location and heritage was the logical site for a museum to display American history at its fascinating best. Although Los Angeles continued to be unresponsive, the creation of this dream museum became one of his major objectives.

In 1903, Francis W. Kelsey, general secretary of the Archaeological Institute of America, asked Lummis to found a society of the Institute in Los Angeles. Despite all its resources and authority, the AIA had been unable to create an enduring chapter west of Wisconsin.

The reply was sheer Lummis.

You folks back East had grandfathers. We hadn't. We have to build our own towns, sewers, car lines, libraries, museums, jails, schools. You could probably dig up fifty people here who could pay ten dollars a year each to help your classical studies in Greece and Rome but I am too busy. You have been going twenty-four years and have a dozen societies. You haven't a museum or even a museum case. You have "added to human knowledge"—but nobody knows it.

We need here a Museum of the Story of Man and if Los Angeles could serve science and the world in this way, under your hallmark, with intelligent benefit and credit to its own people, we would astonish you.

Kelsey must indeed have been the "magnificent Crusader in Science" that Lummis called him, because on being invited to "Americanize" the venerable AIA, he accepted the audacious proposal. Lummis then went after the big men of education and business in the community with characteristic vigor and ruthlessness.

By November of 1903, Lummis had rounded up enough members to hold a founding ceremony. Kelsey came to Los Angeles to celebrate and was the guest of honor at a Lummis Spanish dinner. It was something to experience. The mission-style kitchen at El Alisal, with its maroon-colored walls that rose to a broad venthole, was redolent with roasting peppers, onion, cheese, olives, marjoram, *masa*, and other ingredients of a Spanish California feast. Guests walked into a picture by Ignacio Zuloaga. Easterners found it hard to believe that there could be such a place as the gray stone castle and such a man presiding. Yet Lummis knew how to make them feel at home in this storybook world of dons and troubadours.

It was with high hopes of eventually building his museum that Lummis founded the Southwest Society of the Archaeological Institute of America. Even the name was dear to him.

When I first stumbled upon the Southwest—the stark peaks, the bewitched valleys were as now . . . except that the Old Life had not yet fled from them. Across those incredible declivities, where distance loses itself and the eye is a liar, the pronghorn antelope still drifted like a ghostly scud of great thistledown. . . . In the peaks the cimarron still played ladder with the precipices; in the pineries the grizzly shambled snuffling and in green rincones where val-

ley and foothill came together and a spring issues of their union, there were lonely adobes with a curl of friendly smoke from their potsherd chimneys—gray, flat little homes bald without, but within warm and vocal of the old times when people sang because they Felt Like It.[1]

Stimulated by Lummis' enthusiasm and his singular facility for making science exciting, the Southwest Society was soon the largest of the twenty branches that made up the AIA.

For years Lummis had been battling to prevent certain southern California collections "of almost incomparable importance" from slipping into the hands of out-of-state collectors. At last a fund was raised. Lummis had already managed to persuade the Los Angeles Chamber of Commerce to buy the Palmer-Campbell Collection of early California Indian relics. It was the first scientific archaeological exhibit in California.

His next task was to put pressure on the society and the AIA to recognize the necessity of rescuing the quickly vanishing folk songs.

. . . There were not lacking formal persons in the East to protest, "But that isn't archaeology, you know." To which the obvious and actual reply was: "No, it isn't. But in ten years it will be, and as dead and gone as the rest. Out here we think it would be rather sensible and scientific to catch our archaeology alive.

And that is what the Southwest Society has done, is doing, and will continue to do for so long as there shall remain a still-animate specimen to collect. It is . . . also uncovering and re-articulating the dry bones of the extinct humanities in its great field . . . but the greatest thing it has done in its maiden year has been to trap the Living Thing.[2]

Part of the flavor of the Southwest would have been lost but for the Edison recording phonograph and the persistence with which Lummis sought out persons from all levels who still remembered the old songs. As he hauled his archaic equipment from sheep camp to adobe, he found that aged singers

were already beginning to forget the same songs they had once taught him. Indian children, washerwomen, and members of proud, old California families were all given the opportunity to record for posterity on the wax cylinders. Manuela Garcia recorded no less than 150 songs.[3]

One of the more amusing episodes of the recording project was the salvaging of the old railroad chanty "Jerry Go and Ile that Car." An official of the Santa Fe railroad sent an order over the entire system to track down Jerry at all costs and send in the words. The six stanzas were published in *Out West* with the music in February, 1904. The first stanza is as follows:

> *Come all ye railroad section men*
> *And listen to my song.*
> *It is of Larry O'Sullivan*
> *Who now is dead and gone.*
> *For twenty years a section boss*
> *He never missed a bar—*
> *Oh it's "jint ahead and cinter back,*
> *An Jerry go an ile that car-r-r!"*
> *Refrain: For twenty years etc.*

According to railroad tradition the song was composed in 1881 by a roving Connaught man remembered only as "Riley the Bum."

The organization was not yet a year old when it brought out its first bulletin, proudly illustrated with halftones of the newly purchased Caballeria Collection, thirty-four paintings that had hung in the Franciscan missions of southern California up to the time they were secularized by Mexico in 1834.

Five months later came the great news. Lummis' years of persistent campaigning had resulted in pledges for gifts, loans, and bequests totalling more than fifty thousand dollars. It seemed that his dream of a center for western treasures might be realized. Delighted, Lummis began to plan for his museum as for the destiny of a favorite child.

This was not to be just another museum. It was to be the most beautiful and the most original in existence. And it was to belong to every man, woman, and child in the Southwest. Lummis selected a site that

[1] Charles F. Lummis, "Catching Our Archaeology Alive," *Out West*, Vol. XXII (January, 1905), 35.
[2] *Ibid.*

[3] The kindly Garcias and their fine old adobe house near Ninth and Olive streets were the center of Spanish Californian life in the Los Angeles of that time. Now that area is in the business section of town.

commanded a sweeping view of more than sixty miles of the Sierra Madre and across the city to the sea twenty-five miles away.

Then Henry E. Huntington offered a princely gift, a forty-acre, two-hundred-thousand-dollar piece of property near Eastlake Park. Lummis had to persuade the millionaire as well as the businessmen in the society that it was necessary to pay fifty thousand dollars for one piece of property when another, four times as valuable, could be had for nothing. He marched the members of the executive committee up his hill, showed them the thrilling view, and they reluctantly agreed. Now began the arduous task of raising money to erect the building.

25

"Despite Lack of Modesty"

In 1905 the Los Angeles Library Board had decided that the town needed a male librarian. There was a flurry of protest which developed into five years of storm when it was announced in June of that year that Charles F. Lummis had been selected for the position.

The incumbent was a woman and was capable. At the time women's rights were an issue, and she had staunch allies. Many reasonable people were sincerely convinced that the librarianship was not a man's job —especially not a job for Lummis, who had never set foot in a library school, who wore eccentric corduroy suits, and who was known to drink, to swear on occasion, and who was not only prone to twisting the tails of sacred cows, but even delighted in "bull-dogging" them.

Fully aware of the issues of the situation and in the knowledge that "to many people any change in anything is a Hardship and a Sin," he commented:

The only politics anywhere in the case have been done in an attempt to maintain that any public library of any size is the proper "spoils" of the Women's party . . . as a matter of fact, fatherhood and motherhood are the only inalienable offices of importance that depend on the cleverest of God's accidents. Every other responsibility in the world depends solely on the way the individual discharges it.[1]

Lummis accepted the position on a full-time basis and put in many hours of overtime. He did, however, continue to pursue his numerous other activities in what might be termed his spare time.

[1] Charles F. Lummis, *Out West*, Vol. XXIII, No. 2 (August, 1905), 81.

The apprehension of the staff at having their quiet halls invaded by the fire-breathing eccentric soon changed to pleasant surprise. They found him warmhearted, magnetic, and considerate. He believed that the welfare of the staff was essential to the efficiency of the institution.

Immediately a series of practical and effective reforms were undertaken. Lummis installed revolving desk chairs, drop lights, windows, and typewriter chairs for the staff. Sagging stacks were braced, and boy porters were hired to do heavy work, releasing the higher-paid workers for more suitable jobs. The installation of a pleasant lunch room caused a 50 per cent drop in sick leave, and a raise in the thirty dollar monthly salary brought "immediate increase in efficiency, discipline and effectiveness." (The librarian's salary at that time was $150 a month.) Daily half-hour lectures by the librarian on library work were eagerly attended by the girls who thereupon undertook supplementary study.

"Quietly, steadfastly and continuously the new Librarian has mastered the new routine . . . he has taken advantage of its strength, exposed its weaknesses and proposed their remedies," reported the library board. However, this did not mollify the opposition dedicated to an unrelenting fight to get rid of Lummis.

It was Lummis' 1905 library report which undoubtedly first drew the attention of the country to the realization that something was going on in the Los Angeles Public Library. Althea Warren, a brilliant librarian who long served in the San Diego and Los Angeles public libraries, wrote Turbesé of her own estimate of the Lummis reports. One who has "never read the dry statistical hay which is the usual report of a librarian of a public library [might not] realize how remarkable they are. Nothing approaches them in my mind in library literature for sparkling phrases, vigorous ideas and practical imagination, unless it be Archibald MacLeish's reports while he was Librarian of Congress in the early 1940's." According to the *Report of the Los Angeles Public Library* for 1905,

. . . the consciousness has grown . . . that the first function of any library is not entertainment but instruction. . . . civilization could not well do without that intellectual recreation which masterly fiction gives. The value of excitation by proper books in the development of the youthful mind would be hard to overestimate. But . . . the bony structure of every library should be those departments whose aim is the diffusion of knowledge . . . the reference portion. The greatest libraries in the world and the most useful are the reference libraries. . . .

An aggregation of 120,000 books should be more than a mere overgrown circulating library. It should be a place where scholars can find their tools sharp and ready; where business men can easily learn what is "doing" in their own lines; where those who had looked on books as time-killers or excuses for a "club paper" can be taught the larger usefulness of them. The Los Angeles Library has a magnificent record for clerical efficiency. For scholarship it has none.

In the same report he amused himself and the board of directors at the expense of the Dewey Classification System, since it included under "Fine Arts" such unlikely items as checkers, blindmans buff, skating rinks, and dice. "Philosophy" covered palmistry, humbugs, servant girls, cock fighting, adultery ("Why not under Fine Arts?", he queried), bicycle races, Ralph Waldo Emerson, corner lots, dyspepsia, race suicide, and prizefights. Then under "Religion" he came across such gems as frescoes, Bob Ingersoll, the devil, mortuary art, and witches.

Determined to give the reference department "serious and strenuous upbuilding," Lummis ordered its contents listed according to the various branches of knowledge. These lists were "experted by competent authorities . . . with a list of works we should procure." He instituted a cheap but authoritative system for the evaluation of books. Staff workers

clipped expert estimates from leading reviews of the world and attached them to the books to which they referred.

Long before becoming librarian Lummis had pointed out, "If there is any place where early American history and particularly history of California and the Southwest and of all Spanish America should be studied, it is here."

He soon founded a Department of Western History Material based on clippings from local newspapers, all condensed, classified, and indexed. These gave "as true a picture as the composite press can draw of life as it is lived in the Southwest." As he stated in his library report for 1905:

Within a few years anyone can find out in ten minutes . . . anything that anyone wishes to know about any phase of the growth and life of the community since 1854. [And in addition] the biographical data and portrait of every important man and woman in the history of California to date; gathered from them alive if possible.

The Department of Western History Material is now considered by some authorities to be the most valuable contribution to the Los Angeles Public Library.

Shocked to find that the library lost thousands of books yearly, he made a recommendation in the typical Lummis style. If cattle could be branded against cattle thieves, why not brand books against book thieves? His opponents heard this proposal with consternation. That did not prevent the branding iron from sizzling on the ends of the city's volumes as it had sizzled on the flanks of Don Amado's mustangs. Lummis was so pleased with the branding that he had a brand made up of his own signature and used it on his personal library, carpenter and garden tools, suitcases, and many other personal items.

This was only one of the ideas which caused the American Library Association to regard the untrained interloper with something like horror. So radical! So sensational! "Fancy," they said, "such unacademic declarations of policy!" For example, in Lummis' mind

Public libraries ought first of all to be for scholars and ought first of all to remember that the painters'

apprentice or carpenter or boilermaker or messenger boy who wishes to study something is quite as important a scholar as a Greek professor. . . .

The personal creed, politics or literary taste of a manager of books should not be allowed to play Czar to the users of books. [If an adult wished to read trash] it is probably his large American privilege—though how far they should be entitled to do this at public cost is another matter.

Although Lummis would not have let them into his own house, he restored to circulation the books of St. Elmo, Rider Haggard, Marie Corelli, and others. Also returned to the shelves were the standard works of Mormonism, Christian Science, and the like, and some fifty popular periodicals (including *Scribner's, Century, Harper's, Puck, Life, Punch, Collier's,* and *Leslie's*) previously banished from the reading room —"solely because *too many people used them.*"

"The Library's business is to provide all facilities possible," wrote Lummis, adding that as a library it also had a strong responsibility toward its reading public. As he wrote in his journal in 1908:

. . . I am getting bitten with this new idea for the library and want to make a little poison label which will keep within the law of libel and the etiquette of science and still keep our patrons from leaning on the text books that every library has to have but which are not in fact worth the match to burn them up. If it can be worked out satisfactorily, it will probably be the best of the several inventions I have made in this library.

Miss Melzer and I feel pretty good about our new suggestion cards. . . . We cannot very well say to the worst of our novel readers: "This book is of the worst class that we can possibly keep in the library. We are sorry that you have not any better sense than to read it and that we are obliged to keep it here for people of as little taste as you."

On the other hand we feel a certain responsibility. . . . So we have just had printed cards to tuck into the front of the book and headed: "Have you read these . . . ." listing a couple of dozen really good and interesting modern novels.

For sixteen years the library had been crowded into the musty old Los Angeles City Hall. In 1906 the library board decided to move it. During a previous administration when only six thousand volumes were to be transferred, the library was closed for two months. This time the untrained librarian was able to move over one hundred thousand volumes without closing the library for a single day.

The new headquarters was in the Homer Laughlin Building, and here the librarian's great pride was the roof-garden reading room of sixty-three hundred square feet, the first in America of such extent. Lummis delighted in pointing out its rose hedge, heliotrope, and geranium, its grape arbor eighty by sixteen feet, wisteria, and other vines. There were also fruit and ornamental trees, a fountain, and a provision for smokers. Noting that smokers support a library in as large a proportion as nonsmokers, the smoking librarian gave the cigarette crowd their own section of the sky room.

The more of these new ideas that were adopted, the more offended was the foe. What business had this man doing things so differently from the other librarians? He countered by working harder. Someday perhaps they could be won over. Meantime his girls were encouraged to put more and more into their jobs. In a memo to his staff Lummis wrote:

We have found no millionaires; we cannot expect to compete in books and binding with the richest libraries . . . with their $5,000,000 building, and $5,000,000 stocks. . . . But we can have, and I wish you to help me make, the best library in the world, not only of its size but of any size, in the cheerfulness, courtesy, accuracy, and promptness with which every patron is given what he desires of anything this library has. Don't wait for anyone to wake you up—look for a chance to be helpful. We do not have to ask any rich man to give us that. . . . If anyone becomes impatient with you, increase your own manners. The best capital in the world, in any profession, is consideration. It is also the first duty of all who serve the public. Don't hurry, don't worry and never stop growing.

"The best library in the world" was all Lummis wanted, except, of course, "the most beautiful museum in existence," and a family home that would endure forever!

The irreconcilables in the library took up so much

of Lummis' time with their disobedience, studied insolence, and pressures that his journal "like the guitar and other accomplishments . . . backslided."

Aug. 6. [1908] The tireder I get the easier it seems to me to work. One of the hardest fights I have had since I came into the library and the hardest two hours with the dentist and four or five more things of the same category in the day on top of a night without rest—instead of handicapping me [makes me] feel readier than usual to do something. I sometimes wonder if all that ails me is that I haven't enough to do.

Aug. 7. I remember very well when I would go several blocks out of the way to get into a fight with or without reason. I must be getting old, for I notice the fights and get tired of them and would go at least a half block around to avoid one unless it were a real necessary and righteous scrap. I have had several today and I was right of course (being no longer young and fighting for fun) and the best proof is that I fetched the other fellow over.

His continued activity in his other interests gave his enemies fuel in the fight against him. He was still editing his magazine and despite his own increasing physical ailments, was injecting vitality into the new Southwest Society and museum. To the chagrin of those enemies, however, outside interests did not prevent him from achieving an embarrassing success for the library. As he wrote in his journal:

April 23, 1908. I carried Joy into several departments by telling them to order all the new books they wanted. Our finances are coming out beautifully this year and we have nearly $12,000, a month before June 30. This is better than the deficit that the library has had every year.

Aug. 1908 . . . one of my really good girls pleased me today by reporting the biggest gain in membership in the history of the library in any one month—630— when we were already way ahead of anything else in the country in proportion and ought to expect to slow down in the matter of increment. We have over 36,500 active members.

It was in the summer of 1906 that the American Library Association had its first look at its thorny member. One may imagine the effect on its annual convention when the new librarian of the Los Angeles Public Library marched into its decorous gatherings wearing his corduroys, frontier sombrero, and red Indian belt, and in the midst of the East's summer heat!

Lummis was, of course, still writing the "Lion's Den" and, impassioned westerner that he was, alternating his constant advocacy of his adopted province with sporadic attacks on the East. And so his readers were reminded of

An Eastern summer! What a reminiscence for the Californian—what an experience to renew for them that they have graduated from the Foolish Land where it's as much as one's life is worth to meet one's own weather on the street. It is nearly 18 years since the Lion has participated in this Gehenna on the installment plan. . . . Neither in the tropics nor in the intermediate deserts . . . has he found anything so bad as summer in the land which is sardined with the vast majority of people who confess that they are the smartest in the world. The Morasses of Ecuador or the Mexican Tierra Caliente, the ghastly sands of our Mojave or the Peruvian Atacamba—he would pick any one of these as summer resorts sooner than any city of Indiana, Ohio, New York. . . . Being like all Westerners incorrigibly modest, I learned a lot on that trip East. It would never otherwise do to revisit the . . . region of our escape. But being so, we merely take the East as a joke, love the people who are lovable and never pretend that we gave God the idea of making a Real Country, and say no more of our own luck than seems needful for the spiritual and temporal well-being of such as deserve a better fate than the East.

It was, however, increasingly amazing to me to renew my acquaintance with what I had escaped from. The aghast alarm of dear friends because I would not put on a split-tailed concession to the Grundys (I go out to see what men wear in their heads, not how they decorate their posteriors), the distance at which they had put behind them the manful learning of their fathers, was a constant eye opener to my breezier receptiveness.[2]

2 Charles F. Lummis, *Land of Sunshine*, Vol. XXV, No. 1 (July, 1906), 51–52.

The ALA was surely jolted by the appearance of the western invasion. But Lummis was jolted too, as he wrote in his 1908 library report, to find that a body which has such a vital influence on the culture of Americans had never set eyes on

. . . *the most important quarter of the United States, the arid Southwest . . . that its members were nearly all unfamiliar with the greatest economic problem before the government today, the reclamation of the arid lands; and know nothing personally about those vital phases of American history, geography and development about which they are consulted daily—such as irrigation, orange-growing, fruit-packing, the Pueblo Indians, forest preserves, the Great American Desert, national parks, the Cliff Dwellers, Spanish America and many other things involved in the Southwest.*

It was the ALA Convention that gave Lummis the opportunity to demonstrate his uncanny ability to whip up a happy organization even in the most barren and hostile territory. To the eastern librarians he was the outlandish, hard drinking, uncouth westerner; it was even said that in his own home, when carving at dinner for cultured guests, he had been known to remove his coat!

Watching the faces over the hard collars, Lummis noted a bored look, a crooked smile, or a twinkling eye and soon had a dozen kindred souls gathered at his table. In a witty speech he pointed out that "This national organization of librarians upon whose national convention we are now dancing attendance with more or less reluctant feet—does, with all of its benefits, tend inevitably toward too much seriousness." As a remedy he proposed an association of "Librarians Who are Nevertheless Human." The notion was eagerly accepted, and the starched white shirt of the American Library Association was besmirched with a fraternity known as the Bibliosmiles, its purpose, "to keep the dust off our own top shelves." It was agreed that the group should gather at the annual meeting of the ALA. There should be a seal, badge, grip, high sign, password, anthem, and, instead of dues, a "dew."

California apricot brandy was selected for the "dew." Lummis produced a number of anthems,

sung to his guitar plucking. Most piquant was the password: "Cheer up, ALA."

Another great meeting of the Bibliosmiles was held during the convention the following year, and new members were initiated. It was warmed by much singing and lubricated by generous libations of "dew." Members made impressive orations on such esoteric subjects as "The Sick Best Sellers," "The Six Best Smellers," "How to be Human Though a Librarian," and "Dusting Our Top Shelves."

Back in Los Angeles, Lummis formed a chapter from his own staff. Their meetings were generally held at his fishing shack at San Pedro called "Jib-O-Jib," where the principal activity seems to have been "the devastation of lobsters" washed down with the official "dew," and friendly conversation.

There were dinners at El Alisal to honor visiting members from the East, duly recorded in the House Book under the seal of "The Lonely Order of Librarians Who Are Nevertheless Human," with an Open Book Rampant bearing the legend "Homo Sum and Then Some." The last meeting was in 1920, years after Lummis, himself, had become a Los Angeles Library discard.

Lummis referred to the Bibliosmiles as "the best joke of my ulterior decade." Obviously it was not conceived to endear the founder to the library establishment, and it is not surprising that the journal of the ALA continued hostile. Often the publication found no better way to express resentment than to simply ignore the upstart. Yet, curiously enough, in one of its last editorials on the outland cyclone, it made this magnificent observation, "Despite lack of modesty, the record of actual work seems to be considerable."

"Despite Lack of Modesty!" It would have looked well on his own escutcheon.

At the conclusion of the 1907 ALA meeting, Lummis stopped in Washington for conferences with President Roosevelt and executive meetings of the Archaeological Institute of America. The restrictions imposed by the Department of Agriculture had made it impossible for scientific bodies to conduct archaeological explorations in any region controlled by the department. There was no attempt to keep sheepherders and pot hunters from gophering in these ruins, and nearly all of the hundreds of collections being purchased by museums were being procured from such amateurs or western traders. Yet when a museum or the Southwest Society undertook methodical and scientific exploration, it was harassed and finally driven out of the field by government red tape.

At Lummis' request, Roosevelt presided over a meeting between his secretaries Garfield and Wilson for the government and Lummis, Edgar L. Hewitt, and Professor William H. Holmes of the Smithsonian Institute for science.

Roosevelt began, "Two years ago I started a scientific body, the Southwest Society, on its path of exploration. Now it complains it can't get anywhere because of fences and barbed wire entanglements and obstacles. Let us find out what is the matter."[3]

In a rapid-fire one-hour meeting the president explored the whole question and cut the red tape that had been impeding the investigations. Lummis walked out with an even greater respect for his old schoolmate. The Southwest Society's excavations were extraordinarily successful from that time. "With a trifling amount of money we secured more art objects and other tangible evidence of the ancient civilizations of the Southwest than many expeditions that spent tens of thousands."[4]

[3] Lummis, "As I Remember."
[4] *Ibid.*

THE CONSTANT warfare began to tell. In his diary Lummis wrote:

Aug. 4, 1908 . . . there is a great relief in getting old. Five years ago even, I would have made several killings for what I have heard today; as it is now, I will take the slower and better revenge—namely to force the people that deserve killing into a decent sort of procedure. . . . the longer I live the more I am astonished that a person with a hellish disposition like mine gets along while goodly persons of good temper are always getting into a mess.

Aug. 14. I have had to fight my own way nearly all my life and I think it is of record that I was a fighter. But I have found that it is not necessary to fight everything—and that, in fact, it pays better to leave some of the blame to God instead of taking it all myself. That is the real reason I think—next to the fact that I am old and not very well—that I have learned to be patient.

Old at forty-nine. The pressures under which Lummis lived, the incredible hours he worked, the strenuous emotions, alcohol, battles against hostile associates, and five to ten cigars a day, all were taking their toll.

To him rheumatism, lumbago, dysentery, and the other ailments he suffered were simply a necessary part of the business of growing old. The only thing to do was to take more strong coffee or a sip of apricot brandy or a glass of "juisque" and work a little harder. Yet he came at last to make one concession. As he wrote in his journal on April 21, 1908:

I am afraid that I would make a poor temperance lecturer for whiskey has helped me out when I had no

other friend and to do my enormous amount of work that probably I could not otherwise have done. Furthermore, the fruits of quitting it are very disagreeable for I sleep like a log and too much even after a couple of weeks without a taste. But after this last breakdown, I realized that I was coming to the end of my rope and that I couldn't afford to go any further on artificial strength. I will have to come down to grinding out what work is left in my old hulk without any spurs and must know how much I can stand by myself. So it's me on the water wagon.

Lummis' frontier bones were intimately acquainted with that rude form of transportation, the buckboard. He had whimsically written of it, "Good Lord, deliver us, doesn't she shiver us, rattle-ty-bangaty bones!" Now the water wagon proved an even more uncomfortable conveyance. Some nights he could write in his diary, "No bebo,"—"I don't drink." On others it would be, "No bebo—salvo un poco despues de media-noche"—"I don't drink—except a little after midnight."

This library period marked the beginning of a physical change in Lummis. For the rest of his years there were probably few times when the mere act of living did not call for will power greater than most would find worth exerting.

Many things in Lummis' life were now heading for a crisis. He saw even his own town growing away from him. He confided in his journal,

I used to know everybody in it—not only their faces but their skeletons. I could have disrupted every family in the town and turned upside down everybody or every organization—because newspapering was a good game and I played it to the

limits . . . knew everything . . . going on and didn't abuse my advantage.

Not being afraid to meet his own skeleton face to face, Lummis scandalized those good folk who discreetly kept theirs under lock and key. It could not have been easy, particularly in his position of librarian, to acknowledge an illegitimate child of college days. Until 1908 he had not known of her existence, but once he learned of her, he was as openly proud of this daughter, Bertha, who had suddenly come into his life, as if her parents' union had received a church blessing.

Lummis first met Bertha when he went East to a library convention. He at once invited her to become a part of his family. It did not seem to occur to him that the introduction of a stranger who would supersede her own children might be distasteful to his wife.

It made a holiday for his opponents. Unfriendly newspapers made as much of a scandal as they dared. Like most of his close relationships, this one too was to bear both joy and sorrow.

Bertha's newfound father took her with him on trips through the West, had a room built for her on the estate, and placed her next to him at the great banquets at El Alisal. She became part of a domestic establishment in which Eve tried to feed the multitude with the meager loaves and fishes provided. The feudal sense of hospitality was so strong in Lummis that he never felt too poor or too ill to share with friend or stranger. In the tradition of the West, no one worthy—or unworthy—must be turned away.

Like those hidalgos of old, Lummis surrounded himself with retainers and hangers-on. It began with Amate, the Andalusian troubadour with the troubled past. It went on to Amate's wife, the simpleminded Elena, to Amate's posthumous child, a string of secretaries, a tramp Russian artist, an orphaned Spanish girl violinist, and friends who came by the hour.

Eve resented Bertha, and her resentment increased as her gentle nature was embittered by the situation she had to face. As her husband gained importance, he relegated her to an inferior position in the household. Always there were at least two secretaries inclined to treat her as a prudish and backward country girl. One of these for many years was Gertrude Redit, destined to become the third Mrs. Lummis.

Often a group of guests was ushered to the dinner table at the last minute. As the number increased, Eve in desperation would send an Indian girl out into the yard to chase down and kill another chicken. Then there was the accounting at the end of the month when the master roared over wastefulness and the size of the bills.

Eve, however, had numerous warm friends and she assisted a number of struggling young writers and artists, sometimes with advice, sometimes with a plate of frijoles. She cooked Maynard Dixon's wedding banquet. After she succeeded in introducing Carl Oscar Borg to her friend Phoebe Hearst, the price tag on his pictures changed radically. Mary Austin dedicated *The Land of Little Rain* "To Eve, Comfortress of My Unsuccess."

Often one or two Pueblo Indian boys from Isleta would be working around the place. Eve was fond of them and conversed with them in their Tigua dialect. A favorite was a handsome lad named Copio. In an argument over who was to use a new garden hose, Amate shot him to death. Lummis got Amate off on a plea of self-defense, but, had she been able, Eve would have hanged him with her own hands. As it was, there was one more person at El Alisal for Eve to hate.

Meanwhile Lummis was dreaming of the warm family life of old Spanish California.

I went back to California today—the kind that used to be and that I have tried to hold on to and that we do revive here several times a year. It's the only way to live and I think if I were a little younger I would quit all the civilized jobs and just go back to that independent life which is good to one because one can make it good to everyone else.

More shame to me that I have let go of it; for I used to know it for many years—the only obstacle in my way is having been born under the shadow of the Mayflower with its consequent obligations.

Jan. 1, 1908. If the year could go through like its beginning, I think I should get fat and sassy. From a little after 1 P.M. until about 8:30, I did nothing but eat, drink and be merry. It was the great fiesta at Manuela's [Manuela Garcia] house with Romulo Pico [one of the noted Pico family] as chief of staff. I think our own Spanish dinners are in comparison, but nothing else in California is. She had a big crowd of 36 and the table was very pretty; and all the food the best ever Manuela fixed . . . we had frequent interruptions of song from New Year carols to Capotín and Don Simón . . . the wind-up was the lottery for comadres and compadres—who have the friendly relation of godfathers during the year. I got the same comadre as last year—Manuela's sister Elisa, dear old-fashioned dumpling. This old California custom is quite funny. We celebrated at the end by everybody kissing everybody else. . . .

January 1, 1909. I set forth for Manuela's carrying the guitar. Manuela's dinner was a howling success as usual. Old Don Romulo Pico had on a big apron and was down on his knees at the oven door nursing the turkeys. . . .

We gorged and gorged . . . Don Romulo made a truly wonderful toddy . . . Manuela and Nacho came in singing a New Year's carol in Spanish and from then on during the rest of the two or three hours that the dinner lasted, there was singing, talking and chattering and a mighty good time. . . .[1]

But the man who found such warm enjoyment of these parties and the host who celebrated fiesta days at El Alisal was different from the silent man his children usually knew. Lummis labored to make a home for them such as few possessed; he won the love of hundreds. But the spontaneous affection they might have felt for their father was discouraged by the New England silence which often hid his love. His feudal ideas and the switch he wielded to make his children what he thought they ought to be kept them from knowing him as he really was. They had faint memories of the earlier years when they were cuddlesome and compliant and he had seemed a father full of fascinating songs and stories. But in their hellion years care made him remote and ill health made him short of temper and speech. Even the things he devised to bring them closer made them act like suspicious ponies shying away from a coaxing hand. Yet Lummis held out his hand in many ways. When he first came West

. . . it seemed there was always someone singing at work or at play . . . nightly by dusk or moonlight, twenty or thirty of us would sit in the long corridor, forgetting the hours as we sang our hearts out . . . maybe with Padre Pedro Verdaguer marching up and down conducting; a choir-master with a voice as the Bull of Bashan.[2]

Lummis had taken just one guitar lesson. One was sufficient, he promptly decided. If a song wasn't in the key of G, so much the worse for it. As men had done in simpler times when they must sing or burst, he put everything into his singing. Turbesé recalled those days.

So every night after supper he would settle down with his guitar to sing with us at El Alisal. But his wistful hope that we too would manifest the Latin miracle of happy-heartedness was never realized. He had forgotten that the Del Valles and the Chaveses sang because they were happy. There we sat like members of a chain gang, contributing only a grudging mumble, waiting to be set free—like mules being prodded to the water-hole by a driver who knew only one way to interest the brutes in drinking. It is painful now to remember how we begrudged him even the short half hour of companionship with us he had to spare before the night work took him.

The public seemed to us children to be too much a part of life at El Alisal. Strangers were always coming to gape at the stone castle, pressing their noses against the screens until we felt like inmates of a zoo. Yet we rather enjoyed thinking that there was probably no one else in the city quite like "us Lummises," a distinction paid for by being made fun of by more conventional peers. When school children jeered at us as "Indians" or "Moquis" and made fun of our clothing and names, a more prosaic life seemed not without attractions. I still recall two little girls (one of them was named Zillah!) shrieking with laughter —to think of anyone named Turbesé. Zillah pretended it was the name of her family burro. I also remember keenly when my father had put me in charge on a station platform in Kansas City of his collection of suitcases, two guitars, a typewriter and a horn phonograph. Wearing the gaudy Peruvian cap with ear flaps that he had selected as my headgear, I felt as gloomily conspicuous as a fly speck on a

---

[1] Lummis, "Diary."

[2] Lummis, *Spanish Songs of Old California*, Introduction.

The start of a long trip down the Hance Trail at the Grand Canyon. Pictured are John Hance, the self-styled "greatest single-handed liar in the West" on his famous horse Darby, two secretaries in the employ of Lummis, and Lummis with his youngest son, Keith.

wedding cake. A woman completed my falling apart by stepping up and asking, "Are you traveling with a circus?"

I say it with affection: we Lummises were indeed traveling with a circus. It didn't need a tent and a brass band—only the activities of a man who had so much within himself that one ordinary life was not enough to express it.

There were warm and exciting times at El Alisal when we felt him reaching out and trying to break through to us with expression of the love he felt—the fiestas, especially Christmas and the Fourth of July (such Roman candles and pin wheels and shooting-stars and rockets and strings of firecrackers went off then, with my father at his most glorious!). But the other times outnumbered and obscured them. The *home that he had hungered for was never really his, and never really ours.*

It came to the point where my mother, like Dr. Dorothea, could bear no more. Only a woman of the most mature comprehension—or European upbringing—could have endured what she was called upon to face. It required a supra-natural gift to adjust to the "many men of many minds" who was Lummis.

Dorothea had tried gently to forewarn, but Eve, then very much in love, had resented it. At that time Charlie was writing her from Peru: "Ah, my darling Eve! My true and precious wife! How blessed I am in the long sweet letter wh. I got this morning! You give me new hope and strength and courage, and make me so happy! Truly you *are* my beloved and honored, idolized wife, the beautiful mother of my child, the comfort of my life, the heart of my heart. Truly you . . ." and so on for pages.

Yet her divorce complaint reads, ". . . he swore at her, called her the curse of the house, and on one occasion entered her room and swore at her for two hours, causing her great suffering." It would seem that some of the comments that he made about his own bad disposition were appropriate. In any case, after she left he wanted her back and in later life spoke in her praise.

July 31, 1903

Lummis and two of his children, Turbesé and Jordan, in 1903.

When Lummis finally saw that he must lose Eve, he fought to keep his children. Once standing by a baby's cradle he had been proud to see "a trace of Lummis will in the setting of that chin." Sixteen years later it was not so pleasant to watch that will defying him. Somehow feeling that woman must be loyal to woman, Turbesé, who had been his close companion of baby years, now took the mother's part. He had always been able to dominate life, yet now he was powerless to stop the defection of his own flesh and blood.

27

Life at El Alisal

IN 1909, Eve Lummis left El Alisal with two of her children, Turbesé and Keith, then sixteen and four years old, to stay for a time at the home of her good friend, Phoebe Apperson Hearst.[1] Presently she started divorce proceedings, and Lummis was left with his organizations, his series of secretaries, his castle, and his sycamore. For family he had but the one child he was able to retain, nine-year-old Jordan —Quimu.

Scarred deeply by the loss of those others for whom he had built El Alisal and with his health breaking under the strains he imposed on it, Lummis still tried to make something of what was left. A new pattern of living was designed to drown out his loneliness or at least to disguise it. He entertained more brilliantly than before, wrote with consummate persuasion; his frequent letters to his distant children were warmly affectionate, and his journal and diary made feeble attempts at lightheartedness.

. . . Quimu has been quite an angel today as far as I have observed—and so far as my critical knowledge of angels goes. The way to a man's heart is through his stomach but the way to a boy's conscience is "quite the reverse." A little application of a judicious box-cover is worth all the Sunday school and preachers I know of.

There were other farewells too.

. . . I had to sign the death warrant of dear old Alazan . . . 20 years ago I broke him out of a wild herd of mustangs in New Mexico. Our early acquaintance was what you might call strenuous but he had more sense than some people and it didn't take him very long to find who was in the saddle . . . of all the horses I broke, I loved him best and he was the smartest . . . pretty as a picture. . . . We covered thousands of miles of New Mexico and Arizona in more companionship than generally befalls between man and the better beast. His going cuts about the last link with the old life. If a fool city would allow such things, I would give him a grave here; but in an idiot civilization it is not permitted.

Dec. 23. I hope the last thing I shall ever do will be getting ready for Christmas for someone. . . . There will be a big crowd tomorrow night and we will have the best time that ever was. . . . God is mostly as we make him and it will be our own fault if we don't have a happy Christmas and we will because the whole day and night will be full of love and thought for those that we would like to have with us.

He put up again the pictures of "all the people that ought to be here"—Amado, Bertha, Father, Mamma, Eve, Modjeska[2] and read his "Toast to the Absent."

> Dear God:
>   Have a care of them we love!
> Be about them, where'er they be
> Far or farther or gone above,
> Tell them tonight that we dream them near;
> Give us to know their hearts are here.

---

[1] Eve lived to be ninety-eight. By the time of her death she had a literary reputation of her own. She was a charter member of the Spanish Athenaeum, a member of the Reál Academia Hispano Americana de Ciencias y Artes de Cadiz, the Hispanic Society of America, and the Reál Academia Sevillana de Buenas Letras. She also was awarded the Modella de Honor de la Instruccion Publica de Venezuela and received an honorary Doctor of Letters from the University of Arizona in 1933. She had received only a grammar school education.

[2] Helene Modjeska, the Polish actress, was a frequent visitor at El Alisal.

Wide is the world, but love more wide.
Here shall they sit with us, side by side,
Gentle faces and tender-eyed.
All that ever we held for dear,
God loan us tonight and here![3]

Though suffering with rheumatism and dizziness, he put at the head of his diary "Xmas Feast." Many friends came, there was a twenty-pound turkey, gifts for everyone, and "all were very happy."

Lummis had often regretted that the United States has no law of entail. He had long tried to de-

vise some way of making a lasting home for the family. He and Eve had starved and skimped to create it. He had built it to last against time. Now, with the breakup of the family, he was more determined than ever to safeguard El Alisal against loss or dispersion—against death itself.

Poverty stood in the way. Twice the house itself was in danger of being lost by debt. Twice friends came to the rescue. Finally he worked out what seemed to him the perfect plan for perpetuating the Lummis home. He would convey El Alisal and its

[3] Lummis, *A Bronco Pegasus*, 126.

Thanksgiving at El Alisal in 1909. Lummis prepares to carve as Jordan carries in the bird.

137

collections—the sum of his lifework—to the Southwest Museum which was housing its then meager collections in the Hamburger Department Store and the Pacific Electric Building. He reserved a life tenancy in the house in perpetuity for his children.

His gift, made on February 28, 1910, was hailed as "the most important donation ever made to a Western museum." As Hector Alliot of the Southwest Museum wrote in the museum's bulletin for 1910:

If American archaeology today occupies its deserved place alongside that of classic lands, that, too, is largely the outcome of Lummis' ceaseless endeavors to have preserved the precious mementoes of our land. The Southwest Museum, therefore, created almost wholly by this one man's devotion and enthusiastic scholarship, becomes naturally the fruit of his life's work for his children, his posterity and the people of the great Southwest. . . . The keynote of his life is his love for his children and his children's children and for their sakes all children and a large responsibility toward the community in which he lives. A collector since he was a boy, he has outgrown the collector's selfishness. His children converted him.

At the time there were certain of his offspring who sniffed a bit at this eulogy and felt no sense of elation at the missionary work with which Alliot credited them.

Haunted with memories of the children who used to play there, the house and the old sycamore continually meant more to Lummis. It had been a gratifying thing for the builder to discover in 1903 that it was not only a tree which he loved, but also a tree with a history.

One day after Lummis had begun to live by the big sycamore, an unusual character was brought to him, "a modest, well-mannered, sturdy man, with a Homeric beard and a thatch of hair both so dense as to seem almost bullet-proof. As a matter of fact an Indian arrow in a fight near Camp Mojave had struck him square in the jaw and barely scratched the flesh through that matted beard."[4]

His name was Greek George. He had come west "with the camels." "What camels?" He told the story. In the 1850's Secretary of War Jefferson Davis

[4] Lummis, *Mesa, Cañon, and Pueblo*, 80.

Greek George, the first to sleep under the *alisal*. (Courtesy *Southwest Museum*)

decided to find out if it would be practical to use camels in the Great American Desert. He commissioned Major Henry C. Wayne to buy camels in Syria. George Xaralampo was hired as one of the camel tenders. (Another was Turkish Hadji Ali, whom westerners still speak of as Hi Jolly.)

Greek George paid a second visit to El Alisal. This time he took special note of the sycamore. He walked around and around it; he studied the surrounding land. Then he came back and looked up at the tree.

"Seguro! This is the very one! I thought so the other day when I first came to you but this big stone house and the fountain make it look different. But there is the very hollow where I tucked my alforja [saddlebag] and I slept there in the very lap of the great tree. For when I came here with the camels in

1858 going to Fort Tejon, I camped me under this aliso with my eighteen camels. And now (he put his hand on Lummis' shoulder) I find here a Friend![5]

Lummis named Greek George's tree El Alcalde Mayor after the chief justice of the old Spanish towns. Then in February, 1912, with the playfulness he never lost, he called together wits of Los Angeles to meet him under its branches to hold a kangaroo court. The writ ("to be ignored at your peril") was headed "Court of El Alcalde Mayor." Beneath was the significant warning: POR ACA YO SOY LA LEY ("Here I am the Law")

The purpose of the court was "to try the Garden of Eden for what it has done to mankind. Some later offenders will also be prosecuted." Lovely Mary Garden was one of the later offenders. In 1917 a distinguished lecturer for the Archaeological Institute, Dr. A. H. Sayce of Oxford, England, was a house guest. He was one of the foremost Orientalists and Assyriologists of his day. That did not prevent him from being hailed before El Alcalde's tribunal and charged with the crime of "not knowing an old California good time when he sees it." "A slight withered man, erect and catlike with eyes piercing and unforgettable, Dr. Sayce knew the Far East like the walls of Oxford; but this was his first visit to the Far West."[6]

Sayce was intensely interested in El Alisal and the Southwest Museum. He was a gracious and adaptable guest and enjoyed the unfamiliar Spanish-American dishes, but he had no idea of what was in store for him.

Before we sat down to dinner, I, as the Court—El Alcalde Mayor in person—laid on the table at my right hand a 16-inch doubled-barreled shotgun pistol and at my left a 14-inch Bowie knife. My youthful son [Jordan] was Alguazil [constable] with a huge star on his breast announcing his office and an enormous machete girded to his side.

About a score of men and women of note were at this session of the Shanghai Court. The Prosecuting Attorney was Samuel Storrow. . . . The Defender of the Poor who made a pathetic plea for this stranger in a strange land was Thomas Dockweiler. And the

Chairman of the Jury was the irresistible Lucretia Del Valle, a perfect flower of the California that was.

Dr. Sayce was not permitted to speak in his own defense until after the verdict—our prisoners never were. He was pronounced guilty. When called on to say why sentence should not be pronounced . . . he said . . . that he hadn't known an old California Good Time until he saw it. But now that he did know it, he hoped to have another.

He was then, as I remember, about 70 and just on his way to another trip to the interior of China, quite alone. We have had correspondence since . . . scattering but hinged on gentle memories. Eleven years after this "trial" I had a delightful letter from him again in his beloved Egypt and apparently no older than before.[7]

One February day in 1911 a strange summons went forth from El Alisal, headed from "The Burrow." Under the motto, "Mad as a Ma Chère" were antic bunnies scampering to some destination of mystery. "THE MARCH HARES: Don Quixote XXXIII—Hamlet, II, 2" surrounded an awestruck or moonstruck hare.

Dear Bunny: The hounds are after you and the April Fool's next. Here's the only safe place. Postpone Death, Marriage, Taxes and all other Disasters, particularly your own, and scurry to this warren at Rabbit Time, 5 P.M., March 2. Cabbage at 6. Madness begins later. Others almost as crazy will assist. Bring your birthday with you. If it isn't right, we will remedy it. It's not your fault. Wear your own Hare, Rats barred, Ears up. Check your sorrows at the door and lose the check. Don't get Mad till you have to—but then get good and March. [Signed] The Gray Hare

Thus did the Gray Hare, "maddest of Them All," announce that he had founded the Order of the Mad March Hares, for such friends as shared with him the good fortune of having been born in March.

While we have been distinguished, ever since antiquity, from the Foolishly Sane who befell a careless world in other months, we have never before stood up for ourselves and defied Literature, Luck and the Loco Weed. It is time, therefore, that we

[5] *Ibid.*
[6] Lummis, "As I Remember."

[7] *Ibid.*

QUIEN A BUEN ARBOL SE ARRIMA,

BUENA SOMBRA LE COBIJA

COURT OF

El Alcalde Mayor

POR ACÁ

YO SOY LA LEY

IN THE PUEBLO OF

Our Lady of Angels,

IN THE NAME OF

The Old California Days

You are commanded to reserve ....

from 5 p. m. till the Last Car, for **Jury Duty.**

Among the Notorious Prisoners to be arraigned are:

....

....

....

Contrary to the inhuman and illegal procedure of Gringo Courts, this Judge, this Jury, and these Prisoners and Witnesses will Feed Together; the Introduction of such Evidence being Relevant, Competent and Material to this Case.

Hereof Fail Not, *but make due return of yourself at the appointed time and spot, to render a true and lawful verdict.*

POR MI MANO

CERTIFICO Y DOY FÉE

Yo Alcalde Mayor

ESCRIBANO

An invitation to the court of El Alcalde Mayor.

favored mortals whose birthdays come with Ides of March or thereabouts, should get together, assert our Birthrights and prove that there is Method in it....

...No wonder March is the Master Month in the calendar! Look who started it. I did, March 1, 1859.

Frequently eastern guests were present, and, while their dignity might have been ruffled, they found the occasion memorable with the hilarious "hares" partaking of such genial combinations as the ever-present frijol, red wine, and *hasenpfeffer* while they chanted the Song of the Order:

Godelmighty made the Rabbit
  For the Nashun'l Bird of March
Filled his laigs with jumpin' jacks
  And stiffed his ears with starch;
Spring's already in his blood,
  A-bilin' mighty funny—
Salubrious and Sassy and a-Hoppin' for his honey!
Welsh Rabbit ain't no Rabbit, it's a colic unawares,
But We are March Bunnies—So Who-the-Hippy-Cares?

Now that he could no longer have the family that belonged to him by blood, Lummis replaced them by ones who belonged by adoption. For friends like Maud Allen, Alfred Wallenstein, Thomas Moran, Ed and Lucille Borein, and Will Rogers, he held his famous Lummis "noises"—evenings of music, poetry, good fellowship, and Latin dance.

At a typical noise a guest might have found Rosendo, the blind Mexican musician, playing improvisations on his "rosendolin" (a rectangular instrument of one string played with a glass rod) and the vibrant Spanish dancer, Matildita, a colorful flash of whirling skirts. Perhaps Will Rogers would swing his enchanted loop and Charlie Russell would spell out in the Indian sign language one of the old tales of the rawhide frontier.

In such "Old Timers' Nights—Tenderfeet only by Permission," Lummis could for a little time forget what he had lost. Enchanted, his guests went away quickened by his wisdom, whimsy, and unaging heart. Many found an enriching experience that would last their lives. Some could say, like Monica Shannon, "One Sunday after the rains I came upon a house that spoke out loud of everything that really matters . . . and I went my way full of good things."

One of these who knew and loved El Alisal and its builder put some of these "good things" into a poem.

I know a home built round a lordly tree
Where silver fountains glimmer in the moon;
A spacious hall of wit and minstrelsy,
Of stately saraband and rigadoon;
Where wisdom wears the garments of delight,
Where ballad, lyric, Andalusian grace
Enchant the portals of the summer night . . .
So reigns Don Carlos in his dwelling place.[8]

[8] Henry Herbert Knibbs, "Don Carlos," *Saddle Songs*, 85.

28

Guatemala and New Mexico

CHARLES F. LUMMIS' fiftieth and fifty-first years—1909 and 1910—were among the hardest he had ever known. His family disintegrated, enemies finally forced his resignation from the Los Angeles Public Library, and his health failed. Yet he continued to agree with

. . . that old Kentucky philosopher whom ribald spirits might understand. Someone said to him: "That's pretty bad whiskey, Colonel." And he replied, "Pawdon me, sah. Some whiskey is better than others; but there ain't no bad whiskey." Likewise some days are better than others—but there ain't no bad days. God made them all to come and us to be able to take them as they come.[1]

He was still full of fight, however, busy with the Southwest Society, and he had great plans for the Southwest Museum.

I am like the old Norse Pirate, shot all to pieces, who said: "We'll just lie down and bleed awhile and then get up and fight again." I sure had to lie down and bleed a while tonight. . . . we had the fiercest fight in the history of the Southwest Society. It was not finished unfortunately and I will lose my Sunday and my sick leave. . . .[2]

By 1911 things were jumping again. In March he was asked to go to Guatemala in charge of the expedition of the School of American Research, which was working among the tremendous Mayan ruins of Quirigua. He took his son Quimu as a partner and went into the tropical rain forest. The United Fruit Company had given the School of American Re-search eighty acres of virgin jungle, 150 feet high and so thick that every step had to be cut out with a machete.

In the heart of the 80 acres were the half-buried pyramids of Quirigua, to this day, I believe, the most extraordinary carvings in the highest relief known to Science. It was a tremendous task to clear the 20 acres that the monuments might be brought to the light of day and particularly the pyramids saved from the crumbling roots and from the vast trees that were gripping them and prying them apart.

Using Carib axemen, the trees were felled, stripped and carried away to heaps remote from the monuments, and thus we brought to light the marvelous sculpture which Stephens described and Catherwood made a laudable attempt to draw in 1841. We located the original quarries, two or three miles up the Motagua where these monoliths were split out. How they were brought over the boggy intervening miles and how set up, 1000 or 1500 years ago, is a guess. My own belief is that the builders laid corduroy roads of timber and brought the great blocks on rollers, hauled by innumerable workers pulling on ropes of bejuco [ropes made of vines]. The blocks certainly couldn't have been floated down the river for there wasn't a log in the valley that would float by itself much less carry a 100-ton obelisk. How they upended the shafts is not known, but I surmise that they did it by lifting the head a little at a time and banking up under it with earth until they got it high enough so that a grand pull of several hundred men would set the statue on its feet.

Temples we found, still undestroyed by the Jungle; and their chronology was discovered and translated

[1] Lummis, "Journal."
[2] *Ibid.*

with relative ease. The only trouble with it is that while it has the Great Cycle and the Cycle and the year and the month and the day, there is no Year One....

...The place where a great obelisk or monolith or sculpture should be is where it was made, amid the dust of those whose brains and heart conceived these treasures for all time—not to be shipped away to foreign lands like captives at Rome's chariot wheels. Such a thing as the rape of the Elgin marbles or a Cleopatra's needle would be today impossible.

Today the explorer does as we did in Quirigua. He brings to light and protects the mighty monuments; then with glue-molds make absolutely perfect replicas of the most important, to take home for the edification of such people as are competent to learn. In the fine California Building in Balboa Park in San Diego may be seen the lifelike replicas of the chief monuments of Quirigua, indistinguishable from the originals. And those mighty guardians of the Jungle stand majestic in their ancient home.

The Jungle fever of Guatemala, which kills off the natives like flies and blinds great numbers of them, took toll of our expedition. Dr. Hewett, Jess Nusbaum, Adams and the others all had it in Quirigua—a week or so of "Breakbone" fever which left them so weak that they could not lift a finger. Quimu was the only member of the party who escaped. I was free of those symptoms both there and after my return. But within a month after we came back in May 1911, I found my eyesight failing rapidly. July 24 I looked my last on the light.

It was a good deal of a blow. When I had fought through paralysis I could still see the world and those that I loved. But now from behind this impenetrable curtain the world seemed strange and less friendly. When I could see, even if weak and stumbling, I knew where I was ... I could see people coming and danger.

As Fate would have it, just at this apparently inopportune juncture it became necessary for the Southwest Museum to conduct an expedition and excavations in New Mexico. Dr. Hector Alliot, that rare genius whose services I had secured as Curator for the museum, did not know New Mexico nor the Pueblos. Someone was needed who did. So, Aug. 14, 1911, just 3 weeks after my eyes had failed, we

started blithely for Santa Fe—Dr. Alliot and I, with Quimu as my guide, leader and eyes.[3]

Frank Springer, greatest living authority on fossil crinoids, a ponderous man of 65 who was just recovering from a "hopeless" seige of heart disease, took charge of me when we got to the Rito. He was tireless in his attention; and we devised a perfect method of leading the blind. I put my right hand on his right shoulder and knew absolutely whether he was stepping left, right, up, down, or how, and accommodated myself accordingly.

As I remember the several years of our Summer School in the Rito de los Frijoles as well as at the lofty Pu-ye, in the growing years from 1909 to 1914, all others seem a little childish to me even now. We had such lecturers as Paton of Harvard and Currelly of Ontario and Mitchell Carroll (Gen. Sec. of the Archaeological Institute of America), and F. W. Hodge and Alice Fletcher, the most important woman in American science, Congressman William Lacey of Iowa to whom the country owes more than to any other Congressman for our natural parks and even for our game preserves, John Peabody Harrington, most extraordinary genius on American linguistics, Francis la Flesche, the wise Omaha Indian, protégé of Miss Fletcher, Kenneth M. Chapman, beginning then to be what he is now indisputably, foremost authority on the decoration and symbology of Southwestern ceramics; H. R. Fairclough of Stanford.

Nusbaum and Harrington were two of "our boys" trained in the School, of whom we had every reason to be proud. Nusbaum developed great genius as an architect and builder. We owe to him the "Cathedral in the Desert" in Santa Fe, the great art gallery of the School of American Research. It is a logical composite of the six most important Franciscan churches of old New Mexico; and is in many respects the most interesting single building in the United States.

Among the innumerable cañons of the Southwest, the Rito de los Frijoles, whose aboriginal name was "Tyuonyi," ranks small. But there is not one more

[3] On this train trip it delighted the blind Lummis to terrify the occupants of the men's washroom by shaving with a straight razor while standing on the swaying floor. From then on he never used a mirror and kept count in his diary of the number of "blind shaves" he made. After he recovered his sight, he looked at himself in the mirror only once a year, some time around his birthday.

beautiful, not one that is more an Enchanted Valley than this 1500 ft. gorge, about 4 or 5 miles long, half a mile wide, with steep wooded slopes on the south wall to the top of a level mesa, one of the great "potreros;" and on the north side, the long creamy cliff of Tufa, pitted with weather erosions, but at the foot burrowed thick with the rabbitlike homes of the Ancient People.

Judge A. J. Abbott, a venerable Dartmouth graduate, with his plucky wife, had established a homestead here in a big stone house; and there were several tents for the Summer School; and Mrs. Abbott fed us on lavish vegetables and the most marvelous cobcorn, and biscuits of blessed memory with homemade butter.

The students were young men and women mostly from small Western colleges, one or two from England. Dr. Hewett was director, and we had numerous lectures on all phases of archaeology, from Biblical to Southwestern; and on biology and many other things. We excavated in the Talus Pueblos which were being discovered.

. . . We had field lectures and tent lectures and object lessons in excavation. And every night, save for the occasional summer showers, we had a glorious campfire among the pines, on a little "bench" above the singing brook. There were stories and recitations; but the great majority of the Campfires were for Song. We had wonderful sessions; I knew practically all the Old Favorites, and those who had half forgotten them came back to the memory, and we sang our hearts out under the moonlit sky. Once in a while in a break in the song, there would come a wondrous whisper from the pines a few hundred feet across the brook—old Frank Springer piping away on his flute in delicate mastery.

It was a great encouragement to me that in my blindness I could be of some use beyond my occasional talks on scientific and historical matters; and it is a truth that the old Campfires of Song were also a remembered feature through all the years of the School.

There were tent-houses and comforts, but I never slept but one night under such cover, and then because we arrived late in a rain, I was blind, and there seemed to be nobody to pack our bedrolls up to our cave.

At this first visit I took Quimu's hand and directed him across the stream and along the narrow and steep and slippery footpath leading from cave to cave. I had him describe each cave and told him what clan it belonged to. When we came to a labyrinth of knobs and outliers of Tufa, with the intricate passages to the cliff and around these buttresses, I told him what to look for. Up a precipitous Tufa slope we scrambled into a cave about 10 feet across, and high enough in the middle for me to stand erect in. This had a sort of Mezzanine floor at the left, a cave almost as large, and about 4½ ft. higher, with a large opening between the two. The main cave was my study, all these summers; and I had my sleeping bag there, my big camera, papers, the little Blickensderfer typewriter; and a very large stock of stationery supplies.

The next cave was Quimu's, and all he needed was his sleeping bag. Providentially, on the left side was a window about 14 x 20 inches, through which you could squeeze onto a little Tufa platform outside about 10 ft. from the general surroundings. You could walk along this for 7 or 8 ft. and peer into or climb into a tiny little crypt about 6 ft. long by 3 ft. wide and 4 ft. high. The caves were as clean and dry as the New Mexico air; also naturally very warm, the porous Tufa having drunk the sunlight all day. All the years since, that suite of caves has been mine, shared with such of my children as chanced to be with me.[4]

The distinguished archaeologist, Neil M. Judd, also recalled those caves.

By setting up residence in six of them, Don and I thought to escape daily meetings and evening lectures at the main camp.

Our seclusion was short-lived, however. It lasted only until Charles F. Lummis and his guitar arrived from Los Angeles. As one of the trustees Lummis was entitled to the very best the camp offered, so he moved into a couple of caves just around the corner from ours, lit one of his big black cigars and made himself at home. . . . Lummis was one of those who believed, along with Edison and Steinmetz, that no man needed more than three hours sleep. So he sat

[4] Lummis, "As I Remember."

beside a small fire outside his cave and entertained members of the summer session with old Spanish and cowboy songs until 3:00 a.m. He knew every cowboy and Spanish song ever written, but only one set of chords for the guitar. Despite the rather steep climb up from camp everyone came to hear those songs and they were worth hearing. But what Lummis and the others overlooked on these nightly concerts was that we assistants, unlike trustees, worked from 7:00 in the morning until 5:00 at night.[5]

[5] Neil M. Judd, *Men Met Along the Trail*, 913.

29

"It Was a Marvel
How Truly It Realized My Dream"

RETURNING to Los Angeles in the busy year of 1911, Lummis, despite all the frustrations, continued to direct the affairs of the Southwest Society, and under his guidance as managing secretary the Southwest Museum grew with remarkable speed and solidity. The time was approaching when it would be possible to finance the building of the planned new museum.

During the 1886 Apache campaign I had seen a young lieutenant ride up to a 6-mule team stalled in an arroyo, call to the driver [to get down], himself get off his horse, take the reins and the black snake which the poor muleskinner had been plying with hysterical futility, and simply lift those mules and their load through the heavy sands—less by the crack of the great whip than with the volley of impassioned profanity which rolled from his lungs.

When the time came to elect the first President of the Southwest Museum, it was this man that I chose, Adna R. Chaffee, now Lieutenant General and recently retired Chief of Staff of the Army of the U.S.A.

It was a great joy to work with General Chaffee— grim as a meat axe but gentle at heart as a woman.... Our board was a marvel of promptness and attendance at the meetings every two or three weeks and there was no waste of time with Chaffee in the chair.

A little measure of the gentle heart of this old warrior: at the annual meeting in 1911 he read his president's address which was pointed and comprehensive but as he came toward the end I judged he had a terrible cold. "I have to report the affliction by blindness of our beloved Secretary who has done so much—," and then he actually broke and said with sobs, "Damn it, Charlie, I can't go on—it is too dreadful."

When I first knew him he was said to be the "best cusser in Arizona." When our Southwest Museum finances looked most despondent, I had a brilliant idea. I would get the loan of the great Temple Baptist Church from my friend, Bob Burdette and his wife (one of our Board) and use it for a verbal prizefight— "For Men Only" and challenge General Chaffee to a swearing match.

He had the advantage in Reach and Volume but he could swear only in English; whereas I could throw in several more in Spanish with minor furbelows in French, German and a few Indian tunes.... But alas for the shifting foundations on which we build our hopes! I went to the grim old warrior, very reverently (as I truly felt toward him) but with a sense of humor of the thing and a conviction that we could pack the house at $5 a head. He looked at me and said with the least ghost of a smile, "Charlie, that is a great scheme—but I can't swear anymore." As I looked at him aghast, he added, "I have become a Christian Scientist."

General Chaffee held to his position [as society president] for more than a year after the expiration of his term and at much personal inconvenience in order not to expose the museum to the loss of prestige. It was indeed a serious matter—to cut off so famous a head from so modest a body without danger of bleeding to death.[1]

Another old friend, Norman Bridge, assumed the presidency, and, becoming several times a millionaire through his association with E. L. Doheney, the oil magnate, bequeathed the museum about eight hundred thousand dollars. That, however, was later.

[1] Lummis, "As I Remember."

146

In 1911 the sum of fifty thousand dollars was received from the estate of Carrie M. Jones. When word of this came to the blind dreamer, he knew that the time had come—he could break ground for the Southwest Museum.

Lummis got Quimu to lead him up Museum Hill and began pacing off the ground. Here is where the flagpole is to be set, here the benches to seat the crowd. On November 16, 1911, three hundred citizens, many summoned by Lummis personally, gathered for the ground-breaking—the "most beautiful service I ever saw."

Elizabeth Benton Frémont, daughter of the Pathfinder, turned the first spadeful of earth; General Chaffee was next. Then Lummis thrust the silver trowel into the soil from which his museum was to spring.

One of Lummis' treasures was the first American flag ever to be hoisted in the far West—the Frémont flag. Miss Frémont had given it to him, and it had not been flown since 1842 when John C. Frémont unfurled it on the crest of the Rockies. Now for the first time in sixty-nine years the flag was again waving over California soil.[2]

Sumner P. Hunt, the architect, who had given so much time to the Landmarks Club in reconstructing the missions, was again called on because he had there shown "not only a technical and constructive ability of a high order but a far rarer spiritual insight into the individual character of architecture according to its destiny and function."[3]

Hunt and Lummis had threshed over many plans throughout the years, considering styles that ranged from those of the San Xavier and Santa Barbara Missions to structures resembling the Alhambra. Finally they decided on the ancient Spanish style with its mighty simplicity. Lummis had seen and approved the first elevation. In his mind were pictures from the past that he had dreamed of incorporating in his "most beautiful museum in the world": the caracol tower, the vaulted ceilings, and the staggered windows that he had seen years before in South America before the onset of his blindness.

More or less in desperation, Lummis worked out

an ingenious system, based on a two-foot rule and folds in paper that he could feel with his fingers, by which he was able to make rough drawings approximately to scale that Hunt could follow.

One wonders if more sympathy is due the stubborn amateur who undertook to design the building or the architects and contractors who had to deal with him. By the autumn of 1912 his vision had returned, and almost every entry in the diary is related to the design of the museum and the relentless war over the details.

Oct. 17, 1912. Two-hour fight with Hunt and his office as to the thirty foot windows of the big tower—which he has like the slot windows of an English cathedral. Summon Alliot [the curator] and he sides with them. But I fight it out and insist on the "stagger."

Oct. 18 . . . telling Hunt how the Tower must be built.

Oct. 22 . . . we fight it out on the Torre. They already have some good sketches and I confirm 'em. Fix for lock library rooms. I knock out their girder ceilings and we agree on Barrel Vault ceilings for all halls. Bully session.

Oct. 24 . . . To Hunt's and fight over plans again. Quimu wants caracol tower & I decide on it. They aren't ripe, but I drive it in.

Oct. 25. 1 hr. with Hunt, 2 with Burns and Freese. Nail Quimu's Caracol which we discuss endlessly and engage on everything but battlemented Tower.

Oct. 28. Long fight. Hunt and Burns stick to Episcopal slits and I won't have it. Fix battlementing my way which they approve . . . Alliott fixes front fenestration which tickles H&B and I consent, but I retain my stagger on Pasadena side. New fight on well in caracol—they want caracol but solid (cos expense). Work on barrel vault etc. I stand for BV & Caracol Well.

Nov. 14 (Meeting of the Museum) Hunt and Burns show plans & I fight & get 'em accepted—Caracol and all.

It was one of his greatest triumphs. However, "we could not afford a great tower 125 feet high and 44 feet square just for looks. In all other Caracol or Helix staircases, the stair fills the tower—as in Sir

[2] The tattered flag is now under glass in the library of the Southwest Museum.
[3] Lummis, "As I Remember."

Christopher Wren's masterpiece in St. Paul's with 85 steps."[4]

To provide museum space in a caracol tower was a feat which had never been done before of record. Contractor Kubach declared to the architect that it couldn't be done. "Hell," said Lummis, "It's got to be done."

Hunt translated this to the contractor, "It's up to you; Lummis wants it." C. J. Kubach, an Old World builder, called in the cleverest of his foremen, a diminutive, dynamic Yankee named Henry Newton. Newton also said it couldn't be done. He got the same answer, "It's up to you. Lummis wants it."

A Yankee himself, Lummis often chuckled about Henry Newton and this challenge to "stump" a fellow Yankee.

And this fiery little genius did it as simply as if it were only a matter of established procedure, instead of the first and only thing of its kind in the world. Henry built a huge chimney of sheet iron, 3 ft. in diameter and 125 ft. tall for the shaft. Around this he built up such a forest of falsework that it was almost impossible for a thin man to wriggle through a room. Then one story at a time he "poured" this 125-foot tower, one operation each for the outer wall, the

4 *Ibid.*

floor, the walls of the well, containing the spiral staircase, the landing, the rise and tread of the winding stairs, and the handsome baluster. It was a splendid piece of engineering—and the result will be famous, I think, in perpetuity.[5]

The caracol is a helix in a central shaft, nine feet square, with rooms around it forty feet square. Lummis delighted to point out that it has as much exhibit space, wall and floor, as in all the rest of the great building. The lift is 160 steps, almost double that of St. Paul's.

Sumner Hunt had a real admiration and fondness for Lummis, but it would be illuminating to know what he put down in *his* diary.

"Lummis wants it," carried a great deal of weight with the museum, if not with his family, and the museum was constantly aware of his presence. He brought the reluctant board around to ordering an extra gallery in the Torrance Tower and three in the caracol. He devised a system "by which our wall cases took no floor space whatever, being inset deep in the concrete walls. They were also of a sort never before built and due to conferences with that master cabinet maker, J. Niderer." He chose the museum

5 *Ibid.*

Dr. Bridge and General Chaffee lay the cornerstone for the Southwest Museum, December 6, 1913. (*Courtesy Southwest Museum*)

148

The Southwest Museum, Los Angeles, California.

motto "Mañana Flor de Sus Ayeres" ("Tomorrow the Flower of its Yesterdays").

In many other ways Lummis' mark is stamped in the building on Museum Hill. The flying stairways were from the "wonderful half-ruined monastery" in Arequipa, Peru, and the two great arched exhibition halls or *boveda*, thirty by seventy feet and thirty feet high, are patterned after the room he had in that Peruvian seaport.

By another year the museum building was largely under roof. December 6, 1913, was another historic date. "Lay Corner Stone S.W. Mus.—My Dear Day! About 700 people climb the hill—wonderful representative audience. The ceremony was one of the most impressive and beautiful I have ever seen. Even beats the groundbreaking."[6]

On August 1, 1914, the Southwest Museum was opened to the public. There is a simplicity and balance in the lines that give it a certain timeless grace. The museum El Cabezudo was determined to have stands just where he was determined to have it—up on that hill where he could see it from his own window. He said, "it was a marvel how truly it realized my dream."

[6] Lummis, "Diary."

30

"I Am the West"

MORE THAN ONCE the strange jungle blindness disappeared. Each time Lummis thought he had his sight again. On August 31, 1912, he wrote in his journal:

In blessed Lizzie Kaune's kitchen in Santa Fe. . . . lifted the big black bandage and pried the bad eye open and got dim but recognizable glimpse of my Bertha, my Quimu . . . first human faces I had looked on in 14 months . . . benediction that my first faint glimmer of returning vision and new dawn to the world should be their beloved faces . . . gave me a great heart and patience.

But the blindness returned. He continued holding fast to the "Lummis treatment" of wearing the enemy down. At last in November of 1912 he wrote his friends.

Here's Looking at the World. And particularly at them I love. . . . After 15 months of total blindness I begin to See again; not much but a darned sight better than nothing. And I intend to get ALL my eyes back in time. The friendly bandage still tempers the sunlight but I can now peep out from under. "Old Son" Quimu has led me faithfully and well but now I can find my own way. The Dark is Another World and I had fun exploring it. I was never lonely in that long night for memory and friendship had hung my attic with pictures of gold—but the Glory of the Dawn!

This time his eyesight came back to stay. His family didn't. Neither did the fine physique with which he had played fast and loose.

All through Lummis' life any emotional blow seems to have been reflected in his physical condition. Some thought it shamming. Even those close to him were not in agreement. One thought it was a matter of extraordinary sensitivity. Another who had served him during his blindness felt that Lummis' recovery had come earlier than a dramatic moment in which to tear off the bandages.

The 1899 Velasquez dictionary with the signature *Charles F. Lummis* branded in the page ends does not carry the word *migraine*, nor does the word appear in the 1913 edition of *Webster's*. There is in the Lummis family a strain of this peculiar malady that in severe cases can produce neurological symptoms suggesting paralysis and blindness. However, Eve did not recall that Charles had suffered the frequent headaches usual to the maddening and then little-understood ailment. Another word not yet coined was *psychosomatic*. Yet Lummis' Mexican friends had a phrase by which they put all unanswerable questions in their place: "Quién sabe, Senor?".

There were other frustrations. The secretarial help on which Lummis was dependent was inadequate and a constant problem. Part of this was due to the fact that he expected everyone to work with his own passionate dedication. Why in hell should a secretary want Sundays off? And of all things, to go to church! He saw no reason why a secretary should not be delighted to work for him until all hours of the night and day after day. Nor could he understand why it might seem peculiar to a secretary for her job to include setting the table or pinch hitting as cook, holding a light for him late at night while he dumped a sack of barley into a feed bin for the chickens, or giving him a hand with minor carpentering and plumbing problems.

When Eve finally divorced him it was widely publicized in the newspapers. His new household was frequently turbulent with squabbles between house-keepers and secretaries, with the illness and death of the old troubadour Amate, the tantrums of Amate's simple widow who was a faithful but unpredictable retainer, and the problems of an old man trying to rear the posthumous child, Panchita Amate.

Lummis was still taking his love affairs very seriously. They continued to turn out badly, and each collapse seemed to be followed by some illness. Verse was a vehicle of his emotions. "The Rivals" was written for the little Spanish violinist whose laughter warmed for a time the cold loneliness of the stone house. When she learned that he had publicly dedicated to Mary Garden a poem that he had originally written for her, she packed her bags and left in a rage. "Butterfly of the Shining Wing" was written for one that he nicknamed Ahijada, and the collapse of that affair is indicated in his last letter to her.

Little Ahijada: I shall never believe in anyone again. I now learn that you knew of my blindness in July and never wrote a word for two months. It is now more than two months again since I heard from you —tho you knew I was still blind, suffering greatly and accursed by fate. . . . You were a beautiful picture in my life but I cannot respect anyone so heartless, so careless, so ungrateful. . . .

However happy or unhappy were his amores, he had a real genius for friendship. He shared his friends' joys and sorrows, he counseled them in their troubles, and remembered their anniversaries.

Many times he sent telegrams of rejoicing or condolence when he needed the money to buy food for his own table. On the death of one friend, Frannie K. Hamilton, he wrote:

God has given me a great Wealth of Friends . . . friends who of their own qualities could read some good into me! . . . Anyone who can adopt me for a friend must have a very genius for Friendship for I am rough and gruff and remote, and very slow to contact this disease—which is Dangerous, and beneficial only when it chances to be. . . .

Strangely enough, Lummis was almost equally proud of his enemies. At least of them he wrote: "Old Timers are fond of saying, 'Everybody loves *you!*' Of course, it isn't true for I luckily have a fine corps of well-earned enemies."

However big that fine corps was perhaps even he never knew. But it would be impossible to record all of his friendships with all races, of high or low estate, man and woman, beautiful and ugly. Bandelier must certainly come first. Close behind him comes the chivalric Amado Chaves—and Dr. Dorothea.

Some of his group had a habit of gathering at "that canvas wonderland on Pine Street," William Keith's famous studio in San Francisco. There Lummis had such feasts of spirit and of speech as the flaming geniuses of the Mermaid Tavern knew.

I got deeply acquainted with Keith not later than 1896. His studio was up over the old California Mar-

William Keith, as photographed by Charles Lummis 1898.

ket and there all my leisure was spent—the leisure of a busy man working up an historical series for Harper's Magazine. I have known a number of the painters of this country—Church, Bierstadt, Tom Hill, and many others. All these were fine artists. All had a certain childlike quality. But Keith was the most notable in many ways.

A Scotsman without either of the proverbial attributes of the race, he was neither stingy nor dull to a joke. His studio was a rallying point for several particular friends. . . . Rev. Joseph Worcester, the heavenly-minded Swedenborgian clergyman, had a great effect on Keith's art and was doubtless responsible for much of his later spirituality. One was Theodore H. Hittell, the learned and thorough-going historian of California, whose four huge volumes done by himself and fully indexed have many advantages over the six-volume work on California (out of 39 volumes in all) by the Drummer in Letters, Hubert Howe Bancroft, practically unindexed and of bias in many ways. The other of the exceptional trio was John Muir, the lean, shy Scot, the greatest naturalist this country has ever known but the least magnified because of his inability to "mix," his reluctance for publicity and the crowd, and the strange fact that it was painful for him to write. Sometimes he would hang for a day over a paragraph. And yet when he spoke, in company he liked, Jeremiah's self was no more sonorous a prophet. Almost every day Hittell and Muir got together with Keith for some time and almost daily Dr. Worcester dropped in for a talk with him.

It was an inspiration to watch Keith paint—particularly when he got tired of a picture that had been knocking around the studio for a long time. He would put it on the easel and daub it over with the sculch of his palette until it was dark mud. Then he would take a rag and with a magician's sweep would pull out of the hidden sky a burst of light, with the effect of black clouds about it. Maybe this opening would suit him, maybe it wouldn't. If it didn't, he would daub it out again with black and give a different swipe. Maybe this would be done four or five times. Each time, he would draw back two or three times to get the effect—squinting hard with his near-sighted eyes. When it did suit, he flew at it like a Berserker, alternately wiping with a rag and putting

on color in a perfect fervor of motion. A broadsword fight on the stage is seldom so swift-going.

One day I chanced in just as he was starting one of these palimpsests. I pulled my watch and stood there. He paid no attention to me. In thirty-one minutes exactly he had painted "The Golden Hour," 20 x 36; one of the most beautiful pieces—a broad glade surrounded by noble woods and an atmosphere of molten gold over all. I acquired this painting in my usual way with Keith. In later years, I was compelled to sell it to Henry H. Huntington for $1000.

Sometimes of course pictures lagged with him and he had hard work—sometimes for days—to find an inspiration; but ordinarily he worked in this ecstatic fashion, fairly fighting with the canvas in a delirium of inspiration as to form and color.

I had in those days a very extraordinary collection of opals which I had made mostly in Mexico where I used to rent a mine for a few days, put in as many peons as could work in the shaft under my direction; and have the nuggets cut by lapidaries later. No other precious stone ever attracted me—diamond, ruby, emerald, sapphire. Any of them can be counterfeited so well that only the highest expert can tell the difference. But no one ever counterfeited a good opal—perhaps it is safe to say no one ever will. Its color and light are not dependent on the faceting but are its intrinsic soul. Keith shared my passion for opals; and when I would come up with a new one he would kneel in his bay window in the sunlight to turn it over and over and tears would often come down his face. Frequently he would say, "I have to have this—take any picture you want." So as my stock of opals dwindled, my gallery of Keith paintings increased. The last one, "A Dream of Alaska," was one of his few indulgences in the Mystery of Turner and Moran. It was fully their equal in Mystery, though of course the mists and glaciers had not the Turner colors. But as I had one 28 x 36 painting to bring home with me by train, I left the "Dream of Alaska" in the studio until my next trip—and the earthquake and great fire of 1906 made me a sharer in the vast loss. But even yet, I believe I have more of Keith's "before the fire" than are anywhere else.

I met Thomas Moran, greatest painter of the Grand Cañon and of the Yellowstone, several times in the Cañon—I think the first time in 1886 or 87.

Thomas Moran, as photographed by
Charles Lummis in 1924.

I shall never forget the picture he was, any more than the pictures he made. He was about 6 ft. 2, slender, lithe and straight without stiffness, with a tight jacket, a coonskin cap and a gracious downward beard—as trim and personable a figure as one would find. Through our mutual love for the Southwest and its incomparable scenery, we became really friends; and the affection grew and ripened through nearly forty years.

He was modest but intellectually fearless. His scorn for people too lazy to learn geology before they tried to paint landscapes, or anatomy before they attempted the human figure or the horse was as calm and deep as an Alpine lake. He had served his apprenticeship of infinite patience as a wood-engraver to learn how to draw and to color. He was the only man who ever had any right . . . to paint the Grand Cañon of Arizona—or for that matter the incomparably less impossible Yellowstone. His masterpieces of both these masterpieces of God are in the National Capitol.

When he came to California to live and settled in Santa Barbara, the old friendship took new vigor. The death years before of his companion-wife—herself an etcher of rare grace and skill—had singularly orphaned him—and at the same time it developed beside him and for him a noble and beautiful character, his only daughter, Ruth. A girl of strong intellect, strong character, an uncommon ability for the stage, and with many suitors, she survived the shock of her mother's death by becoming not only daughter but mother to her single-hearted and unworldly father. The great work of the last 20 years of his life we owe almost as much to Ruth Moran as to the painter himself. She cared for him, sheltered him, was his companion, his business agent, his guardian, everything. I have known but one comparable case, that of the daughter and first-born of the Pathfinder and Jessie Benton; Elizabeth Benton Frémont, who gave up her whole life to be the Angel of the Hearth for her marvelous mother.

Sometimes Moran and Ruth visited me at Alisal; sometimes I visited them in Santa Barbara; and always it was beautiful. In 1922 at 85½ years, he painted just a souvenir for me, a glorious 18 x 30 oil of the Grand Cañon; and a year later, at 86, stood easily at the table, and put in my Home Book such a water

color of the Green River Cliffs as would grace the proudest art exhibit. At my last visits, he was bedridden and very weak; with his long white beard, still plentiful hair, and clear vivid eyes, he looked more like a disembodied spirit than anything. . . .

He had Turner's passion and weird genius for color and Turner's marvelous power of Amethystine Mystery; and particularly in some of his later paintings he surpassed, in color and in mystery, anything except the very best of the man whom Ruskin made an idol. And Moran had a far more thorough training in drawing and incomparably more knowledge of landscape and geology; and his drawing was truer than any painter who has worked in America, with the possible exception of William Keith, also skilled in almost a lifetime of preparation by his years as a wood engraver.

Both these men also painted at first literally, transcribed real estate as it were, until they had earned the right to create. And when they had earned that right, they used it nobly. They took no liberties with the Eternal Possible. I have seen Keith make one sweeping downstroke and there was a tree—and you didn't need to guess or be told whether it was a eucalypt or an oak or a pine. It was True—but it had taken him forty years to be able to do that.[1]

Among the "Lummis bunch" were the Hittells of San Francisco. The head of the family was Theodore H., the California historian, a grand old man of omniscient eye, domed forehead, and Michaelangelo beard. Lummis' diary records many a visit at the historic Hittell home at 808 Turk Street.

Dinner and long evening with the Hittells and fine Katzenjammer—Katie[2] and I always able to fight. Little old-fashioned red-cheeked bit of Pennsylvania Dutch pertinacity, who always wore a brown bolero length jacket and a skirt of corduroy with a bunch of keys at the belt—she kept the same costume throughout the years. Miss Katie was a great walker (she belonged to the Sierra Club and walked their 25–30 miles up to the day she died), a gallant defender of all her ideas and prejudices, as quaint, as pungent, and as dear to me as the wonderful little

---

[1] Lummis, "As I Remember."
[2] Catherine Hittell, daughter of Theodore H. Hittell. She was a frequent contributor to the *Land of Sunshine*.

green sage cheeses she used to serve at the end of the spicy meals down in the ground floor dining room.

Turbesé was a frequent visitor to the house and remembered it well.

Even to a child the Hittell dining room was an exciting place. What child would not be enthralled by its curios, its tall shuttered windows, its fine old china, its Chinese 'boy'; I loved to pore over its old world children's books. The head of the family had one of the broadest minds in California history. Working in his study with his manuscripts and his meerschaum, or swinging down Turk Street in his high silk hat and opera cape, he seemed to me the perfect expression of historic San Francisco. Though a man of wealth, he retained the unwasteful Pennsylvania way, and stored a jar of 'spills' on the mantelpiece to use instead of matches. It was my secret fancy that he kept track of how many unthrifty matches the family squandered.

The "boys," Carlos and Frank, were men of thirty and thirty-seven years when Lummis visited the family in 1898. To his delight it was a household that liked to argue. They argued about poetry, politics, California history, Frémont, the influence of the missions on the state, and the "good old days." Only dear old Mrs. Hittell kept a core of tranquility amid the turbulence.

The Hittell home (later restored to Victorian elegance by two English brothers, now torn down to make way for "progress") was once the scene of a near catastrophe. One of "808's" most captivating visitors was Miss Emily, the daughter of General Coey and later Mrs. Franklin H. Hittell. She was a girl of great sparkle and vitality. Fond of Lummis and of a good joke, she thought it would be fun to dress up like him and recite a waggish takeoff called "Down East Out West." There came an awful moment when she wasn't so certain that she'd had a bright idea.

My name is Lummis—I'm the West;
For culture I don't give a hang
I hate the puny East, although
I can't conceal my Yankee twang.

My trousers they are corduroy,
Ditto my jacket and my vest,
For I'm the wild and woolly boy;
My name is Lummis—I'm the West.

I am the mountains and the sea,
I am the salty plains between;
You've seen the orange crop? That's me;
I did it with my magazine.

My monthly Indian reports,
Drier than old Mojave's breast
Where the uncultured jackass sports;
My name is Lummis—I'm the West.

Who first beheld the Indian race?
Columbus, say you?—Tisn't true!
I was the first to see his face—
I've had him copyrighted, too.

I'm local color—Sitting Bull—
Tracy the Bandit—Teddy's guest—
The atmosphere is full of Me.
Charles F. Lummis, who's the West.[3]

[3] George Wharton James used this poem in an article about *Out West* in *Overland Monthly* in May, 1923, alleging that it had been published in a San Francisco weekly, "but the author . . . I have never been able to find."

31

MANY of Lummis' friendships centered around Santa Barbara. There lived Alexander Harmer, the artist, with his wife and two beautiful daughters. Other families well known to the history and society of the region were a comfort and inspiration to him, the de la Guerras, the Dibblees, the Crams, and the Del Valles. Above all he admired Dona Ysabel del Valle.

. . . the marvelous and renowned mother, the "Senora Moreno" of "Ramona"—although Mrs. Jackson got only the administrative skill and not the wonderful womanhood in her very few hours at Camulos. That noble old dame was an orphan asylum in herself and Camulos was always full of children she was bringing up. I have myself known her more than once to walk miles on a rainy winter's night on muddy roads to be with some poor Indian woman in her hours of trial.

As early as 1888, Lummis had published a small booklet titled "The Home of Ramona."[1] It described Helen Hunt Jackson's visit to Camulos, and with ten photographs demonstrated that this was the scene she was describing in her famous book.

An enchanting woman Lummis delighted to visit was Elizabeth Bacon Custer, widow of General Custer. For Charlotte Perkins Stetson Gilman, Lummis had a warm and great admiration. He relished her

. . . eye for tradition that was merciless and her sarcasm of a quality I do not just remember elsewhere —so cool, unbitter and inevitable that the "two-edged sword" to which one critic has likened her

seems all too bungling. She is rather a razor—and decidedly not a "safety." It is of that edge which leaves many to walk on and talk on without a suspicion that it has divorced their heads from their logical shoulders. . . .[2]

To him, Jessie Benton Frémont was "the most interesting woman I ever met—as she was the most famous in America for a long time. . . ."

To the great dancer, Maud Allan, Lummis gave the Grecian name Antílope, after our desert antelope that drift "like thistledown before the wind." (He found conventional classic dancing "that peculiar capering with the knee seeking the chin, the dancers drinking out of 2-pronged Pan's Pipes which no such dancers ever appear to blow into.")

David Starr Jordan was a favorite subject.

I became acquainted with him very soon after Senator Stanford picked him as Founding President of the young university founded by the senator and his wife in . . . memory of their lost only son. They were homely old people, who would likely be termed Babbitt by the Menckens of today; and their tenderness for the lost boy led them to do some things which would be "funny" if they were not pathetic. But they endowed the college as no other university had been endowed before, with $30,000,000. They picked, in my judgment, the head of this new institution with more intelligence, more instinct, or more good luck, or all three, than any other college has elected. And the acid test of their actual bigness was that they gave him a free hand in all matters academic.

[1] The subject was also dealt with exhaustively in *Out West* (December, 1903), 575–96. The article, signed by "Carlyle C. Davis," seems to have been written by Lummis.

[2] Lummis, "As I Remember."

Doña Ysabel del Valle, whom Lummis described as "an orphan asylum in herself." (*Courtesy Southwest Museum*)

Jordan took a great interest in Lummis and his publications. In one six-page handwritten letter Jordan dedicated three pages to scholarly criticism of the use of the word *dormidera* referring to the California poppy in *Out West*.

Jordan was a member of a group that Lummis led to the pueblo of Acoma and Katzímo (the Enchanted Mesa). The trip is described in his autobiography *The Days of a Man*.

. . . Lummis, by the way, although eastern-born and Harvard bred, also is one of California's unique

. . . It is my deliberate judgment that his achievement is unparallelled in the history of education. . . . He knew them all [as Lummis walked through the Quad with President Jordan] and spoke to them all, in his rather awkward way—like a mountain bowing —but there was an atmosphere of friendliness that seemed to me as astonishing as it was beautiful. . . . When a man was admitted to Stanford he was waited on by a committee of the Student Governing Body (which I think had its first successful inauguration here) and given sailing directions as to what was expected of a Stanford man. . . . I feel deeply confident that no other college president has ever influenced so many young men and women with his own thought, his own sanity, his own plain human nature and his high love for scholarship, as David Starr Jordan.[3]

[3] *Ibid.*

Elizabeth Benton Frémont, daughter of the Pathfinder, seated in front of the Frémont Flag, the first American flag to fly in the far West. Photograph by Charles Lummis.

and original characters. Active and versatile, Western to the core, he has attempted without hesitation, any feat, physical or mental, which touched his fancy. . . .

In the course of our six days at Acoma, we travelled several strange and narrow ways . . . our leader, himself [Lummis] went up and down the long-abandoned and practically impassable north trail, twisting over bulging precipices—a feat never before accomplished by a white man.

. . . The rattler—Crotalus atrox—[abounds]. . . . During our walk about the foot of Katzímo we fre-

Joaquin Miller, the eccentric poet, as photographed by Charles Lummis in 1900. (*Courtesy Southwest Museum*)

David Starr Jordan, one of Lummis' closest friends, for whom he named his oldest son. (*Courtesy Southwest Museum*)

quently caught sight of a snake coiled in the entrance of a [prairie] dog hole. Accordingly we drew a big one out in the usual way by employing an umbrella handle. Pinning it down with a notched stick behind its head, Lummis then seized it by the nape of the neck and held it before the camera, his face carved by mixed emotions, a study in physiognomy.[4]

After speaking of the Penitent Brothers (*Penitentes*), which they did not see, Jordan continued,

[4] David Starr Jordan, *The Days of a Man*, Vol. I, 621.

"They were not in season—but an impenitent brother [Lummis] drove us back at a scandalously rattling speed shortening the 13 miles by taking each arroyo seco at a jump."[5]

With all the affection Lummis bore his friends, he often saw the humor of their foibles. He berated "the blanc-mange mentality which in America could not see Joaquin Miller's poetry for his boots and in England saw his poetry mostly *through* his boots." But he chuckled in his journal over a visit Joaquin paid to him while he was librarian.

. . . at noon old Joaquin Miller came up with his "glad boots" and all the rest of him. He is fun—but he would hate to think so. He promises to come down to the Jib-o-Jib, and there I will have more fun with him still. [This from the Lion in corduroys and red Indian belt!]

Joaquin was in the library again today pursuing his historical researches in the way he pursues his kind of research. I think he does better as a poet—where facts don't bother him at all. I found him today possessed of the most fearful and wonderful notion as to Gen. Kearney's "battle" of San Pasqual. This was the bloodiest battle ever fought in California—and 18 men were killed. But Joaquin seems to insist on the notion that this engagement took place near Pasadena, which was indeed a San Pascual ranch but it is about 100 miles from the San Pascual Valley in which the deadly doings were held. I had a time to change his mind today—for it takes a long time. He lives a good deal inside his head and doesn't seem to hear when you tell him what he asks for. If I see him

tomorrow I will try to find out whether it reached his seat of learning or not.

For "his boys"—Edward Borein, Eugene Manlove Rhodes, and Maynard Dixon—Lummis had a special affection. He hammered away at them about their abilities and their responsibilities as portrayers of the real old West. They loved him, even when disagreeing with some pronouncement. Many times they acknowledged their debt to him. Among "his boys" Lummis also counted Hugh Gibson, whose career he followed from his earliest years in diplomacy to his becoming minister to Poland and ambassador to Belgium.

For almost thirty years the red House Book lay on a table in the *Zaguan*, and as writers, artists, musicians, and outstanding personalities from all over the world came to partake of the wit and wisdom of El Alisal, they left testimonial on its pages.

One wonders when perusing the House Book how Lummis was able to scrub up the indigent and

Maynard Dixon, as photographed by Charles Lummis in 1900. (*Courtesy Southwest Museum*)

[5] *Ibid.*, 634. Lummis recalled this trip in his journal, referring to the same date twenty-nine years earlier. "I had to stand up in the front door to drive, the others had to sit in the bed of the wagon. And Dr. Jordan was very humorous about the famous driving of Hank Monk who was the stage driver that conveyed Horace Greeley 50 years ago and I decided I would give him a little Hank Monk of his own. So when we started back from Cubero I fed those mules with the black snake whip until I got them into a dead run and didn't let 'em stop from it. The road was a pretty bad one, chiefly because along sloping sides of hardpan the wagon would slew around sometimes until it almost hit the mules in the face and it took some steersmanship to keep it from tipping over. Over rocks and gullies and skids and down and up precipitous arroyos I skinned those mules. Wanted to make Dr. Jordan call a halt but he was game tho rather pale. And Mrs. Jordan was game too. In fact nobody peeped—but we made those 12 miles in 55 minutes; and Dr. Jordan said frankly and generously that he thought Hank Monk had been greatly exaggerated."

illiterate old camel driver Greek George and seat him at a Spanish dinner on December 13, 1903, with the actress and countess Helene Modjeska, Frances Fisher Browne, editor of the *Dial*, and a dozen other prominent figures. Who else would have done it!

The visit of the Duke of Alba, Lummis' *Querido Amigo*, was a special event. They were *hermanos* in the Order of Isabella. It was duly recorded in the diary on October 12, 1924.

It was 5:15 before the Duque de Alba and Douglas Fairbanks and young Carrizosa (son of the Marquis of Merito) arrived, preceded a little by Carroll of the Times *and Litchfield, photographer. They had speeded ahead of the ducal party from the Expedition Park and the county Museum where, of course, Bryan had clung to them like a bull-pup to a root, particularly in reference to the authenticity of an Immaculate Conception by Murillo; kept them there so late that the Duquesa and Mary Pickford had to go home. But the Duke and Douglas made up for any Lost Ladies. They were both genuinely delighted with the house, the Museo, the woodpecker's nest and much delighted with my photo of Ibañez[6] which I had displayed next to that of Alfonso. [I said] I don't know how you stand with my friend, Don Vicente. Alba said "Bully! I am enormously fond of him. I carry messages between him and the King."*

The visit of Vicente Blasco Ibañez was also recorded.

Jan. 29 1920, Plaza 12:15. Meet Ibañez & Padin a la puerta—fueron paseandose. Convidan almorzar. Ibañez 1/3 fried chicken, 2 raw eggs. P, fish and chicken; I, oyster stew. Bully talk. Marco's chauffeur nos halle 1:30 y espera fuera. Vamos Marco's auto al Alisal. Chauffeur Ray Setien nos espera. Ibañez encantado de la casa, fuera y dentro. Los retratos, pinturas, cosas antiguas, carpenterias etc. Traigo mi camera grande, con su permiso y hago 2 inst (shutter

bulb hardened) & 2 times. Then Setien 2 of Ibañez & me; all 3 in House Book.

A few days later Lummis, Will Rogers, Gene Rhodes, and Ibañez went to the Mission San Juan Capistrano together. This great happening called forth a poem, "The Four Horsemen of the Eucalypts" published in *A Bronco Pegasus*, which concluded:

> *Will Rogers of the impulsive rope,*
> *Philosopher and Lincoln wit;*
> *Gene Rhodes whose Southwest stories lope*
> *A gait no other seems to hit;*
> *Vesuvian Ibañez, too,*
>
> *That rode 'em hard in Argentine,*
> *Then roped a top-hoss in Who's Who—*
> *With jails and duels in between.*
> *So there's your Three—*
> *And me.*

That same night there was a dinner at El Alisal, small for those days with only thirty-five guests, but properly entered in the House Book.

Ibañez returned to his beloved Spain, but three of the "Horsemen" frequently got together. Whenever they did it was a celebration, especially when they were joined by Charlie Russell. Lummis took delight in describing each celebration in his diary.

Aug. 11, 1917 It was a nice looking dinner and a very good one. I wish the lamb had been a centipede. . . . [Mariska] sang bully and so did Hesse-Sprott. . . . Then I dragged Ed Borein in from the corruption of the court and stuck him at one side of the table about midway and wound him up and then he told them stories for more than an hour and had everyone laughing their noses off. And when they all quit about 11 or so we sat around and swapped lies a little longer. I chased Borein to his bunk and we have turned out quite a bunch of dictation in spite of the untimely hour.

Jan. 2, 1920 [journal] Eugene Rhodes and his fine old mother got along a little after 5 and we had a bully visit. He looks no older than years ago but something has happened to his teeth so that his speech is very difficult to discriminate being as bad as Harmer's inability. Then Will Rogers and his wife dropped in and met Eugene for the first time but with many

[6] Vicente Blasco Ibañez, author of numerous novels, had also been the leader of the revolutionary opposition to the government of Spain for many years. He had been incarcerated off and on since the age of eighteen for these activities and had been exiled at different times to France, Italy, and Argentina, from where he continued to direct the revolutionary movement. Eve Lummis, under the pen name Frances Douglas, translated several of his novels, including *The Four Horsemen of the Apocalypse* and *Blood and Sand*.

The "Four Horsemen"—Will Rogers, Eugene Manlove Rhodes, Vicente Blasco Ibañez, and Charles Lummis—at the Mission San Juan Capistrano.

bonds because they are going to film two or three of his stories. He has seen Will Rogers on the stage and in the east so they were quite ready to meet. And we had the usual official supper of the albondiga and the brown frijol done in Elena's incomparable way and eaten in vast profusion by each of the whole crowd and some of my Satsuma jam in which Mrs. Rogers claimed partnership as I was putting it up the last time she was here and I gave her a taste of the making. And we had a good homely human talk . . . it was a great thing to get these two old timers started and they kept each other in constant action. They are both original and droll as all good cowboys are and it was such a circus as you couldn't get anywhere for money for they were totally unself-conscious and natural. Will had been in that desert-stamping ground of Tularosa, [N.M.] which Eugene thinks is the finest place in the world; and it was a long matching of numerous cowmen and old characters, although both of them put together haven't a tenth part of Ed Borein's narrative genius. We all wished he had been there—he and Will are close pals and Eugene has heard so much of him that he feels sort of acquainted too. And remarks by Eugene about Senator Penrose started me on reminiscences about that wonderful college mate of mine and our devilments which the cowboys thought quite as funny and wild and wooly as anything on the range. Will was going to take us all to see his new picture, "Jubilo," but he got so fascinated with the jabber that he passed it up and said later he just couldn't tear away to take us to any old theatre where he couldn't talk and he had enjoyed the evening more than anything in years. He had a pretty good dose of it from 5 until 11:30. And all wrote in the House Book . . . and Will took them all home in his wonderful $9000 car.

June 7, 1920 Gene viene 5 wi. mother. Take him over to Sis and Dr. wi. taste of hassenpfeffer. George there. Then Maud Allen, lovely, and her charming tiny old mother . . . then near 7, Will Rogers and wife and Charlie Russell and wife, then ¾ hr. delay for supper—just heating the albondiga loaf. Hassenpfeffer, frijoles and spuds. Annie and Q. good dinner, barely enough. Lumsden jam and Laura coke. Will Rogers a scream on his travel and sea sickness. Russell funny too and tells story bully in sign language. Wife

interpreting. Rhodes droll, too. Maude, funny stories of her slip on chalk.

The March Hares assembled for the eleventh time on March 6, 1921. Of the ninety-four guests who signed the House Book, Serafin Pla and his wife Edith made two. It was about their fiftieth party at El Alisal since their friendship with Lummis had begun in 1914. Edith qualified because she was born February 27—close enough, and because she was beautiful and she could sing. Her husband qualified because he was her husband, he was Spanish, and he, too, was a singer.

Fifty-three years later, looking at the same page in the House Book, she remembered that celebration and recalled the charm of those gatherings.

Oh, Charlie Russell was there! He had such a sense of humor. His voice was low and rumbling, he sort of grunted, but he told his tales in Indian sign language, his wife interpreting. In the middle of a story he would make a certain sign and she would blush furiously, saying, "Charlie, I'm not going to say that." Wooden faced he would repeat the gesture. "Now, Charlie you stop. I won't say it and if you keep on talking like that I won't come here any more!"

I would sing in English and Italian and Serafin would sing in Spanish. He first went around turning off the lights, one by one, then standing by the last that was still lit, would begin to sing. Often it was "Estrellita." When he was in the mood for a sad song he would pick one of Dr. Lummis' favorites, "La Cancion del Prisionero," the song of the Spanish prisoner who was asked what he would do with his life could he begin again, da capo. "I would not want to," he replied, "Because she would betray me again and I would kill her again!"

Serafin had a rich, resonant voice like Pinza. Dr. Lummis loved him. He was awfully thin, all bones. I used to tell him that his voice got its resonance from rattling around in those bones.

When the musicians were leaving the party we would talk about Dr. Lummis and someone would always say, "That old man has a lot of nerve to get out there and sing and play the guitar. He can't sing and he can't play the guitar." I would say, "He likes to sing and he does what he likes."

Charlie Lummis, Charlie Russell, and Nancy and Harold Lloyd. (*Courtesy Southwest Museum*)

But no one invited ever failed to come. One did not say no to Dr. Lummis. And there were people who wanted to come for years but were never invited."

One day Lummis happened to run across Ed Borein in downtown Los Angeles. Ed happily announced that he was to be married that day. Lummis recorded the event in his journal.

June 27, 1921 With them to the Hall of Records for the license, then [decided] that the wedding dinner should be at the Alisal instead of in town, Ed stipu- *lating he should bring the steaks and cook them. So I marketed and erranded and hurried home by 5 and gathered in a poor little wedding cake, the largest in the vicinity. Rev. Lane arrived early with his wife and three infant children, one in arms. Says he takes them everywhere. I gave away the bride and Ed went through the ordeal admirably. Then the aforesaid wedding feast—of onions and spuds and string beans and fried bananas and two wedding cakes. Ed cooked us a huge and del. steak in master fashion.*

The House Book was ready and Ed had a sudden inspiration. Lucille had declared she would not say "obey" but she did it just the same very musically. And Ed worked on a page of the House Book about 20 minutes and then displayed his jolly cartoon. . . . It is one of the best sketches in that priceless book.

Of many visitors there is only brief comment. On January 20, 1903, there is this entry in the diary. "Fredk. Remington and wife and Sutherland and wife, visitan 2:15–4:30. Los enseno mucho. Muy contentos. Remington escribe in House Book and Pony Tracks." The following day, however, the *Times* carried the story from Remington's point of view.

. . . *Mr. Remington spent the afternoon at the home of Charles F. Lummis, and upon returning to his hotel was so enthusiastic over what he had seen that he peremptorily refused to talk about anything or anybody but Mr. Lummis' house and Mr. Lummis, himself.*

"He is one of the greatest men in the country to-day," went on the famous portrayer of frontier life. "Positively I never met a man just like him. He's a genius—that's what he is. His philosophy of life is simply great. That he is an artist, you have but to go over his home—a home that I envy—to be convinced of the fact. He built the house with his own hands. . . . It's every bit hand work."

"Mr. Remington," ventured his interviewer, "Are you planning to bring out any new types in your drawings?"

"Yes sir, Lummis is a wonderful man," continued the artist, seemingly unmindful of the reporter's query. "And the worst of it is you don't half appreciate him. If he wasn't right in your midst I dare say you would rave over him as you do over other men with far less talent than he possesses. . . ."

1903 was a busy year at El Alisal and some names were merely mentioned in Lummis' diary.

Mar. 21, 1903—Stewart Edward White (author of The Blazed Trail *and* The Westerners) *me visita 2 horas. Escribe in House Book and autogs. his two books.*

Nov. 3, 1912—Clarence Darrow and wife; Miss Coffin, Hughes and Ed Grafton vienen 6 to 10 y bully talk.

No one will ever know the subject of the conversation. As they arrived at six they must have partaken of the *albondiga* loaf ("seasoned hamburger") and the frijol. Also claret. The host was drinking pretty hard those days and felt that hospitality demanded a drink for every guest even though they might be abstainers. He would, therefore, sometimes pour a glass for each and, as he disposed of them, make a charming toast on behalf of the nondrinkers.

He was moved, however, on February 23, 1923, when

Amado Chaves came out. . . . Amado, my oldest friend in New Mexico and 72 years old, looks younger than I do. Hardly a gray hair! And his face is ruddy and his eyes bright. Consuelo (daughter) is 20 and looks a great deal like her mother. They were here to supper and both wrote in the house book.[7]

Musicians and heroes also charmed him.

Oct. 31, 1909 Sousa came out . . . namely John Philip Sousa, the greatest bandmaster in the world . . . with Charlie Edson. He had been told that he would not see California unless he saw the Place. He obediently came . . . wanted to hear the Indian music so I played him about 20 records on the phonograph and he was deeply delighted. Then we got in Amate who played five or six of his imitations which he plays so well. Then we came up to the den for awhile and had a nice visit and Sousa wrote in the house book a bar of his last march.

July 31, 1927. Capt. Richard P. Hobson, the hero who sunk the Merrimac in the Spanish-American War . . . and blocked the entrance to Santiago Harbor, thereby bottling up the Spanish fleet, came out safternoon with his fascinating wife and fine Dot and flapper niece. They were here an hour, greatly interested. All in home book.[8]

During those thirty years El Alisal was a busy place. In 1918, for instance, the *Museo* was filled at least twenty-three times with assemblages of fifty or more guests. The entries in the House Book are not chronological. Between the crowded signatures guests injected witticisms, bits of their philosophy,

[7] Lummis, "Journal."
[8] *Ibid.*

verses, and expressions of esteem. Compulsively the artists squeezed in miniature examples of their skill. The gracious and somewhat mystical Carl Oscar Borg reduced the great tree at Camulos and the party held under it to the size of a special delivery stamp, while on another page his imagination drifted back to the beloved plains and mesas of New Mexico. Charlie Russell scattered his steer-head trademark throughout the book, and his protégé, Joe De Yong, favored saddles and packhorses. Ed Borein, although he had put in three full-page drawings, also slipped in among the autographs a few of his own minute caballos.

During many of these years, Maynard Dixon was living in San Francisco and not attending the great festivities. In 1915, ten years after his wedding there, he came back to the house. His little daughter, Constance, embellished the book with her own "thunderbird," while on the opposite page he made a beautiful tribute.

Memories of the Apache campaign were stirred by a visit from General Leonard Wood. The diary notes: "Oct. 24, 1912 . . . to Alexandria. Wood not in but his aide Captain Frank Ross McCoy, me trata muy bien. Wood llega 3:50 y Billie Manning! Grand reunion. Wood will come at 9."

Hollywood personalities were constantly dropping in. "Jan. 8, 1927 . . . Then came Frank Hill, Brooklyn Librarian and his niece, Mrs. Noah Beery and Noah himself, the famous "heavy" of the movies, and we had a really bully visit for more than an hour. All very deeply interested in the place and the notorious villain begged a long branch of lemon verbena which he wants to try to slip."[9]

Carl Sandburg drew biting comment: "Jan. 29, 1927 . . . then Carl Sandburg and Mr. Denning visited an hour and a half; young Zeitlin [a poet] being the most impressed and benefited because the least full of himself."[10] Edwin Markham irritated his host by taking it upon himself to invite a guest to the party and by arriving three-quarters of an hour late. The diary for April 9, 1927 reads in part:

[Markham] very jolly, in fact master of blarney that's almost rodomontade. Mrs. F. [current house-keeper] has fine dinner . . . I put on Charro suit. Markham starts House Book . . . Sol Cohen, violin . . . Carrie Jacobs Bond 2 monologues, Alma Real 3 songs, Leon Rice 2, Markham in Serra chair reads ¾ hour, his poetry and Lincoln. Ben Field (whom Markham had invited) some rot, Miss Cline, some rotter; Harry Knibbs, 2 corkers, I about ten [verses] of Geronimo and Old and New. Knibbs says G. best read tonight . . . all til midnight. M. great with ladies.

Lummis was still angry when he got around to dictating his journal.

. . . Markham had never been here before. He was as much impressed as by anything he can be outside of Markham. I handed him my little copy of "The Man etc." and he finds it the actual first edition and showed me the word that proves it, says it's extremely scarce and the last copy he knows of sold for $65. It wasn't worth it! . . . Joaquin Miller did this sort of thing far more dexterously. He was as gallant to the ladies but with tuberose bouquets instead of brickbats and with a Grand Air Markham never mastered. I do not know when I have seen a man so full of himself; and while he is big-hearted & lovable this egotism is very wearing.

In earlier days John Burroughs had come in for some cuts particularly after breaking a dinner date. "We had to hire him a hen so that he could study Nature. At least that's what he claims he writes about." Eventually Lummis became quite fond of the "Sage of Slabsides." Burroughs visited the house on numerous occasions accompanied by his biographer, Clara Barrus, and A. C. Vroman, known for his Indian photography. On February 21, 1920:

Albondiga loaf, frijol, coffee, spuds, pie, Burroughs— bran and hot water. About 75 in all (67 register). Tessie, piano, fine; Marie Duvril canta bien, song by Miss Conan Doyle at piano. Pla sings fine, Leon Rice, divinely, Grace Jess, exquisitely—"Raggly-Taggly Gypsies" & Vine cycle. La beso. Unc. John charmed. Will Rogers rope, gun—monologue and all, marvelous. Unc. John says never such an evening. Everyone tickled. All after 12.[11]

9 Ibid.
10 Ibid.

11 Ibid.

Facing the Mystery. John Burroughs, as photographed by Charles Lummis in 1921, six days before Burroughs' death.

In 1921, a few days before Burrough's death, Lummis took a magnificent picture of the bearded old man which he called "Facing the Mystery."

The House Book bears many flattering comments on the house, its treasures, and its master. None expressed the feeling of those who loved and admired Lummis better than the words of the Scottish short-story writer, Lorna Moon.

Dear Minstrel and Bard: Of the white silk hair and the clay-red eagle face, it is yours to be always greater than anything you may do, to be always bigger than any relic you may leave behind; so stay long with us to warm us in your glow. For writers there be by the thousands, and singers are as the sands of the seashore, but a radiant soul is to be held preciously upon the palm like an opal.

In order to reproduce in facsimile the following pages from the House Book, the descriptions of the plates are given below.

PLATE I — A sketch and poem by the famed writer and illustrator Ernest Thompson Seton.

PLATE II — Remarks and signatures of the Boks and Doubledays, of writing and publishing fame. Visiting El Alisal in 1903, they described it as having rooms which "every museum must envy."

PLATE III — Lummis kissing the girls at Camulos, a pencil sketch by Alexander F. Harmer.

PLATE IV — Messages, written on two separate occasions, from American musician Arthur Farwell.

PLATE V — An ink drawing by Carl Oscar Borg.

PLATE VI — A message from Cincinnatus Heine Miller, better known as Joaquin Miller. It was well known that Miller's handwriting was nearly illegible—sometimes even to himself. The message reads, "In the strong home of the strong man—stalwart house of the great strong lover—a writer shall strive & stand."

PLATE VII — The menu and signatures of the "guests" at one of the sessions of the Court of the Alcade Mayor. Included among the guests was the Sage of Emporia, William Allen White, the famed writer and journalist.

PLATE VIII — A note from John Muir, naturalist, writer, conservationalist, and one of Lummis' most esteemed friends.

PLATE IX — A pen sketch by Edward Borein made shortly after his wedding ceremony at El Alisal.

PLATE X — Notes from visitors to El Alisal, including a brief remark from poet and Lincoln biographer Carl Sandburg.

PLATE XI — A sketch by Neil M. Judd recalling his expedition to New Mexico with Lummis for the Southwest Museum in 1910.

PLATE XII — Signatures of those attending a party in honor of Charles M. Russell. Included are Ed Borein, Eugene Manlove Rhodes, Arthur Farwell, and Bertha Lummis Bush.

PLATE XIII — In 1923, exhausted from overwork, Lummis held this final "noise" before traveling to Camulos for a rest. Among the guests were the Indian singer Tsianina, Canadian poet Bliss Carman, and American composer Charles Wakefield Cadman.

PLATE XIV — A celebration for Turbesé and her husband, Frank Fiske. Lummis' comment at the bottom of the page describes the evening's festivities.

PLATE XV — A pen sketch by Frederic Remington.

PLATE XVI — The signature of Zintka Lanuni Colby and her story as told by Charles Lummis make this one of the most poignant entries in the House Book.

PLATE XVII — Signatures of members of the Federation of Music Clubs and other friends, including Charles M. Russell and Joe De Yong.

PLATES XVIII AND XIX — On facing pages of the House Book appears this sketch by Maynard Dixon and the drawing of a thunderbird by his daughter, Constance.

PLATE XX — A pen sketch by one of Lummis' "boys," Ed Borein.

PLATE XXI — Visitors to El Alisal on November 2, 1912, included the attorney Clarence Darrow.

PLATE XXII — Among the many people from the music world who visited Charles Lummis and signed his guest book was the American bandmaster and composer John Philip Sousa.

PLATE XXIII — Signatures and notes from fiction writer Stewart Edward White and writer and critic Willard Huntington Wright.

PLATE XXIV — A note from James Willard Schultz, a western writer. Schultz married a Blackfoot Indian woman and was adopted into the tribe and given the name Apikuni.

PLATE XXV — Notes and signatures from William Lloyd Garrison, the son of the abolitionist; American naturalist John Burroughs; and photographer and book collector A. C. Vroman.

PLATE XXVI — A bit of music and a message from Leopold Godowsky, pianist and composer.

PLATE XXVII — An entry commemorating the 1920 meeting of the March Hares, Lummis' organization that celebrated March birthdays. Included is a lively poem by "The Gray Hare," Charles F. Lummis.

PLATES XXVIII AND XXIX — Signatures of the guests attending a party in honor of Bibliosmile Frank P. Hill, the librarian of the Brooklyn (New York) Public Library. Included are Marco Newmark, Eugene Manlove Rhodes, and Charles M. Russell.

PLATES XXX AND XXXI — In 1923, Lummis, ill and exhausted, journeyed to Camulos to rest. He took the House Book with him. While he was there, a feast was given in his honor by his very close friends Charles H. Cram and Ysabel del Valle Cram. Among those present were his daughter and son-in-law, Turbesé and Frank Fiske; his son Jordan Lummis; his wife, Gertrude Lummis; Ed Borein; Marco Newmark; Henry H. Knibbs; Carl Oscar Borg, and J. B. Lippincott.

PLATE XXXII — Signatures of guests attending a small feast at El Alisal in February, 1920. Among the guests were all four of the "Four Horsemen"—Charles F. Lummis, Will Rogers, Eugene Manlove Rhodes, and the famous Spanish novelist Vicente Blasco Ibañez.

Old Montezuma made a Guild of all his Men of brains
Who got their inspiration on the mountains or the plains
And some were Rulers, some were Priests, & some were Craftsmen skilled
But all had given the world *ideas* that entered in this Guild.
The Thunder-bird, their emblem dwelt, where clouds & peaks confused
And the only test of membership was, <u>What has he produced</u>.

Now Royal Montezuma's gone, his Empire turned to dust
But who shall say the Bird has flown or that the Guild is lost
No, no, the inspiration of the Great West never flags
The Spirit in the Thunder-bird still haunts its ancient Crags
The Guild still lives, its tribute gives, refined by memories sad
And when the Brethren meet [as now] They know it <u>and are glad</u>

Alisal
Los Angeles   Ernest Thompson Seton
5 May 1901.

PLATE I

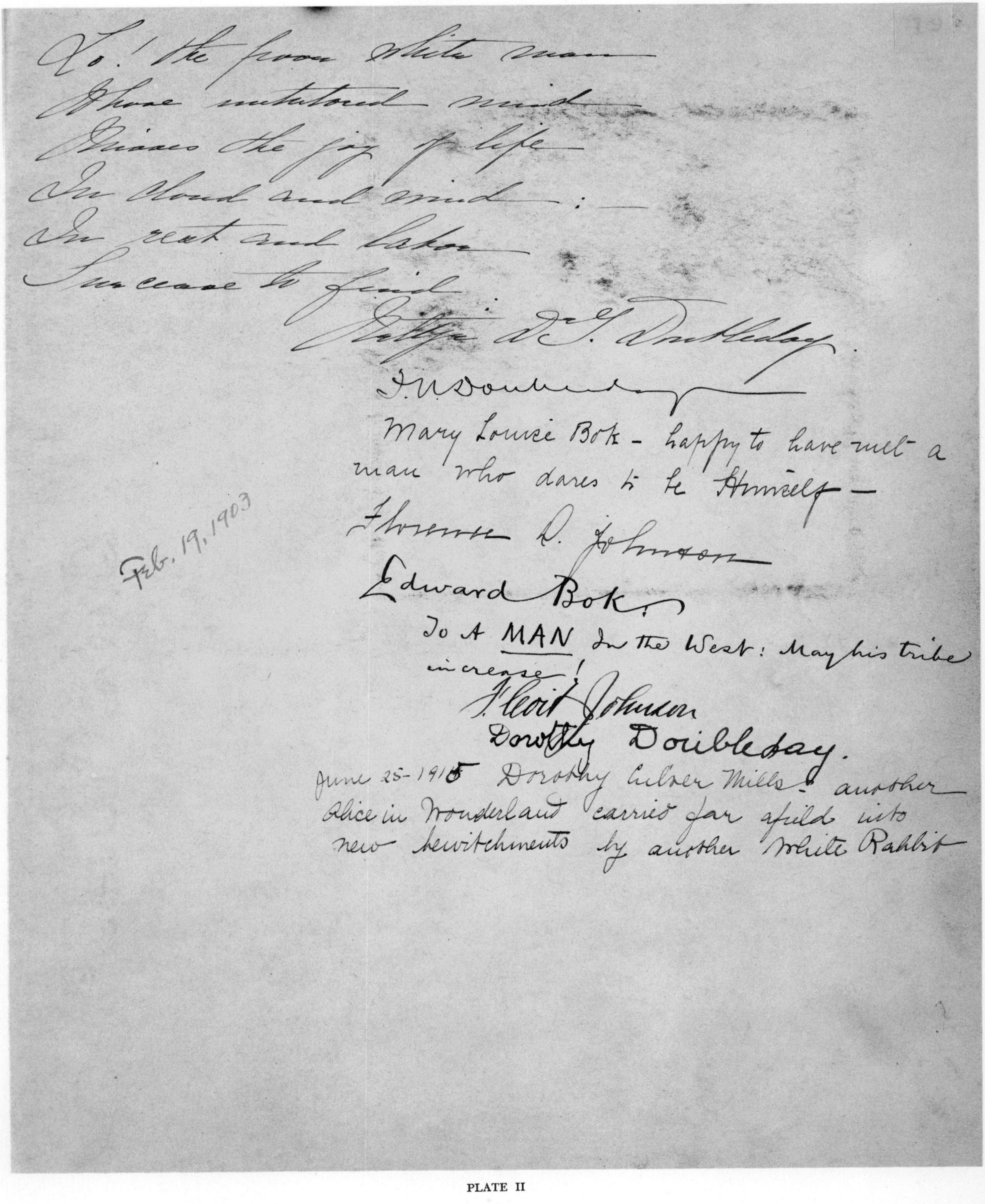

Lo! the poor White man
Whose untutored mind
Divines the joy of life
In cloud and wind; —
In rest and labor
Surcease to find.

Nelson D. J. Doubleday.

F. N. Doubleday

Mary Louise Bok — happy to have met a
man who dares to be Himself —

Florence R. Johnson

Edward Bok.

To A **MAN** In the West: May his tribe
increase!

F. Coit Johnson

Dorothy Doubleday.

Feb. 19, 1903

June 25-1915 Dorothy Culver Mills — another
Alice in Wonderland carried far afield into
new bewitchments by another White Rabbit

PLATE II

"Ed Quisero!" Chas. F. Lummis Collecting toll in Santa Barbara

Alexander F. Harmer

May 10th 1923.

PLATE III

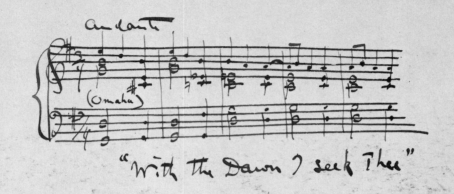

Andante

(Omaha)

"With the Dawn I seek Thee"

"Camerado. I give you my hand"

Arthur Farwell.

January 17-1904.

December 11 - 1919

After fifteen years — found much (including
the constancy of the warm friendship of C.F.L.) —
but am still seeking.

Up with the birth of day Out on the trackless way —

Arthur Farwell

To remember one of the proud moments of my life, —
When I meet the author of my boyhood's love
a "The King of the Bronchos"

Sept 16. 1924

Reginald L. Pole.

PLATE IV

PLATE V

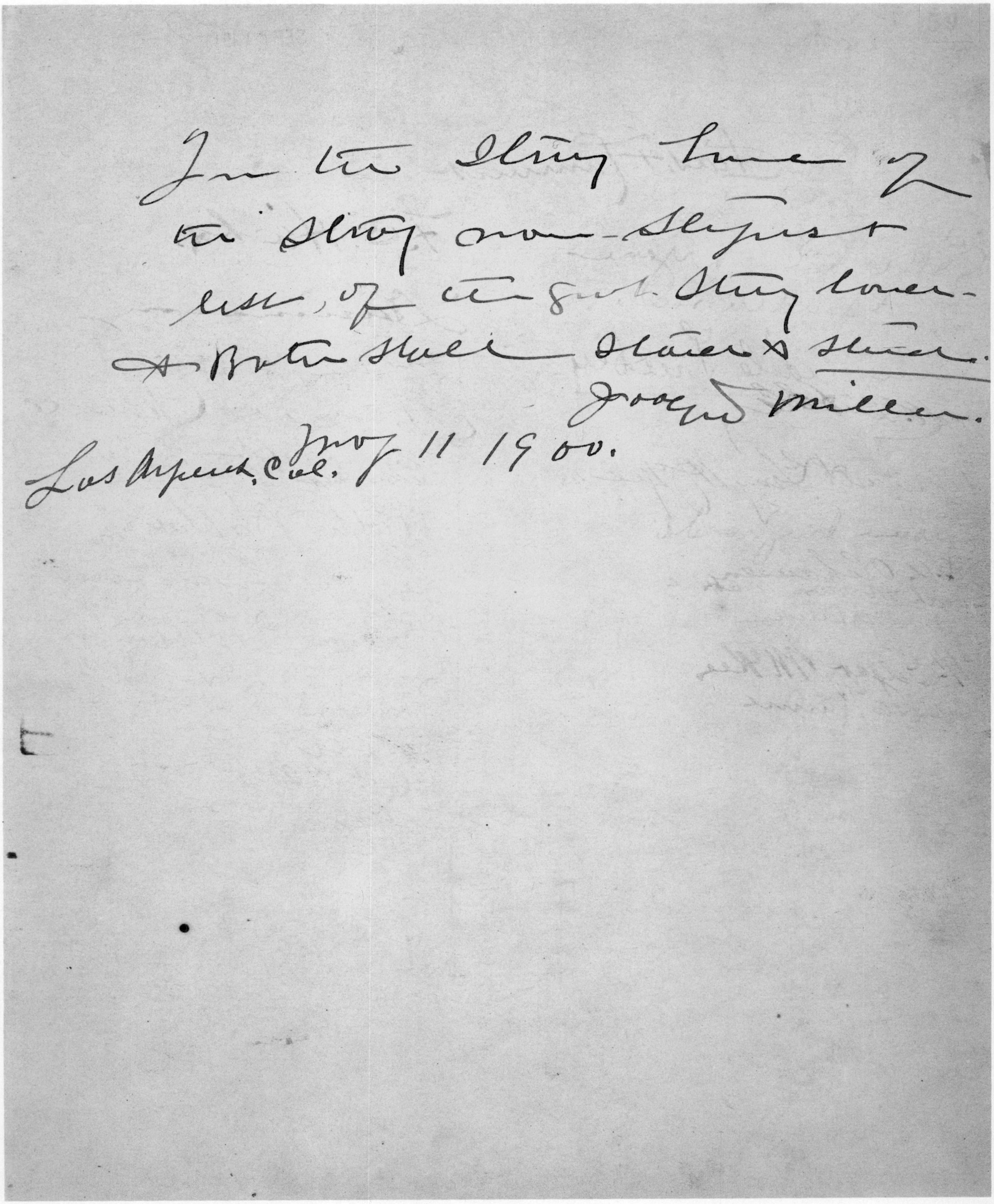

In the strong hours of [illegible] strong man — strongest of all good strong lover — A Better Hall [illegible] — strive.

Joaquin Miller.

Los Angeles, Cal, May 11 1900.

PLATE VI

Court of the Alcalde Mayor, May 22, 1913
To try various Hardened & Notorious Sinners.
The Court & jury (being hardened also) will eat
& Associate with the Sinners, & try to look like them.
Chas. F. Lummis—

Caroline H. W. Fales.
J. O. Koepfli,
+ his mark
witness, Chas. F. Lummis—
Anna McC. Backley
Susanna C. Ott
Ernest R. Noster
(Little Willie)
Violet Estelle Baer
a cinder—

Walter B. Ridgeway.
Mrs. Edith A. Collende
Mrs. Algy Edwin Lillicrap San Diego, Calif.
F. W. Ott of the Legislature
Laura Miller

Albaricoque
á los argentes.
*
Vino Blanco
hasta Acabar.
*
Corre El Gallo
Frijol á la
Yanqui
Asparagos
Nebucadnazor
Charqui
á la Campaña
Papas al
Infalible
Ensalada
Que Angry Joe
Fruta
Prohibida.

Juliette B. Koepfli
W. A. White Emporia Kansas
Manuela C. Garcia
Y. A. Garcia
Ruth Anne Baldwin
Jerome Reynolds

Grace Adele Greeley
Mrs. William Mac Laughlin
W. H. Gates Not of the
Legislature
Chas. Cassat Davis—

PLATE VII

*going to the mountains
is going home.*

John Muir

June, 1905.

Helen Muir

Wanda Muir

Ernest A. Gardner — 26. Apr. 1919

PLATE VIII

PLATE IX

I am one who would willingly be instructed
in the religion of joy, and who regrets
that she has not longer known its
prophet.
                    Elia W. Peattie.
                    May 4, 1902

My Dear Mr. Lummis:
         Have you here a touch of the sentiment that gives one
a pleasant dream. Here is gathered a congregation of
souls that is available to him that hath a soul.
                    Cordially,
                    W. Lightfoot Visscher.
January 22
1914.

Jan 29, 1927
"The place of great phantoms be for you."   —   Carl Sandburg - Chicago

I shall remember having put my hands
         upon the wood of your doors   Jake Zeitlin.
                                              Jan. 1927

I rode in on the tail of Carl's kite — to an afternoon I shall
         always remember —   C. S. Henning.

PLATE X

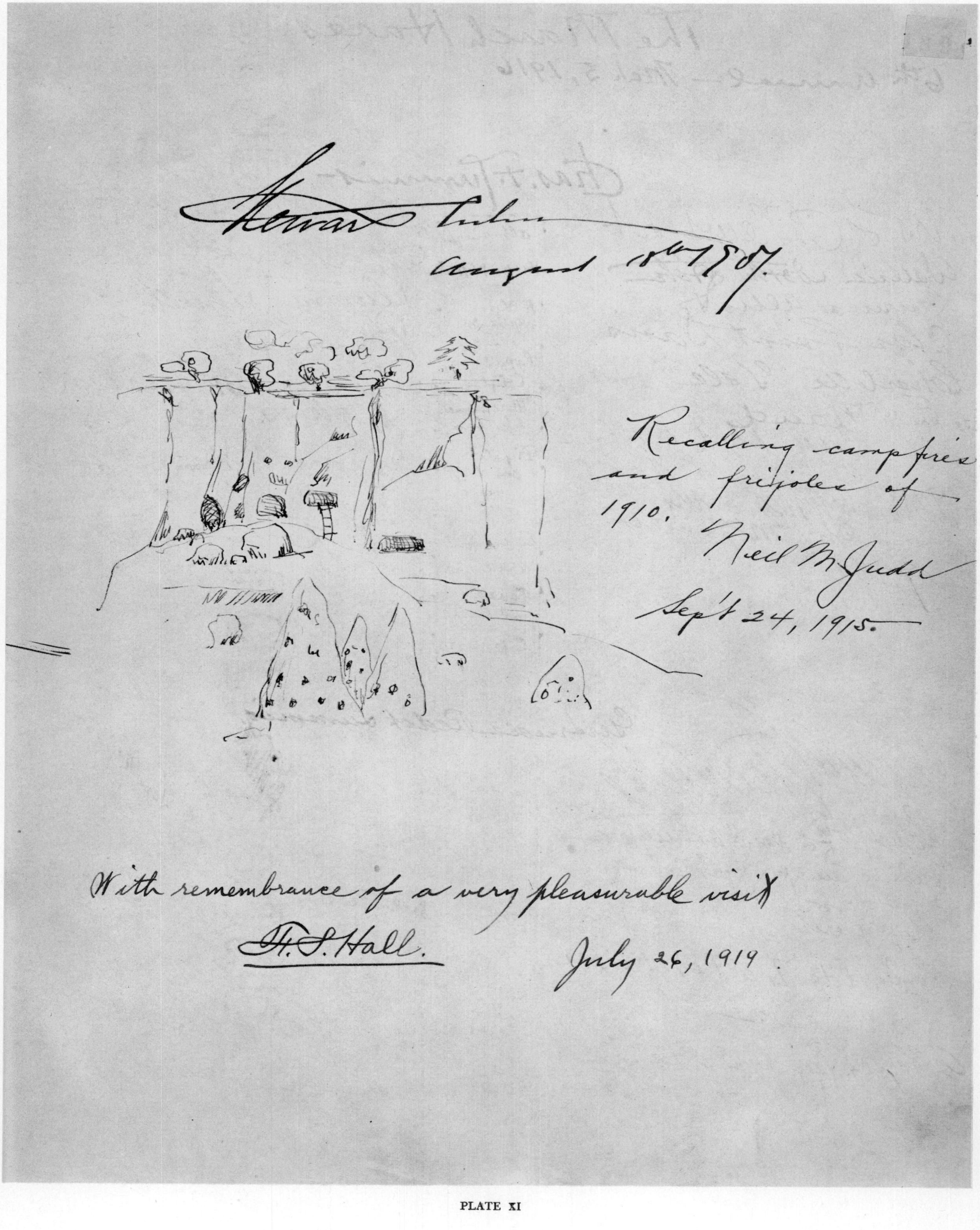

Stewart Culin
August 18 1887.

Recalling camp fires
and frijoles of
1910.
Neil M. Judd
Sep't 24, 1915.

With remembrance of a very pleasurable visit
F. S. Hall.
July 26, 1914.

PLATE XI

Feb. 26, 1922

Welcome Back to
    Charlie Russell
who paints the Indian His Pony & the Buffalo
as no one Else: How!

C. M. Russell and Wife   Chas. F. Lummis-
Ed Borein and Wife   Great Falls Montana.
                              Santa Barbara
Lucile E. Borein
Adam Hull Shirk   Peter Badger
Anna Shirk   Julia M. Rhodes
Alma Snyder   Bertha Lummis Bush
Edith Ryan   Corinne J. Crosley
Nancy C. Russell   Joseph Swickass
Rozel O. Butler   Arthur Farwell
Alice M. Greer   M. Louise Blakely
Raymond K. Bevier   Arthur Farwell
S. S. Badger   Mabel F. Nourse
E. M. Rhodes   Serafin Diaz
John W. Sherman
Brenda Fowler Sherman   E. Louis Emma
Helen Goldberg — Helene C. Morgan
Sylvia Goldberg   Lucille Emma
Maxwell Ryder   Caroline H. W. Foster
Paul A. Vickers   Carl J. von Bibra
Myra Belle Vickers.   F. v. Bibra
Mae Belle Bacon.   Annie Milner
A. D. Hunter.

PLATE XII

Gone since May 14, last (p. 148)

Writing "Some Strange Corners of Our Country" — and
long on the Frontier of the Other Country — this Noise is
a Spree before I go back to my Rest Cure at Blest Carmelos.
Jan 9, 1923. Chas. F. Lummis — And see who's here!
And first of all, that lovely flower of the First Americans, dear Tsianina.
and Bliss Carman — a Surviving Poet.

It is with pleasure I sign my name in a book belonging to
Charles F. Lummis, a friend of mine and my people — Tsianina.

Unworthy of being in this company, but glad all the same,
as becomes a lover of this land, of sincere friendships, and
all beautiful things. Bliss Carman

Forever grateful in being in the house of my friend —
a house where rare fellowship and true comradarie
has reigned.   Charles Wakefield Cadman

Mrs. C. S. Woods

Mrs. S. McKelvy Woods   Swickley, Pennsylvania

S. McKelvy Woods   Glendale. Cal.

Mrs. Ida B. Davis.   Myra Belle Vickers

                                       Mildred Masser
Alberta Reeder Davis.
                                       Otto Gloetz.
Sarene Reeder Davis.
                                       Fred Court
M. Louisa Blakely
        GALE   Josef Zwick ard
Wae B. Lumsden (Baby)
Henry Saub   Carl von Bibra,

F. von Bibra   Mabelle Havens
Justin E. Bush
Otto J. Zahn

PLATE XIII

For Turbesé & Frank (Fiske)
The Little Daughter & the New Son
at their first Home-coming together. May 21, 1916

Chas. F. Lummis — Turbesé Lummis Fiske
Grace Adele Freeley — Frank Fiske
  Katherine J. von Blon.
Alberta Reeder Davis. Isabel Gilchrist Monteith
Lucene Reeder Davis Mrs J. Albert Davis,
Bernhard Mollenhauer I am not Davis
Emma Porter Makinson Mrs Evrard
Mary B. Lummis Evrard
Keith Lummis Henri La Bonté
Mrs S.E.S. McNaughton W M Goodwin
L. C. Makinson Jennie Hagan Goodwin
Oline D. Bondies Mrs M. E. Steinfeldt
Mrs Harry Bondies "Texas" Charlotte L. T. Brooks
Snow Longley "Charles Wakefield Cadman
Mrs Minnie C. Thom Esm. Alfred Wallenstein
John L. von Blon
Tiny Mae B. Lumsden
A. L. Longley
W C Bondies —

Lettie Anna Newport
Clara Lumsden Whittaker

Penelope Cuthbert —
Lanier Bartlett
Fannie Mollenhauer
Charlotte Gale

Peripatetic Grub
also Liquids
with their Hounds and Alberta & Lorance
from "Baragalupi" & the Mollenhauer with
two "violins" "violin & cello; & ErNand & Inora
to the piano & Madame Purisima; & Gladman
Our Clara & MissMakinson to his soups"; &
La Bonté, singing "Elle "Kaffin" (Von Blon) & Our
to piano & cello — Adele with papa & his
Jones, & with Mrs Makinson to her
own, & "Song of the Sun" let al-
And the Congregation "papa.
ternately by Henri & "papa.

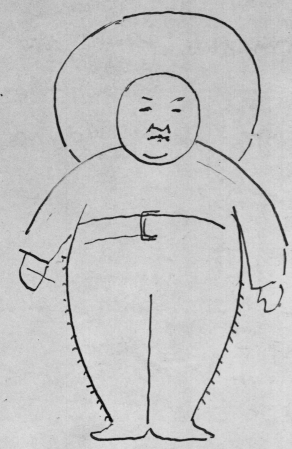

"The Broncho Buster"

Frederic Remington

After a great day at Lummis' —
1903

Jan. 2[

PLATE XV

Zintka L. Colby.
May 1ˢᵗ 1902.

Zintka Lanuni Colby.
(Lost Bird.)

[Marguerite Zitkala Noni; one of the survivors of the
Wounded Knee massacre by U.S. troops, Dec. 29, 1890.
See The Ghost Dance Religion, Jas. Mooney, U.S. Govt. Reports,
1896; p. 876, et seq. Her photo in 1891, p. 878.
    This little child, then about 4 mos. old, was found Jan. 1, 1891,
(three days after the "battle") in her dead mother's arms; she was
half frozen, & the only one that lived of the several children
found on the battlefield after three days in a Dakota blizzard.
The troops left the wounded — the Indian wounded — three
days before even looking for them. This baby was
adopted by Gen. Colby, then commanding the Nebraska
State troops; & came to see me with Mrs. Colby on the
above date. Her real name is unknown; but the
Indian women in camp named her, after this rescue,
Zitkala Noni = Little Lost Bird; & the name has been
retained tho' somewhat corrupted.   C.F.L.
                    March 26. 1912

Zintka Lanuni Colby now
        Mrs Chas. Davis.
    Returned at above date grown to
womanhood Compliments of Mr & Mrs Chas.
                                Davis.

PLATE XVI

April 15, 1924

To The National Federation of Music Clubs

Art, like the Soul, is of many lives—
And longer than Life is long—
Form and Color and Wedded Sound—
But the Flower of its flowers is Song.

Chas. F. Lummis—

With sincere and lasting gratitude for this most wonderful evening. Beautiful experiences never die.

Lucile M. Lyons
President N. F. M. C.

Bessie Bartlett Frankel. First Vice Pres, N. F. M. C

With sincere appreciation of a wonderful man!

Cecil Frankel In reflected glory.

Mrs. Ida B. Davis
Alberta Reeder Davis.
Lorena Reeder Davis

Alexander Bevani

Helene Constance Morgan

Frank Fiske

Wishing to be as unique as these surroundings
Louise Hughes Nulty

Leon F. Rice

Victor A. ...

Harold R Skeath

Harley Hamilton

Constance Balfour

C M Russell

Nancy C Russell

Emelie ...

Serafin Plá

Joe De Yong

C. A. Edson

Lis Lund

"Tiny" Bard.

Mrs E Walzen

Cecil Norton Winchester

Eugenie Powell

Grace Mrd Jess

Elsie Wagerson

Jane E. Harley

Sage Christopher

Myra Belle Vickers

Carlita Yates

Otto Ploetz

Merle Armitage

Alice Walzen Yates

Ethel Groves
New York City.

PLATE XVII

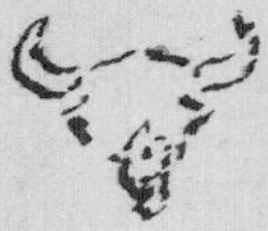

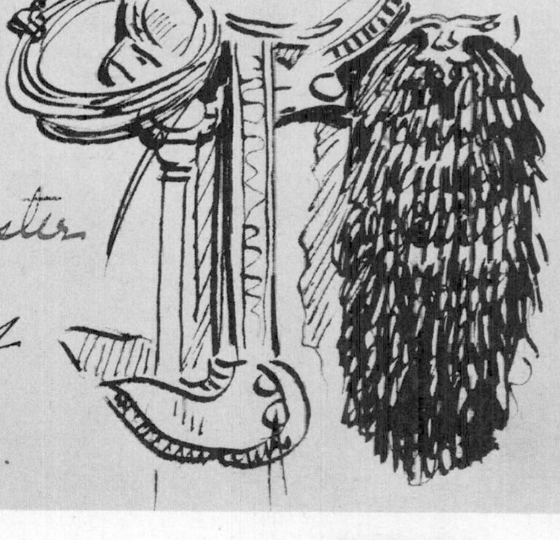

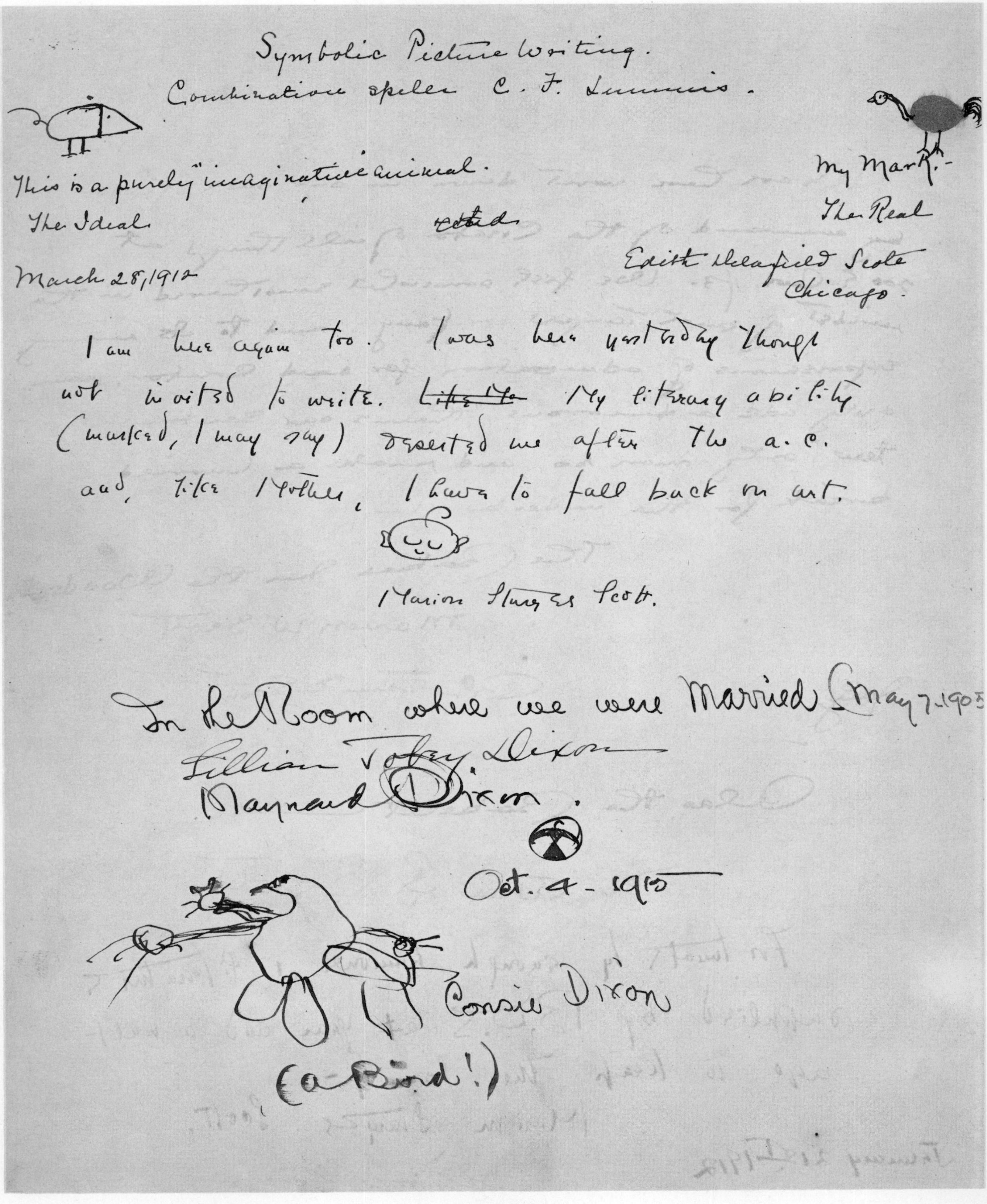

Symbolic Picture Writing.
Combination speller C. F. Lummis.

This is a purely "imaginative" animal.
The Ideal.

My Mark. —
The Real

March 28, 1912

Edith Wheafield Scott
Chicago.

I am here again too. I was here yesterday though
not invited to write. ~~Little Me~~ My literary ability
(marked, I may say) deserted me after the a.c.
and, like Mother, I have to fall back on art.

Marion Sturges Scott.

In the Room where we were Married (May 7, 1905

Lillian Tobey Dixon
Maynard Dixon.

Oct. 4 - 1915

Consie Dixon

(a Bird!)

PLATE XVIII

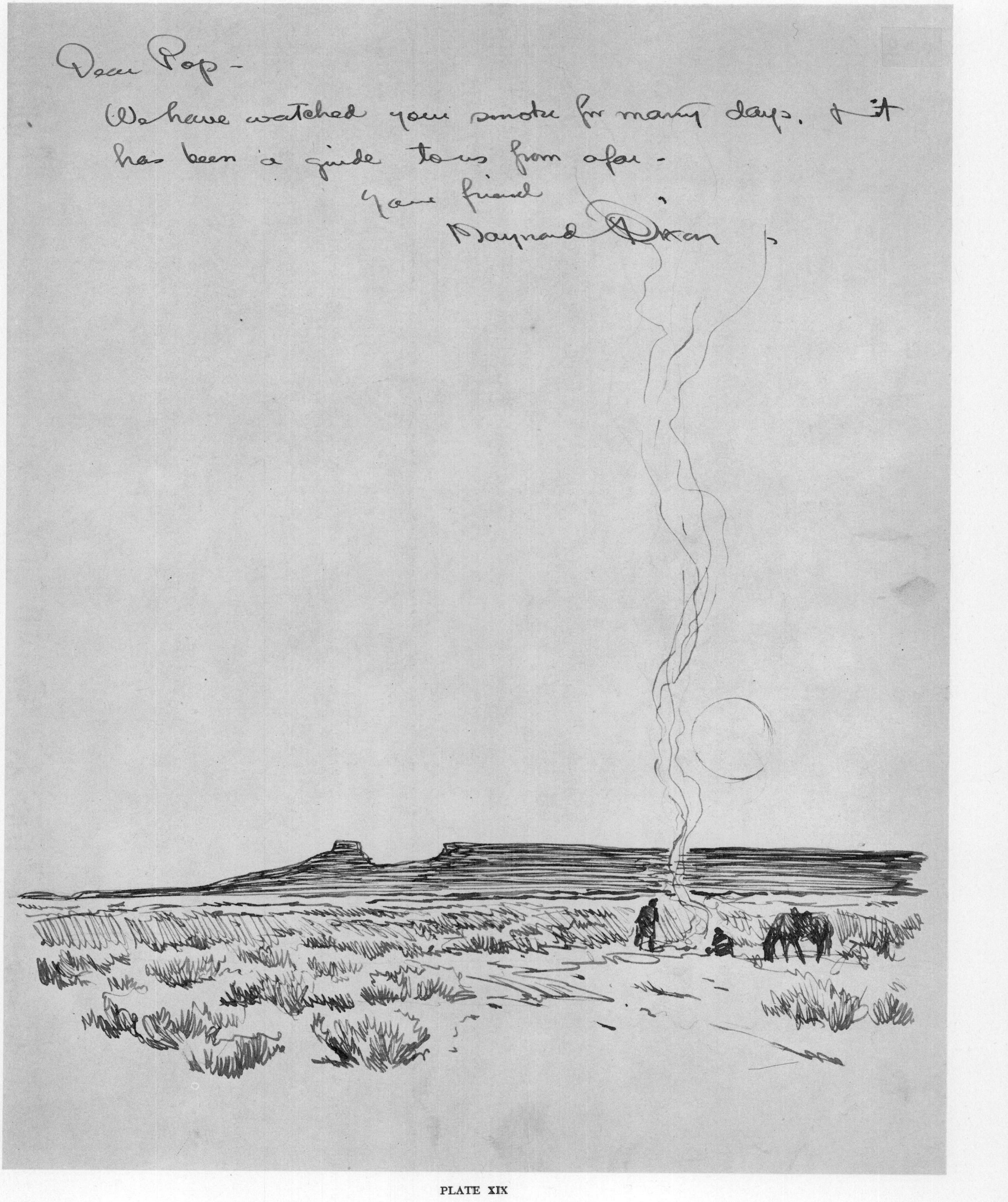

Dear Pop –
    We have watched your smoke for many days. & it
has been a guide to us from afar –
            Your friend
                Maynard Dixon

PLATE XIX

A Vaquero of San Jose del Cabo

For Lummis; the man
who started me out
on a hard trail
Edward Borein.

Sept 3 —15 —

PLATE XX

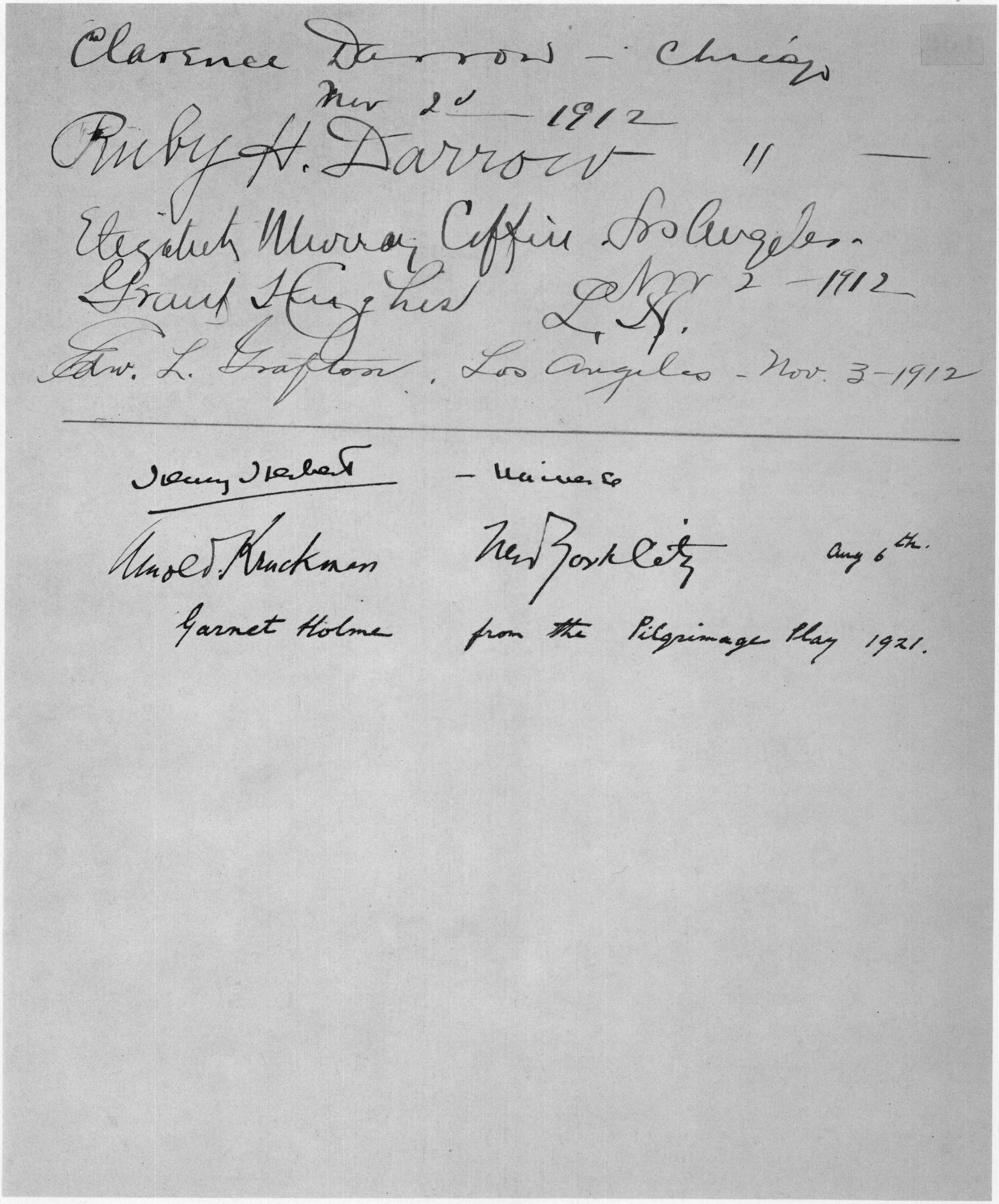

Clarence Darrow – Chicago
Nov 2d – 1912
Ruby H. Darrow "
Elizabeth Murray Coffin Los Angeles.
Grant Hughes L.N. Nov 2 – 1912
L. N.
Edw. L. Grafton, Los Angeles – Nov. 3 – 1912

Henry Herbert – Universe
Arnold Kruckman New York City Aug 6th.
Garnet Holme from the Pilgrimage Play 1921.

PLATE XXI

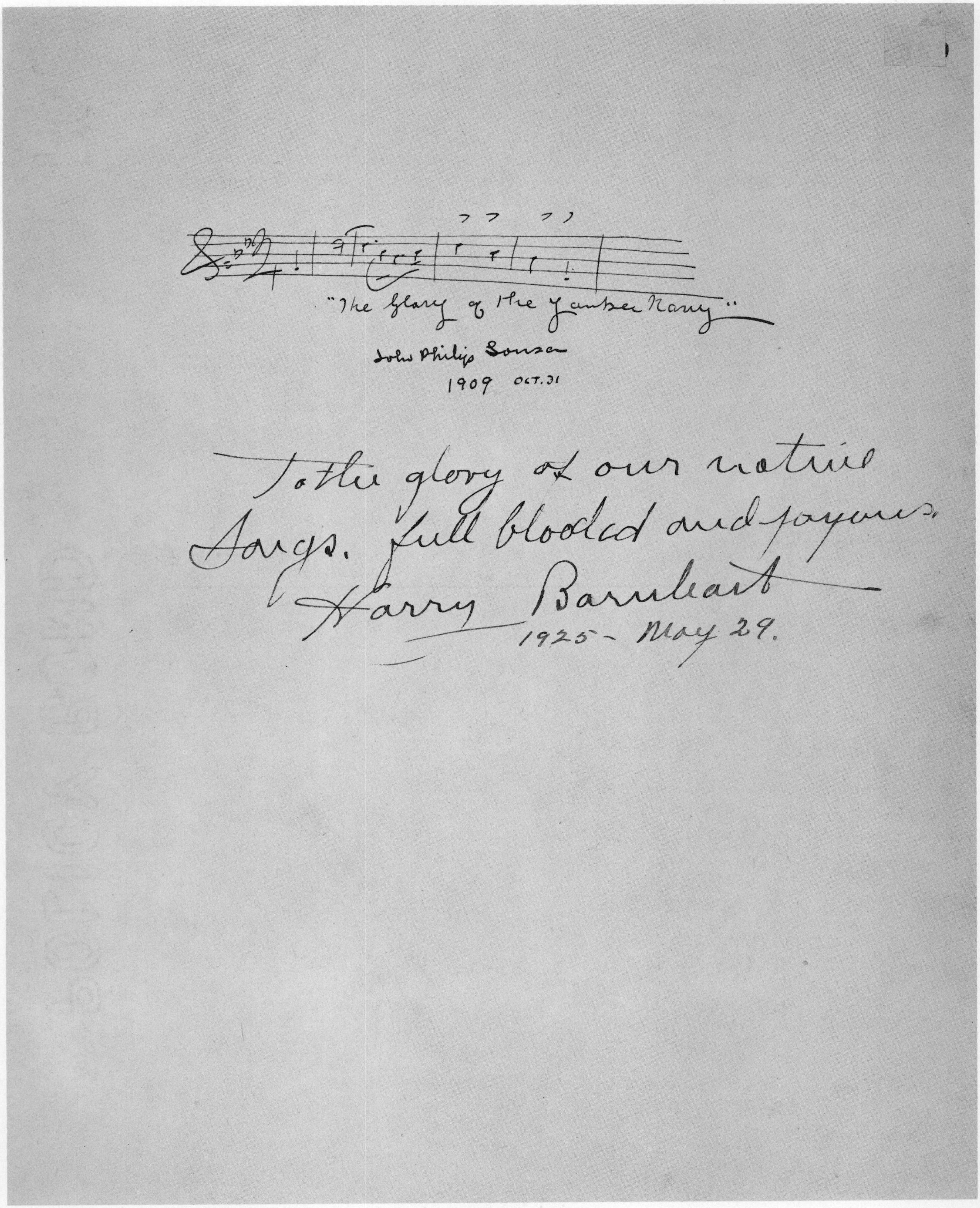

"The Glory of the Yankee Navy"

John Philip Sousa
1909 Oct. 31

To the glory of our native
songs, full blooded and joyous.

Harry Barnhart
1925 - May 29.

PLATE XXII

Here's to the man who says he's never busy, but who gets more

done in a week than ever I will, and who speaks fluently the

language of Our Tribe

Stewart Edward White

March 21, 1903.

Tonight has been one of those
rare civilized interludes which
help make bearable this
uncivilized age.

Willard Huntington Wright

Mar. 17, 1918.

PLATE XXIII

May you live forever
and enjoy the most
interesting house, I believe
that was ever built by man.

Easter Sunday
April 12, 1903   [signature]

/ To Charles F. Lummis
Thanks! Thanks!

Api kui'!
(James Willard Schultz
Kut ai pim ah ki
no caught woman
(Celia H. Schultz)   )

Home, May 4, 1916.

With happy remembrances of the
old Warner's Ranch days of 1903 —
and the ever increasing regards.
Affectionately —

Feby 23/1919.   James E. Jenkins.

PLATE XXIV

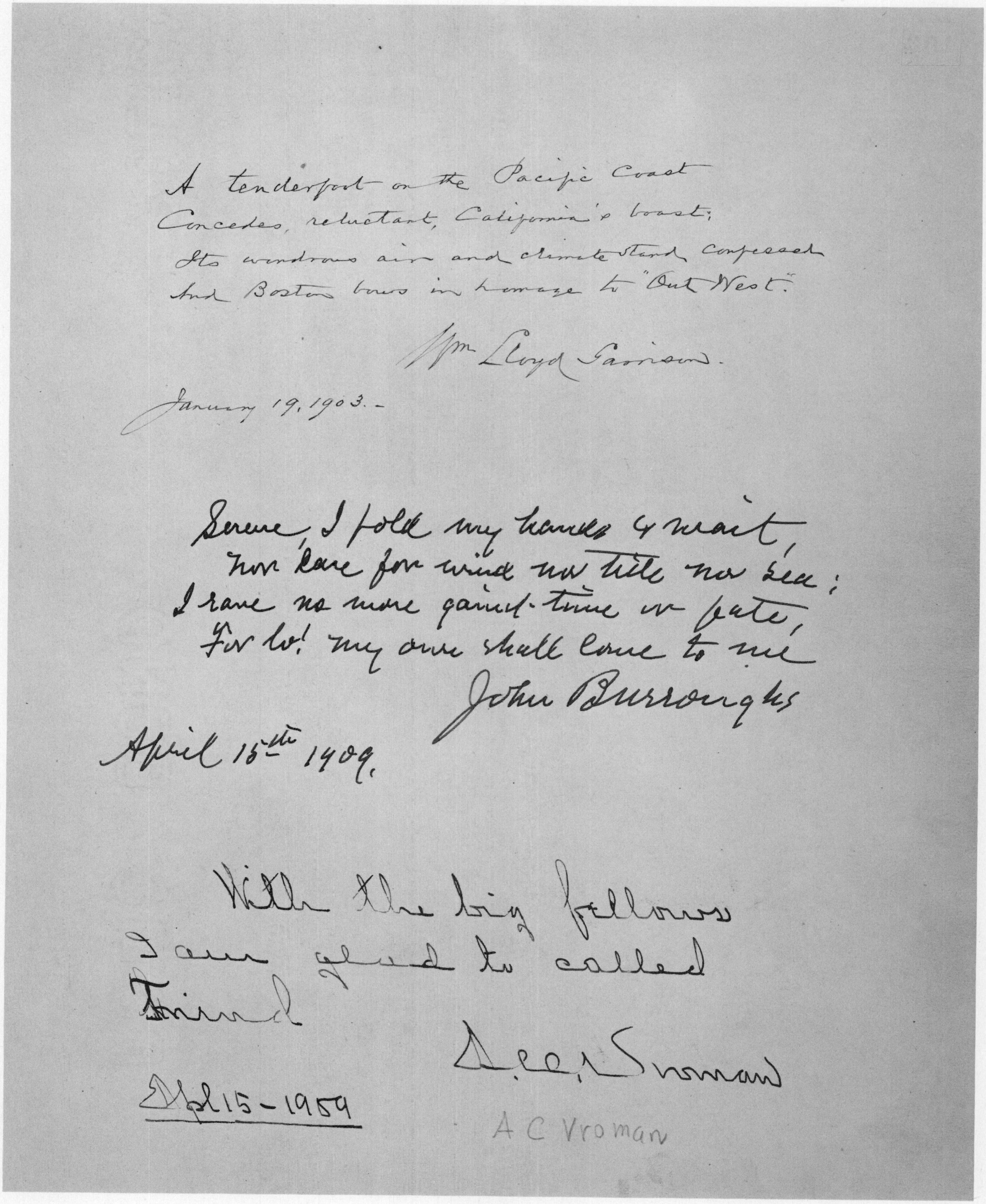

A tenderfoot on the Pacific Coast
Concedes, reluctant, California's boast;
Its wondrous air and climate stand confessed
And Boston bows in homage to "Out West."

Wm Lloyd Garrison.

January 19, 1903.—

Serene, I fold my hands & wait,
Nor care for wind nor tide nor sea;
I rave no more gainst time or fate,
For lo! my own shall come to me

John Burroughs

April 15th 1909.

With the big fellows
I am glad to called
Friend

A. C. Vroman

Apl 15 - 1909

A C Vroman

PLATE XXV

Leopold Godowsky

etc. to be had at
Schlesinger (Berlin)
for 25 cents.

In remembrance of my first visit to
the unique home of the remarkable and only
Chas F. Lummis. Leopold Godowsky

June 22nd 1919

PLATE XXVI

"Mad as a Ma Chere"

The Annual Madness – 1920 – MCH: 6

"Tho' this be Madness,
    yet there's Methodists in it." Ham-and.

THE MARCH HARES
DON QUIJOTE, XXXIII = HAMLET II 2
1911

Air: "Live a-Humble"

Godlemighty made the Rabbit
    For the Nash'nal Bird of March –
Filled his laigs with jumpin'-jacks
    And stiffed his ears with starch;
Spring's already in his blood,
    A-bilin' mighty funny –

Salubrious ☉ Sassy ☉ a-Hoppin' for his Honey.
Welsh Rabbit ain't no Rabbit, it's a colic unawares –
But We are March Bunnies – So Who-the-Hippy cares?
    The Gray Hare   Chas. F. Lummis –

Mariska Aldrich Travis –
    one of them!

Arthur Lee Willard., Captain, US Navy,
    US Stn. Mexico.

J J Kareny Lieut Comdr MC USN

Jennie Hagan Goodwin   W. A. Goodwin

Emmett S. Davis .   Lucy Laubersheimer

Leon Rice   Theresa Ernst. – Los Angeles –

Marco R Newmark

W. Francis Gates   Occasionally on the
    list of the elect?

Virka Purdun Richey –   Don Field

R. H. Burnham   Grace Adèle Freeley –

Osee E. Seldert.   Mae B Lumsden (Baby)

Edna A. Bassett.   Dr Louis Graeter

Jenie Rice   Mary Tatum.

     Carlyle B Lumsden

April 4. 1920 — Sollum Easter Services for That Beloved Bibliosmile Frank P. Hill

v. pp. 79, 196, 294

A RALLY OF LIBRARIANS WHO ARE NEVERTHELESS HUMAN — THE BIBLIOSMILES AND THEN SOME — HOMO SUM — FOUNDED 1907

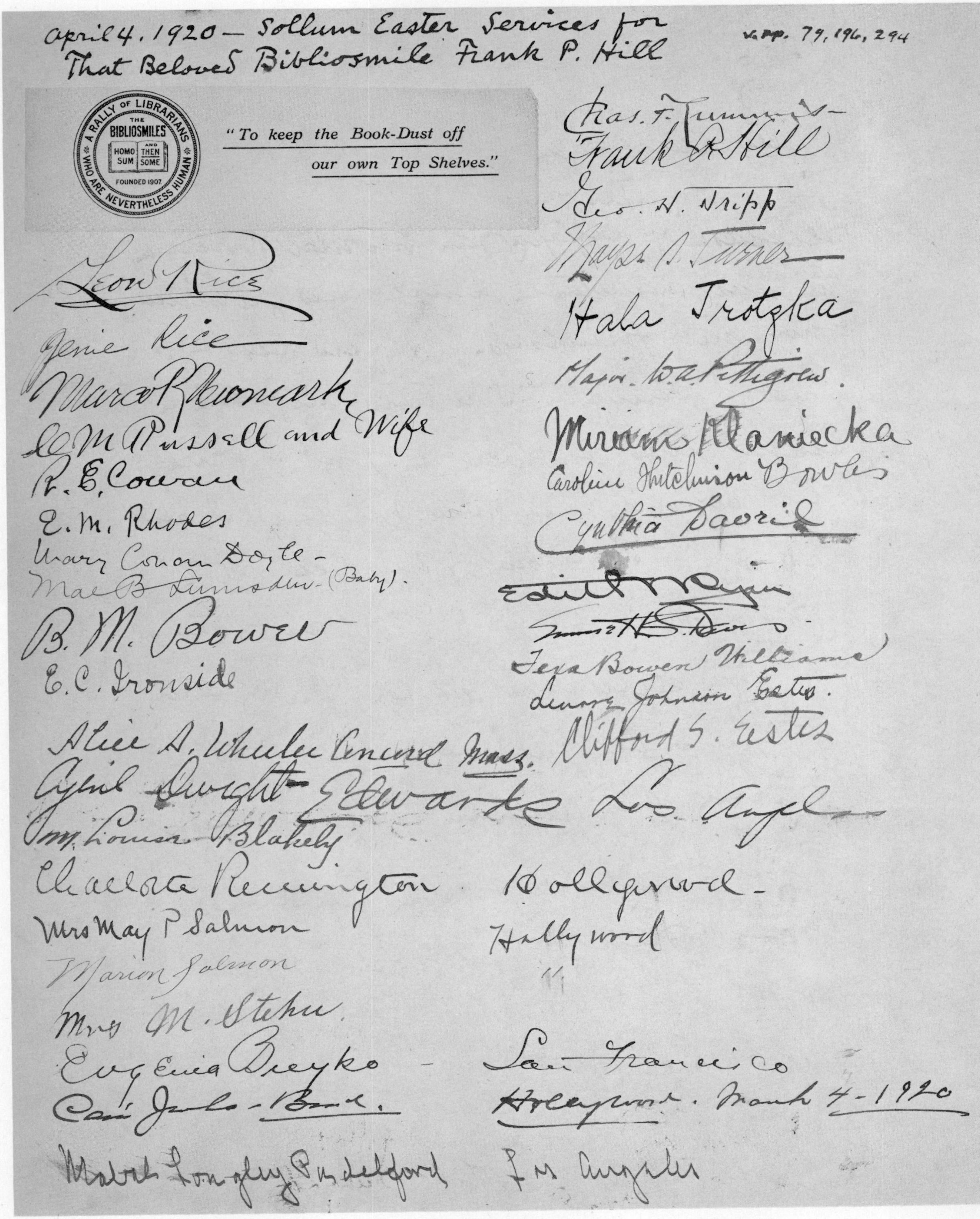

"To keep the Book-Dust off our own Top Shelves."

Chas. F. Lummis —
Frank P. Hill
Geo. H. Tripp
Hayes B. Turner
Hala Trotzka
Major W. A. Pettigrew.
Miriam Slaniecka
Caroline Hutchinson Bowles
Cynthia Daoril
Edith Wagner
Emmett H. B. Davis
Tessa Bowen Williams
Lenore Johnson Estes.
Clifford S. Estes

Leon Rice
Jenie Rice
Marco R. Newmark
C. M. Russell and Wife
R. E. Cowan
E. M. Rhodes
Mary Conan Doyle —
Mae B. Lumsden — (Baby).
B. M. Bower
E. C. Ironside
Alice A. Wheeler Concord Mass.
April Dwight Edwards Los Angeles
Mrs. Louise Blakely
Charlotte Remington Hollywood —
Mrs May P. Salmon Hollywood
Marion Salmon "
Mrs M. Stehn.
Evgenia Breyko — San Francisco
Carrie Jacobs-Bond. Hollywood. March 4-1920
Mabel Longley Pindelford Los Angeles

PLATE XXVIII

Marietta Aldrich Davis

Carolin H. W. Foster

Elizabeth Waggoner

Marguerite Mac Calip

Mary Tatum

Helen C. Morgan

Teresa L. Troconiz

H. T. Morgan

Julia S. Ritter

Julia Manton Rhoder

Another perfect day.

Ruth Smith Braun

We plant, we reap, we sow
a mess of seeds
In ignorance, — then know

Robert Sorrell Elson

"Peggy" Robinson

Oscar Mauser

David Schwartz M.D.

Pearl Jones

H. Paul Larson

Evanston Ill

Anna Goodman

Annie Milner

Jeanette Rubin

Munza Cheminasky Schwartz

Myrtle W. Hoek

Ford Sees

Edith L. Pla

Rosalie M. Stoll

3m Langton Prager — Hollywood

Gladys E. Blackwell

Hollywood

Mabel W. Burch (your heavenly twin.)

Kathryn Giddings Hollywood

PLATE XXIX

May 27, 1923   The "Resurrection Barbecue."
Camulos Rancho

This Home-Book has never before been away from El Alisal — but it ⊕ I are At Home in Camulos, too.

Few return from so far down the Valley of the Shadow as I have fared in the last year — but few have such friends to win them back, or such a paradise for healing.

Thirty-eight years ago, fresh from my "Tramp Across the Continent," I first came to Camulos. I thought it then — I think it now — the loneliest spot on Earth. So, when a deadly breakdown felled me last June, it was here I took Sanctuary. And here I have won back to life. To celebrate my pretty-much recovery, this Barbecue is given by Chas. H. Cram ⊕ Ysabel del Valle Cram, the dear, long-time friends to whose loving-kindness ⊕ unfailing care I owe my life.

In all the world I could find no fitter place for such a celebration than this last, best Home of the Patriarchal California-that-was; and with these staunch friends who have loyally kept alive the best traditions of Camulos.

Chas. F. Lummis —   Chas. H. Cram.   "Ysabel del V. Cram"

Joseph Scott,   Bert Sprotte.   Basil Ruysdael

    "Edith L. Pla.

Anna Rujena Sprotte —   M. J. Kendall
still and ever Liebling's Kind
    Ruth B. Moran
Ida J. Mells   Gertrude M. Girvan
M. H. Newmark   Doris Overman
Marco R. Newmark   Mary Louise Overman
    Marguerite R. Tew.   Frieda Peycke
    Wynona Breazeale Johnson —   Samuel Storrow
    Fiskie L. Fiske
Jordan Lummis.   Otto Ploetz.
Anna E. Blake (formerly Mrs. J. M. Griffith)
    Annie Milner   Mrs. Ida B. Davis.
Marie Tanduchief   Alberta Reeder Davis.
Ruth M. Hiestand.
Mrs. Samuel Storrow   Loren Reeder Davis
    Jessie Lucille Gibbs.   Ida Julia Knibbs.
    Myra Belle Vickers.   Henry Herbert Knibbs
    Geo. Townsend Cole

PLATE XXX

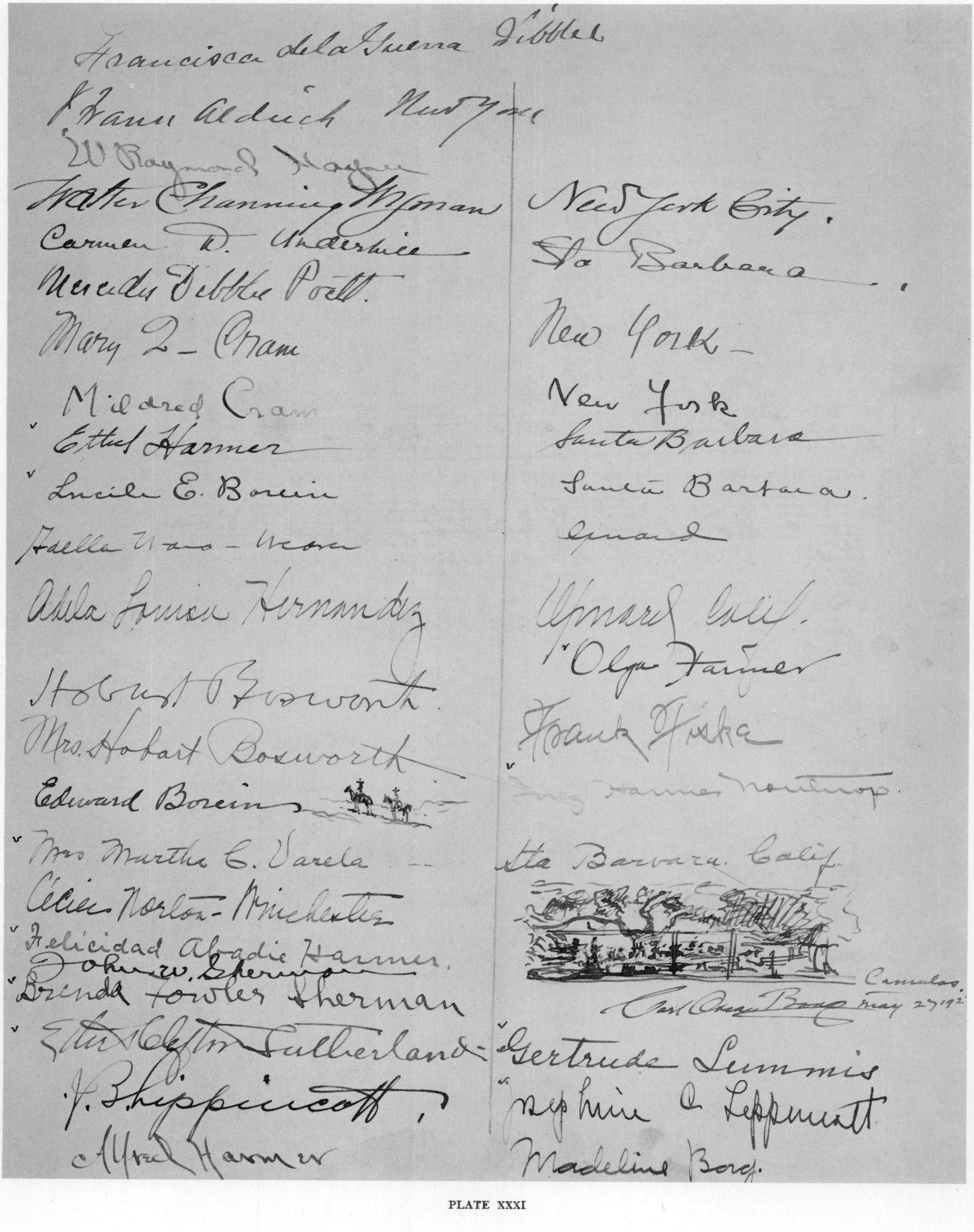

Francisca dela Guerra Dibblee

P. Frano Aldrich   New York

W. Raymond Mayen

Walter Channing Wyman   New York City.

Carmen D. Underhill   Sta Barbara

Merenda Dibblee Poett.   New York —

Mary L. Cram   New York

Mildred Cram   Santa Barbara

Ethel Harmer   Santa Barbara.

Lucile E. Borein   Oxnard

Faella Ware-Moore

Adela Louisa Hernandez   Oxnard Calif.

Olga Harmer

Hobart Bosworth.

Frank Fiske

Mrs. Hobart Bosworth

Inez Harmer Northrop.

Edward Borein

Mrs. Martha E. Varela   Sta Barbara. Calif.

Celia Norton-Winchester

Felicidad Abadie Harmer.

John W. Sherman

Brenda Fowler Sherman   Carl Oscar Borg may 27 '12

Edna Clifton Sutherland   Gertrude Lummis

J. B. Lippincott   Josephine A. Lippincott

Alfred Harmer   Madeline Borg.

PLATE XXXI

Feb 2 1920

Un tributo al Gran Maestro Don Vicente Blasco Ibañez
Novelista sin par, Campeon indomable del inmortal genio
Español, su alma, sus ideales, su aristocracia, su humanidad,
sea en misma España, Madre Civilizadora de las Americas, sea entre
sus hijos Neo-Mundiales. Una bienvenida y un cariño de California,
flor de las hijas de España.

Fras. F. Lummis—

Profundamente agradecido,
paso estos elogios á la madre
España, pues solamente ella los
merece.

Vicente Blasco
Ibañez

Con sincero agrade
cimiento por mis a-
tenciones recibidas
del ilustre historiador
José Padín

My dear Gamaliel:

This page is not large
enough for the account of my debt to you.
Sincerely E. M. Rhodes.

Will Rogers.
Outsiders will get in
as you will notice
by the above name.

Elsie del Valle—
Magdalena R. Miller.
Victoria W. Menjies.
Teresa L. Troconiz
Madeleine Etchemendy.
M. F. del Valle
F. Menjies
Sra. Feliciana de Y. de Pedroarena

Isidora Pedroarena

Marianne J. Etchemendy

Mary Tatum.

Flora P. Hogbin

Alfred C. Hogbin

Caroline H. W. Foster.

Marguerite MacKaly

Victoria Juarez Wolfskill.

Henry Dains

PLATE XXXII

CHARACTERISTICS which made El Cabezudo magnificent on some battlefields also made him a difficult man to work with in the confining quarters of a museum.

Some of the people connected with the Southwest Museum had, for a respectable number of hours, sat in a class in archaeology, ethnology, or a related subject and had a certificate authorizing them to apply the appropriate titles to themselves. Another group was made up of affluent individuals who could add to their laurels as patrons of science by supporting the museum, and they felt that what they paid for belonged to them.

Few of either group had ridden late on a rainy afternoon into a New Mexico sheep camp to pass the evening around the fire singing with the Mexican herders, to spend the night smelling the wet leather of the saddle and the rich odor of the wet saddle blanket, and to listen to the strange, half-human cries of restless sheep. Lummis' only claim to the titles of archaeologist and ethnologist was a lifetime of work at these trades. As to his wealth—a respectable church mouse would have scorned it. There was no question in his mind about the ownership of the museum—it was his. He had conceived it, been in attendance at its birth, and nourished it. The fact that he had been able to persuade others to pay for it was immaterial, and he gave them no special consideration.

Although Lummis did protest that with age he was growing more patient and less aggressive, this was not apparent to outsiders. Some even felt that concerning matters western and archaeological he was no less than arrogant.

At one point the curator, D. F. Palmer, presented

twelve charges against him demanding that he be ousted as secretary. Among them were that Lummis sought to coerce, intimidate, and humiliate the curator and destroy his professional reputation; that he deliberately manipulated the minutes of the executive committee; that his reports on cash expenditures were inaccurate and that he exaggerated the value of museum property; and that he encouraged vandalism and supported despoliation of the archaeological remains of the Southwest. A final astonishing charge was that Lummis was sacrificing the Southwest Museum by promoting a "rival" museum in Santa Fe, New Mexico.

The committee appointed to examine the charges decided that the two personalities were incompatible. Because the committee felt that Lummis was an indispensable factor in the upbuilding of the museum, it recommended that Palmer resign.

Friction continued, however. Lummis' plans for a series of subsidiary museums through the Southwest were unpopular in many quarters. Finally, "I resigned as Secretary of the Southwest Museum March 11, 1915 on the plea of dear friends on the board who thought that Money Interests were more important. . . ."[1]

Certain men had demanded that Lummis be ousted, men he had interested in the museum. They had money; the museum needed their help. For its sake Lummis had to give up all connection with it, forego any part in the institution he had founded and loved, relinquish this last child also to other hands. He called it "the greatest disappointment of my life."

With the philosophy he had forged out of life,

[1] Lummis, "Diary."

Lummis determined to make the most of what his opponents had left to him—his Southwest Society from which the museum had grown. Two years later even this was taken from him.

1917, 30th. After months in which the Millionaire Wolves have been trying to suppress the Southwest Society which I am about to incorporate, Alliot has arranged conference for me with [Jared] Torrance, who refuses to remain Pres. of S.W. Museum if I continue S.W. Secretary. After sweating great drops of blood, I have surrendered my own name "Southwest." I was the first person to use that term of this region in science or literature—I have compromised on "Institute of the West"; long talk with Torrance at Raymond Hotel; he greatly relieved at my change of name . . . he will be the first to join the new corporation as a member (and does send in his $10 fee).[2]

Although Lummis called Torrance "most cordial and friendly," a few years later Torrance forced the new association to disincorporate also.

For those to whom Lummis seemed almost a legendary being, it was a bewildering thing to see life crowd him now to the wall, to see it force him to surrender one by one what he loved most—family, museum, and organizations that owed their existence to him.

The hope that he might yet find domestic happiness—even the wistful hope that he might again become a father—led him in 1915 to marry his little English secretary, Gertrude Redit.

He set himself to trying "to cultivate the things which I most lacked, which was mostly patience." During this period he wrote some lively material for the Los Angeles *Times* called "I Guess So" and "Chili Con Carnage." But much of what he had once poured into literary work now went into interest and concern for the needs and lives of his friends.

In February, 1919, Lummis had to meet a new tragedy, the death of his beloved friend Hector Alliot, his own choice for curator of the museum. "Hector Lionheart. . . . Fearless and tender, brilliant but poised . . . with a woman's heart, the frankness of a child, the brain of a philosopher—and a Soul of Fire."

Lummis felt this new threat to his museum. "The Curator is the soul. The Museum is as he is—a mere carcass (as many museums are) or a living entity." The Southwest Museum could not function without a curator. With rare humility he reminded the trustees how the museum got its start and what had made it a museum.

There must once again be a curator to carry on the work Alliot had begun: "someone who is not cold-blooded nor yet light-headed; practical but not materialistic; someone who can both Do and Dream; someone who has 'business sense' and yet sense enough to know that the Soul is not mere 'Business.'"

No one could fill Alliot's shoes. It was as a stopgap that Lummis offered himself: "I should not expect his salary—I am not worth what he was. A bare living at taking care of 'My Baby' would be all that I desire."

He thought that by this time—four years since the museum's break with him—the old enmities would have died. But he had to face the fact that the trustees still would have none of him.

The man whose vision had conceived a great museum for a frontier town, whose energy had brought it into being, and whose genius had embellished it, had outlived the community's need for him.

[2] Lummis, "Journal."

MORE AND MORE the rapidly aging man became occupied with his vast correspondence, his multitude of friends, his numerous pets,[1] and his daily, type-written journal, which ran to many pages and was widely circulated among his intimates. Lummis' health was failing, and a cataract was destroying his eyesight.

In 1922 the long-patient Century Company demanded that he complete at once the book he had promised them, an updated version of *Some Strange Corners of Our Country*. What had once been done so easily now required great effort. During part of the struggle to complete the book, Lummis had the help of a secretary who had worked with David Starr Jordan on his autobiography. She promptly became "Daughter-Heart" and the cause of friction with his wife Gertrude. The strain of completing the book in the midst of domestic controversy brought Lummis down from 148 pounds to less than 100. There was a time when his doctor thought he could not survive.

An invitation to Camulos undoubtedly saved his life. In that golden, unhurried valley he knew again the healing joy of living among those who loved him. It was many months before he felt strong enough to face the dissensions and frustrations of home.

On March 1, 1923, Lummis' sixty-fourth birthday, the Southwest Museum celebrated Founder's Day. Letters and telegrams poured in from all over the world, and friends thronged to the museum to pay him honor. After all the years of museum silence, it was "just as though one of my own flesh and blood had proffered some beautiful filial act." In his diary one can still sense the surge of his heart. "Ed Ayer, come all the way from Chicago! Sam Storrow speaks. Says as Joe [Scott] how much all love me. And to prove it, many have subscr. so I never have to worry about my home again—taxes, assessments, mortgage!"

At the climax of the program all were led down to the Arizona Room. Joseph Scott gave one of his moving orations. When a veil was thrown aside at the entrance to the caracol, a bronze tablet could be seen.

The frail, old Lion moved closer until his weakened eyes could read.

To
CHARLES FLETCHER LUMMIS
IN HONOR OF HIS WORK
AS FOUNDER OF
THE SOUTHWEST MUSEUM
THE TRUSTEES DEDICATE
THIS TOWER NAMING IT
THE LUMMIS CARACOL TOWER

How did this make him feel? ". . . very proud, very humble, that such a beautiful and noble tower should bear my name." It gave him new courage to dream. Why might he not be "of still further service to this great child which has outgrown me?" As he wrote to Marco H. Newmark: "The beauties and the glories [of Founders Day] are all lovely jewels, but they are not Life (which to me means work). What I want

---

[1] During his years in Los Angeles, Lummis had a startling inventory of pets: A young eagle, an owl, two six-foot rattlesnakes, a young buck, and a three-month-old wildcat. At various times the "Alisal orphan asylum" sheltered fireflies; chickens (Caruso and his feathered harem); a burro; a hornpout which came to his master's whistle; a long procession of cats which included Peter, a male, Repeater, a female, and Mu, with his bird-warning collar. There were numerous horned toads, the flying squirrels Scinropterus and Pteromys (Si and Terry), and the dogs *Suanu* ("Little Man") and *Tejon*. Wrote Lummis with obvious glee: "Now I AM getting contented—the orphan asylum is really about ripe. A multitude of rabbits and a swarm of hornpout, the noble trio of bullfrogs . . . turtles . . . the crowning orphans, 6 tiny lobsters!"

to Do. I'm full of books, and am to have a wonderful chance to work them out of my system. I want to do for the museum all they will let me do."

Shortly thereafter Lummis was invited to visit friends in Santa Barbara. In the fragrant courtyards and historic adobes of that Spanish California town he fell naturally into the Santa Barbara style of living. Swapping tales with its courtly Dons, serenaded by its great ladies (still beautiful in their elegance and grace), watching their dark-eyed granddaughters sway through the old Spanish dances, he knew he must live to help them keep this way of life.

At a barbecue of the Los Alamos Club at the Las Cruces Ranch, Lummis gave this gospel to them, "Save the Old." Guests jumped to their feet, named him their only honorary member, and induced him to publish the talk. He wrote three "red hot" articles for the *Santa Barbara Morning Press* which were later published in 1957 as the pamphlet, "Stand Fast, Santa Barbara!" It was reprinted every year by the paper's former owner, and the new owner promised to continue the practice.

. . . for 300 years the very word [California] has been a name to conjure with. . . . Its magic grew taller with the heroic era of the Missions, then the glorious Patriarchal pastoral period—the happiest, the most generous, the most hospitable, the most lovable life ever lived on this continent.

To this centuried Romance, Santa Barbara is legitimate and favorite heiress. . . . Will she follow the rest, and cast the rich pearls of her dowry before the swine of blundering materialism—or will she stand erect and queenly and alone in the purple beauty of her Romance?

Shortly thereafter Lummis felt strong enough to return to El Alisal "loaded for B'ar," fired with his thought of all the things he wanted to do, and especially to save the old Spanish songs. He was counting on the help of his treasured secretary, but he had not reckoned on "Gre," his wife. She could not live in the same house with the promised helper. In one month he lost eight pounds. His eyes grew much worse. Even his humor wobbled slightly: "Gre has painted the iron bed she got from Bertha an incredible lavender lake or mauve. Tell her it can't come in house—I'll get new paint. She demurs, but I insist.

She admits it isn't the color she expected."[2] The marriage wasn't either.

After eight years he was importuning her to have in the home a secretary she could not stomach. There was no one to point out in gentle irony that sixteen years ago she herself had been the indigestible ingredient.

Finally the matter brought on a separation. "Haven't any more life to waste." He plunged into the work of translating the Spanish songs. The work took a heavy toll on him, and his eyes gave him much pain. But in 1923, with Arthur Farwell doing the harmonizing and Ed Borein designing the cover, the first volume of fourteen songs was published, titled *Spanish Songs of Old California.* Fifty years later the volume was still selling.

Lummis referred to his secretary as *Sempre Leal,* ("Always Faithful"). She helped him carry heavy rolls of roofing paper, clean out the squirrel cage, soak his corn, carry the snake box with the two gopher snakes, and tidy the workroom. She found material which had been lost for years, arranged the work table for action and stimulated his "rusty brain." He made such progress that he felt she would help him regain the health he had lost.

May 7, 1924 was "Lummis Night at the Gamut Club."[3] To honor "the best loved man in Los Angeles" . . . they carried me around the room on their shoulders, singing "Jolly Good Fellow" and men all over the room got up and read from various of my books and made all sorts of speeches. . . .

Then he sat down before the club guest register, picked up a pen, and in a tremulous hand wrote:

> *May 7, 1924*
> *Life has come full for me,*
> *Full of being and doing*
> *Out in the open and free.*
> *I have met what any dares*
> *Played with and tamed the fire,*
> *Taught my sorrows to lick my hand,*
> *My pleasure to know the rein.*

And I have learned the proportions of things. Tonight one of the . . . most beautiful of a long life is

---

[2] Lummis, "Diary."
[3] A social club of the bon vivants of Los Angeles of that time.

far richer than it would have been in the younger years when I should have fancied this magnificent tribute was just for me. It is richer because I now realize with high comfort and joy that the things I love are so dear to you, my dear fellow Gamuteers. That means that these shall not die. God bless & keep you & keep the Gamut Spirit burning!

Charles F. Lummis[4]

He came home that night to find Sempre Leal's room stripped, the furniture and the secretary gone. Some of his treasures (autographed letters and the like) had also vanished with her.

In those days Lummis personally shopped for the family groceries. The small figure of an aging man, his face not so red now, dragging a little wagon behind him, was often seen in the markets along Pasa-

[4] Courtesy Carl S. Dentzel, director, Southwest Museum.

dena Avenue. To friends who protested at his spending so much of his time and strength on the trivial tasks of the household, he replied,

. . . maybe I am lucky to be able to be happy with these things instead of falling down in a Noble Despair because I cannot do the Big Things that are still in me if I can get them out. . . . The only thing that can possibly bring me back to my old place in the field of letters will be to keep this old body of mine in working trim. The petty little carpenterings, marketings and other domestic activities have brought me back physically from the abyss to a tolerably presentable status. They have kept my mind from going to sleep—for the little ingenuities of doing these things are enough to make anybody's brain get busy. They have added to the comfort of the home and to the pleasure of those that I love and they have kept me happy, serene and—by God—Master.[5]

[5] Lummis, "Journal."

34

A Dream Lost

THE EXTENSIVE Lummis collections together with El Alisal and the surrounding city block, all of which had been given to the Southwest Museum in 1910, were returned to Lummis in 1917 after the friction between him and the museum personnel developed. Lummis' great wish that the house be preserved as a museum and a home for his descendants nonetheless remained. He also retained an affection for the handsome building on the nearby hill that he still considered his "youngest child." He secured waivers from his children and settled Gertrude's claim by giving her his remaining Keith paintings. He then continued negotiations with Sam Storrow, an old and trusted friend and a director of the museum.

On December 17, 1923, he wrote in his journal:

Sam Storrow comes for me 12.30 (out fr. town on purpose). To fine lunch at Rector's, 4th St. Discutimos mucho, he to get my idea. Relieved that G (Gertrude) is out of it, and not to be tangled; and the children agreeable. SW Museum (now on its feet) to maintain this as the Lummis Foundation. I and my children to have life right absolutely. Educational Museum, keep the land (free from taxes), pay me $100 a month as Curator, and to name my successor. To revert if they don't fulfill conditions. He has rich men who will build an art gallery and other laboratories keeping Alisal the capital note in the plan. Can get wonderful collections. . . . Back to office and I sign two deeds to him to hold for museum —Real and personal. Lovely to me.

Assured that his terms had been accepted, Lummis was satisfied. But in 1926 he finally succeeded in obtaining a copy of the directors' resolution setting forth the actual terms of acceptance. It was a crushing blow to learn that no provisions had been made for his children after his death and that it had been resolved, among other things, "that said house will not be demolished or materially changed during the lifetime of said Charles F. Lummis. . . ."

With his failing strength he started one last battle to save El Alisal. He wrote to the museum directors in June, 1926.

Now I will ask you to observe that the "Resolutions" adopted by the Board have no legal value whatever. They are not worth the paper they are written on. There is no return or compensation for my gift. In place of providing for my family so long as there should be one, you would be absolutely free to turn my children out the day after my death.

You would also be free to tear down, or alter or to "materially change" a house whose architecture is part of my life and my brains and my love and my hands. . . .

Nothing but dynamite will demolish or materially change this house during my lifetime; and I rather think it will be found "consistent with the purposes of the Southwest Museum," which I founded, to retain this property along the lines I indicated long ago.

You will be glad with me that I lived long enough to discover this status. If I had died without knowing my whole life would have been thwarted—at least in its vital issues of science and honor; my human children would have been robbed of their birthright; my youngest child, this corporation, would have been unwillingly and unintentionally in the position of having defrauded its Father and Founder of all that was dearest to him.

To James A. B. Scherer, the director, went the following:

. . . I hope you will realize that I am in earnest. Another might say Desperate . . . but I never Despair. But I have waited far beyond common sense or even Faith—or even decency to my children.

I am Done—not for anger, but because I realize that unless I secure effective action At Once it will be too late; that I shall have been left a betrayer of my own children and my own ideals. And unless Death "draws first" that won't happen; for I shall devote my last efforts to rescue the Holy Grail I confided to kindly but careless hands.

Thus once more, dear Dr Scherer I ask your active assistance. . . .

To Henry O'Melveny:

. . . and as you never failed me before, I am sure you will help me now—when I find the whole effort . . . of my life has been frustrated—of course unintentionally. If I thought it intentional I would say Betrayed. But I am sure there is as good faith on the other side as mine if less thoughtfulness and sacrifice, and you will have no difficulty in bringing about a solution which will save the honor of the museum and save me from dying disappointed and dishonored.

With all the persuasion at his command he pleaded with whomever might be able to rescue him, but the directors turned a deaf ear to the founder. They agreed with Lummis' original position that divided among his children the collections would be scattered and the mortgaged property lost. They felt that it would be illegal as well as impractical to commit the museum to the task of keeping a home for endless generations of descendants. On receiving the property, the directors had paid off the mortgage[1] and granted Lummis an annuity of one hundred dollars monthly. Besides they had returned the property to him once before.

Yet El Alisal was not disposed of immediately after his death. Various members of the second and third generation lived there for years, and some were even given a small stipend as custodians. It was not until February 24, 1939, after a long, hard period of depression, that the Executive Committee of the Southwest Museum resolved that it could no longer maintain the home and that it must be offered for sale.

Good fortune intervened. Precisely at this time the city fathers of Los Angeles decided that it was necessary to purchase a portion of the property for the Arroyo Seco Freeway, causing the museum to delay the sale of the entire estate.

Meanwhile a group of good ladies, old friends, admirers, and concerned citizens organized to protect the beleaguered El Alisal. Their enthusiasm swept up clubs, civic organizations, and influential public figures to the end that the entire property was acquired by the city and later by the state and is now protected as a California state monument. At this time, most appropriately, it is the headquarters of the Southern California Historical Society.

It would have been nice if the old man could have known.

As it was, the realization that he was legally helpless pushed him close to the breaking point. Edgar Hewett rescued him temporarily by arranging a return to his land of *poco tiempo*. A few months past sixty-seven, with cataracts on both eyes, Lummis looked eighty when he arrived in Santa Fe.

---

[1] The mortgage had a worthy origin. In 1903, Bandelier had been forbidden to leave Peru until his debts were cleared. To rescue his old friend, Lummis borrowed twenty-five hundred dollars on his property. Bandelier, poorer and sadder in business matters even than Lummis, was only able to make occasional payments. The mortgage remained and grew with the property until the Southwest Museum finally cleared it.

35

A Last Long Look at Sunshine and Adobe

IN HIS very last years Lummis was able to make two trips to New Mexico, the land that had thrown such an enchantment on him in his early and vigorous youth that strengthened him as he declined. A chronicle of everything that was crowded into these two short visits during the summers of 1926 and 1927 would make a book by itself.

It might be worthwhile here to take a glimpse at the equipment with which Lummis traditionally traveled.

. . . the big camera with its plate holders, etc., Mr. Fuch's [tailor] brown corduroys, 2 doz. 5 x 8 plates in the big fiber suitcase . . . the strong Gladstone with the big bunch of stationery—letterheads, second sheets, yellow Ms. journal, onion skin for Journal, envelopes, etc. Also mended my big pocketbook for tickets, etc.—Also trying to find cigar boxes to fit Journal paper and blue prints, etc.—and other containers for other things that can't be sent loose . . . stationery, Ms. Journal, clips, 2 or 3 reference books, etc. Also did up the little guitar "acomita"; also 2 umbrellas & the 2 tripods & the Alforja in a stout roll . . . B [secretary] jotted down the list while I packed the Gladstone, the fiber, the cowhide suitcase & the Stattler: so I will know what is in each—but she laughed much at my equipment. It takes a good deal for me to work a month or more . . . I put some old straps around the lunch box and with pieces of copper wire tied on a wooden handle. . . . It is a mighty formidable array of 12 pieces, 3 to check . . . some heavy as lead.[1]

"Like a man thirsting for water," he set out for New Mexico. Every old landmark seemed to promise "health and new years waiting to my credit." But the old man coming home again to his New Mexico was not the lion of the past great days.

"And now was this Lummis, this little man, hardly able to drag himself to our door?" asked the *Santa Fe New Mexican.* "Yet two things disease had not touched, his crisp speech and alert eye."

He would not let weakness of heart or dimness of vision keep him from climbing and working and digging right alongside the younger men. "I am not going to be found dead in a camp or a house or a tent—not when my caves are still there."

The *Santa Fe New Mexican* continued to report on his visit.

He missed not a performance of the Fiesta.

And when they rolled out of town on the annual archaeological trip of 1000 miles to ancient sites and living pueblos he lost that humped over, cadaverous look. Every foot of the country . . . was familiar ground to him, some of it quite unchanged since he had last explored it, afoot or astride, with Bandelier, nearly forty years before. Revisiting wrought wonders. Before the joyous end he clambered up the difficult Old Trail to Acoma . . . chipper as a boy. And when he emerged from the warm embrace of an Indian friend of other days, "Don Carlos" was himself again.

Men with whom he had worked for New Mexico told him that she had need of him still—as when young and aflame he had helped to bring her to the nation's knowledge. Surely he would be given the strength and the years to serve her still more.

Once again the Board of the Museum of New

---

[1] Lummis, "Journal."

Mexico and the School of American Research welcomed him into their councils. When they were one day deciding where to put the memorial tablet to the venerated Alice Fletcher, Edgar Hewett told Lummis that he too would sometime be there in bronze.

Hewett soon asked Lummis if he would dare risk a one-thousand-mile auto trip in a "scientific round-up." Would he! No bullier way to die. So off they went up the wild Embudo rapids, over *faldas* of the Sangre de Cristo, across the Red River and other lovely valleys, "over the superb Cuesta with its marvelous vistas," and to old Fort Garland, where in 1884 Lummis had had his last beaver trapping. Storekeeper Hoagland "guessed the young fellow you saw here then might have been Johnny Meader—he lives here yet."

John Henry Meader, the old trapper Lummis met on his way west in 1885 and visited again at Fort Garland, Colorado, in 1926. (*Courtesy Southwest Museum*)

The whole caravan stopped while Hewett and Lummis walked to the neat cabin where they were welcomed by an old man of seventy-five with whiskers to his belt and eight inches wide. Lummis asked, "Were you trapping here in 1884?"

"I sure was, and never been away from here since."

"Remember a young fellow in knickerbockers and red stockings, tramping from Cincinnati to California, who stayed and trapped with you, and when he left, you walked 20 miles down the road with him for company?" Before he was halfway through the big beard began to split.

"You him?" And they had a hug.[2]

After leaving Fort Garland, Lummis, Hewett, and the caravan

went to Mesa Verde, Colorado; to Cliff Palace, Sun Temple, and I went up and down the big cliffs today as much as any of them, though my rotten eyesight made me slow.

They urged Tsianina to sing in the hotel tonight. She refused. "But to any of you who want to hear me enough to get up at 5:00 in the morning and come to the Rim, I shall sing the Zuñi Sunrise Hymn from under the arch of the cave of Spruce Tree House."

Up at 5:00, no shave, rushed to the Rim. To my wonder, every soul on the Mesa was there perched on the very brink of the cañon. Before the mighty ruins of the cave about 400 ft. across from us, and about 200 ft. below, under the great clam shell brow of that cliff, stood Tsianina in her beautiful buckskins. A minute before the sun she began to sing that noble Indian invocation. We could hear every note and syllable perfectly. It was exquisite and awesome.[3]

On the east slope of the Continental Divide Lummis saw from miles away "the strange tower of Pueblo Alto, Kin-a-a, wh. I discovered in 1888. Still tall & gray above its ruins."

At Gallup, New Mexico, he and Tsianina, an Indian singer and the idol of the town, were welcomed in the "almost palatial home of Clint Cotton, one of the most delightful I was ever in."

Clint and I have been friends for more than 40 years. Since royal old Lorenzo Hubbell lost fortune

2 *Ibid.*
3 *Ibid.*

Tsianina, the famous Indian singer, at Balcony House, New Mexico, in 1926. Photograph by Charles Lummis. (*Courtesy Southwest Museum*)

Lummis with Tsianina and Santiago Naranjo, on his last visit to New Mexico, 1926.

and health, Cotton is the last of the Patriarchs and it's a beautiful life. He made his fortune as an Indian trader, is now a wholesale merchant. His adobe store is 450 ft. long & 70 ft. wide!

Fine dinner. . . . Then we visited on the 140 ft. porch. . . . It's an indescribable joy to see again the Old Timers & the Old Scenes! . . . Clint showed us his great chest of Navajo blankets, gathered in 40 years trading I was doubly glad to see them. I still have the One Best & the best five in the world, he can't touch 'em. Below that he has me hopelessly skinned.[4]

At the ancient pueblo of Zuñi, wrote Lummis, "the great six-story pyramid house I used to photograph has practically disappeared." Part of Lummis' "resurrection medicine" was the Gallup Indian Ceremonials.

[Mike Kirk] quenchless cowboy-trader-impresario-poet-dreamer . . . conceived and founded and brought about the beautiful inter-tribal ceremonials here and has run them for five years. . . .

Fully 500 Indians in their gala, over 200 covered wagons, &c. Everything purely Indian, no Spanish feature whatever in those 3 days. Horse races, breaking horses, all kinds of foot races (including one like the Chase of the Chongo—v. Land of Poco Tiempo), the Whib race (2 sides, 3 men each, running a 10 mile race & driving a small stick ahead with the toes).

Tsianina sang beautifully, She headed the parade, queenly on a gallant horse. And Hoskey Noswood, handsome young Navajo of Shiprock Agency, sang mighty well, a delightful baritone . . . (Evening). Best seats in press box had been reserved for me for the season. The Indians lit the bonfires with the fire-drills . . . Pablo Abeita, Quimu's godfather, made a very able and sarcastic speech in English. He was a picture! Such dignity and grace! I had met him and Comadre Maria, his wife, on the street & there were great ceremonial embraces.[5]

Watching by firelight such dances as the Comanche dance of the Zuñi, the Taos Snowbird, and the famous Ye-b-chai of the Navajo, again it almost seemed to Lummis as if some of their primal strength came into him. Possibly it did—the next day came the "Squaw Dance" of the Navajo women.

They climbed up into the grandstand & seized each a Gringo of her choice with a death grip on his coat & dragged him to the arena, where he had to dance with her till he gave her 50¢ or more when he was released. She always danced behind her partner still clutching him, so he didn't see her at all. A young Maruca (I think put up to it by young Cotton) laid hold on my coat and carried me off. Though so weak, I stepped wide and handsome in a mighty war dance, to the delight of Indians and Multitude. Gave my lady 4 bits when out of wind & clambered back to my seat. But in a few minutes an old maruca lifted a 10 year old girl over the rail. She hid down behind it, but her mother urged and she made a scared dash for me, seized me with no uncertain grab and fairly drug me to the arena. I stepped prettier & higher than ever & went back to recover my wind.

By now there were full 2000 persons in the great ring, 30 deep, swaying and milling—a vast Flower of a thousand colors—such a wonder as I never saw, And Ancient Joe Crazy Horse, one of the Zuñi Delight-Makers, entertained the crowd several times inimitably.[6]

For nearly fifty years Don Amado Chaves had been the dearest part of Santa Fe to Lummis. In the aristocratic Spanish tradition Don Amado had established a summer home on the Pecos River, some fifty miles from town. There the old friends met for the last time. There also Lummis caught his last fish, and in the tradition of all fishermen he boasted:

I clambered out 2 different ways up side canons & each day caught trout, tho' it's 2 months too late, far too cold and streams too low. Also streams are very brushy & I can't see a twig 5 ft. in front of me & keep tangling my line and losing leaders. But I used to know trout better than anything; so in spite of handicaps I always got some—to the surprise of the natives. And it did me more good than anything.[7]

There were powwows with many other old companions: Gene Rhodes, John Collier, then the Commissioner of Indian Affairs, Ernest Thompson Seton,

[4] Ibid.
[5] Ibid.

[6] Ibid.
[7] Ibid.

and a host of others. And so his heart was "kept warm by old friends & old scenes & the settings that have served me in my life work." The Indians, too, were full of joy that their Charlie Lo-mis had come back to them.

After a day with John Collier at a conference with the Indians at the Pueblo of Santo Domingo, Sotero Ortiz, president of the Indian Council, moved for a vote of thanks to God for sparing Lummis' life thus far and to Lummis for helping them. Lummis was less impressed by the fact that the Indians should vote thanks to God than he was by the more remarkable occurrence of a unanimous vote from a group of Indians. Touched, he thanked them in both Spanish and English. When the meeting broke up, each Indian shook his hand and wished him well. Some of the old ones embraced him and made a ceremonial prayer over him.

Lummis revisited the aged Sisters of Charity who had nursed him in his paralysis, and the eighty-seven-year-old parish priest, John Raper, who was an old friend from Chillicothe, Ohio.

. . . a beautiful talk. He again told me about the wonderful old times when I was the "young giant of Chillicothe." He remembers to this day my "wonderful back" and my prowess as a boxer and wrestler and baseball pitcher and other things. Ran into dear old Santiago Naranjo[8] in a flaming sunset shirt of silkaline & Jicarilla beaded leggins and his beaver-skin hair "ribbons" & we had a little chat . . . met Sheldon Parsons, one of the real artists here—& looking it with his Vandyke beard & big hat. He walked around the Plaza with us, while the band concert went on & the walk was crowded with happy carefree paisanos & many Indians.[9]

While Lummis was still in Santa Fe, a series of critical problems had come to the culmination between the Pueblo Indians and the government, problems that no one seemed able to solve. The Indians decided to "send for Lummis. Whatever he tells us, we will do."

The *Santa Fe New Mexican* covered the story.

Lummis an Aide in Securing Entente. The U.S.

Pueblo Indian . . . first instance so far known where all the pueblos have been represented in a tribal gathering. . . .

Chairman [Frank] Paisano said that the meeting of the Indians last night had been greatly helped by the advice and help of Charles Lummis, veteran writer, historian and friend of the Indian. He said it was the finest talk ever made before an Indian council and that the speaker "had taken their hearts."

In part [Lummis] said: "I told my Indians . . . that if a man is my friend I want to know him and if he is my enemy I do not want him in the back in the dark. I did not blame them for their distrust of the white people in general or the Indian Department. Human nature does not change but administrations do. They can not blame the officials justly for mistakes (which have been many) if they do not say what they want from them. I told them that the disagreements among the Indians themselves, one man telling them one thing and the next man telling another, had been hard on the officials. But now the government asks you to get together and tell it what you want. . . .

"I, myself, came here suspicious that this council would do away with the old council of the Indians. But instead . . . it is only emphasizing the need of them. It isn't the government that is trapping you— you are trapping the government into hearing your wants and having their pledges given before all these witnesses. If they do not live up to their pledges and keep good faith, you have nothing to lose.

"We Indians know the need of the councils and the old councils will be of invaluable help to this new council."

In Isleta again Lummis was met by rejoicing Indians, and at Ojo de la Casa by that brave frontier woman, Alice Rea, Eve's elder sister, most of whose years had been given to the service of others.

Found Al in fine shape, tho' she is now 71 [she lived to be ninety-four]. Lean as ever & a war map of wrinkles but with the old fire & the old twinkle in her eyes & unmistakable trace of her former beauty. She was very glad to see us. The house is a long low 7-room cabin roughly chinked with mud outside, but inside very well plastered by Alice, Al's dot, in a pleasing creamy tone wh she got by mixing yeso ["lime"] with adobe mud. Their door and window

[8] See "Elder of Immemorial Kha-po," in *A Bronco Pegasus.*
[9] Lummis, "Journal."

trim is the prettiest color I ever saw in an adobe, a cheerful Nile green. . . .

A novelist who could write the story of the life of this fine old frontierswoman in all its hardship and privation & danger & self-control, self-denial & patient heroism, would have a marvelous field. A young woman from Conn., whose mother died very early & who brought up her three younger sisters as a mother (and one brother, too) and married a rather brainy Englishman—but hopelessly English—and took care of him and his child & her 2 sisters in Isleta for many years, standing the poverty entailed by his laziness and the nagging of his nature; then moving up to the top of the 10,500 ft. Bosque Peak in 1890, & living there for a dozen or 15 years always with many family cares & always with poverty & deprivation & hard manual labor—she used to do the plowing as well as lighter work.

In Isleta Cacique Dolores Jojola—the noble old man whom I left apparently dying last December—now was out making adobes to repair his pretty little home among the cottonwoods and fruit trees. I told him that I wanted his picture—I doubt if it has ever been made. But he consented saying "as it was me." . . . Pablo who is a striking type, refused to let me photograph him though we have been friends for many years. He never did have his picture "took."[10]

If the Dark Angel had said to Lummis, "This much you have time for and no more," surely these places on the earth's face would have been his choice.

Near the end of his stay Lummis went "to the foot of the rock part of the Horse Trail; then thro' the gap between the 2 mesas, where Villagran, the Soldier Poet, made his wonderful leap in 1598."

Lummis did not dream that these were his last glimpses of New Mexico. Or did he? Toward the end of his last visit he wrote in his journal:

[10] *Ibid.*

Pablo Abeita, a longtime friend of Lummis', whom he visited at Isleta, New Mexico, in 1927. (*Courtesy Southwest Museum*)

Over a month ago at home I had the impression that a spider or something bit me on the left cheek bone, ¾ of an inch under the eye, wh has kept a little bulbous swelling there ever since; not painful but not quite normal. In the last two days this feeling of distention has spread to the left half of my upper lip so that it is entirely numb. Think I will see Dr. Massie about it tomorrow.

216

RETURNING to Los Angeles in the autumn of 1927, Lummis went to his old friend and neighbor, Dr. Laubershimer, about his "uncomfortable mug."

The spider bite and paralyzed lip on the left side didn't interest him at all, but the right eye . . . gave him "grave concern." Signs of a tumor. . . .

T. [Turbesé] tuned both guitars and we sang "Lone Starry Hours," "Quelele," etc. . . . I imagine before morning we shall have an increase in the Lummis census. I hope it will be Charles Jordan, of course, for I wish to see the name go on. But neither will we drown it in the other event.[1]

His second grandchild was a girl, but he was nonetheless proud of her.[2]

Doctors continued to study the suspected tumor. On November 9, Lummis wrote:

Well, I have my ticket and destination—but not the train time as yet! I was never late for a train but once in my life—but I think perhaps I will miss a few on this road. . . . I know of a lot more things I want to do at this end of the line than at the other. . . . the verdict "malignant" . . . said it was a bad case. . . .

Down to 6th and Spring & trotted around 4 blocks to get some sweet peas for my home folks. . . . Phoned blessed MH [Marco Newmark]. . . . He is a good more worried than I am, nothing serious worries me. Little needless things irritate me but anything that can't be helped is just as easy as rain.[3]

That night, smiling quietly, he broke the news to his family. To them it was paralyzing. For him it meant "hurry."

Lummis was still very much in the center of the stage. He picked up the script for the last act with confidence, almost with gusto. He returned eagerly to his long-neglected craft, hoping to produce as much as possible before the final curtain. But:

Al's [Alice Rea's] scrapbook is the First Order of business. If I don't get it to her at once she is apt to be snowed in at her mountain ranch and not get it for months. . . . And then it is the Spanish Pioneers (new edition) to a finish. And maybe some collateral work. My next trick after the Pioneers will be to finish the 2nd book of Songs. I don't want to leave that undone.[4]

For a long while he had been working on a poem based on his own experiences in the Apache War. Also with this "Ballad of Geronimo," he had a secret dream.[5]

Got a fleabite and phoned Harry Knibbs about Geronimo & the other truck I would like to shake into a book of verse. . . . A great deal . . . will depend on Harry Knibbs, one of the half dozen real poets left in this country. . . .

The book of poems if not most important, will sort of ease my mind. . . . And I sure would want to make another and a more familiar and personal book on New Mexico. However, we Can't Have Everything to Please Us . . . as the grieving parents of little Johnny remarked.[6]

[1] Lummis, "Diary."
[2] Betty Jane Lummis, the second daughter of Jordan Lummis, later Mrs. Mark Groves.
[3] Lummis, "Journal."

[4] *Ibid.*
[5] See "Man-Who-Yawns," *A Bronco Pegasus,* 35.
[6] Lummis, "Journal."

Those who had sometimes felt the discomfort that could result from Lummis' relish for the dramatic now were witnesses to the unsensational way in which he met the inevitable. He wrote in his journal: "To the X-ray clinic. Dr. Soiland (charming man) . . . had me pretty well sized up. I am really nice looking seen through the back of my head. . . ."

Edgar Hewett later recalled the conversation when Lummis rather facetiously broke the news to him that he had only a short time to live.

I said, "Are you sure nothing can be done?"

"Oh, yes," he replied, "The medico says he can give me a little more time by cutting off a considerable part of my mug."

"Fine," says I, "The more of your mug he cuts off, the better looking you'll be. On second thought, have him cut off the whole head. Then you will be a fairly good-looking man."

"Uh-huh, it wouldn't do much good in your case. The place where your head had been wouldn't be any emptier than it is now."

Although Lummis had respect for all religions and a special fondness for the Catholic Church, he was not a follower of any nor did he have any sustaining faith in a life after death. Yet years before he had written in the *Land of Sunshine*:

"An Old Subscriber" seems really concerned to know "why the Lion mentions God so often and how the Lion comes to know so much about God?"

Confidentially now, the Lion does not know much about God—although he has friends who do. . . . The Lion used to know, until he got too many friends. . . . The Lion's embarrassment came when . . . he began to learn that the Human Race is human instead of only a few streets in Boston; and that while God agreed with all these people, they did not agree with one another. It is at least disconcerting, after twenty odd years of New England certitude that English is the only language understood in Heaven . . . that God is a Methodist and is really sorry for Baptists and Universalists and doesn't recognize the "Romish" church at all . . . it is disconcerting, I say, to find out later on equally good authority that the Almighty is a Catholic, a Democrat, and understands prayers in Spanish, French and Parsee without an interpreter.

. . . The Lion has had to give up putting Wanamaker clothing upon the Infinite. He is no longer even dead sure that God is an Anglo-Saxon. But he is surer than ever of a rather more important fact.

There are a great many things I do not know about God. But this little I do know—for He tells me. God is not my belly, nor my pocket, nor my ignorance, nor my lusts. He is not a chance to rob my neighbor, nor an excuse to do what I like nor a scapegoat for dodging my duty. Whatever else he is, He is the something bigger and better than I. He is what I must climb to, not what I can fall into. He is the Right.

And the reason He is frequently mentioned here, in the crude methods of speech He outfitted me with, is that I believe it is better to look up than down—or in the mirror. "God" in these pages means simply— but literally—The Best We Know. Scientifically, that is what it means anywhere. And The Best We Know is a good enough standard to apply to whatsoever case.[7]

Lummis never claimed pain or the verdict as excuses for slowing down. Those close to him saw the impatient one becoming patient, the master of sarcasm becoming tender. One of his hardest jobs was to say " 'No' to people and causes that have a certain claim on my sympathies though not on my time." Asked to speak at a small Mexican grammar school, the man whose days were becoming so few said "I wouldn't miss it for anything."

I expect I shall be the first person in the U.S. to tell them not to be bulldozed by the Gringos nor let themselves be looked down upon; and to give them a few fistfuls of history to fling back in the face of any shallow parvenu Yankee that tried to high-hat them.

. . . I felt that these paisanos were entitled to this kind of talk and it was a comfort to give it to them. And they liked it. At the end I sang El Viejo ("I am an ancient of 90 long years. . . . what things I have seen, Don Simón! . . .") And that liked them also.[8]

Many of Lummis' old friends took the time to send expressions of affection and sympathy. Charlie Russell's widow, Nancy, said what many felt. "Your

7 Charles F. Lummis, *Land of Sunshine*, Vol. XII, No. 6 (May, 1900), 378.
8 Lummis, "Journal."

philosophy is marvellous to me. The sunshine and happiness that you are able to radiate under the trying things is one of the most wonderful things I have ever encountered."

The pace of his activities seemed to increase rather than slacken. The diary was maintained, the journal was filled with memories, letters went out to his friends, and work on the books and poems progressed.

On May 18, 1928, Lummis was invited to the Women's Athletic Club to hear a talk by James A. B. Scherer, the director of the Southwest Museum. It had been just one year since Lummis had made the following characteristically devastating criticism of one of the director's projects.

May 7, 1927

Dear Dr. Scherer:

I am delighted that the Southwest Museum is to have an official and regular publication, and I have read thoroughly and with much interest Vol. I, No. 1 *of* The Masterkey. . . .

But it seems to me that the official publication of such an institution of learning, and with your splendid "Declaration of Policy," should be very scrupulous and very safe. I find in this first issue many things which seriously distress me and which certainly are not worthy of the institution. To be told that the old Spanish ranchos "presented a most animated scene, with brightly dressed LEPERS dashing about in the costume worn in Granada 500 years before" is not reassuring. There is no such word in the Spanish language as "lasaros"; it is "lazaros"; and that means lepers. Undoubtedly, the young lady wanted to speak of the cowboys who threw the Lazo, which we have anglicized as Lasso; but all vaqueros are lassoers and they were not counted a distinct class; the name for the one who throws the lasso particularly is not "Lazero," but "Lazador." Furthermore, you doubtless need not be reminded "that 500 years before" any epoch in pastoral California, Granada was a Moorish city, not conquered by the Spanish until the year of Columbus's discovery. And it is a dead moral certainty that no Moors were running around Granada in any costume remotely resembling anything worn in California.

All Spaniards, *in Spanish America, were "Gente de razon,"—and not merely "the blue-blooded ones."*

Corn was not ground "in metates" but on them. Chicken meat was not put in enchiladas, but in tamales. "The rest of the population" certainly did not "take the food standing." Spain did not "crush all initiative in her subjects." If the cattle "required small attention," why were there so many vaqueros? Of course the cattle were herded all the time. The small ranches were not "ranchitas" but "ranchitos". The "patrona" certainly did not act as "comadre to a foundling of the province"—probably your writer means madrina, godmother. The godmother was comadre to the mother of the child. A "merienda" is not a picnic. The article about the Casa de Adobe is sympathetic, but marred by these other glaring ineptitudes. On page 25 I am pained to find the word "artifacts." I paid my attention to this astonishing ignorance in my last book, Mesa, Cañon and Pueblo and will commend you to pages 290–291.

This was but the first of four pages of similar material covering everything in the *Masterkey* from Indian weaving to the area included in the Southwest and ending with a defense of his previously mentioned theory that man is indigenous to the New World.

If this letter had caused Director Scherer any wounds, time must have healed them, for the journal for May 18, 1928, reads: ". . . Dr. Scherer talks charmingly . . . many beautiful tributes to 'that great old man there' (me). Says 'artifects' clearly and grins at me and I say 'Thank you.' "

Eventually the pain increased. For four months, "hating these palliatives," he fought it off with nothing stronger than whisky. At last he allowed himself "an aspirin before I could go to sleep . . . first time I've yielded although Dr. Laubie told me not to try to bull it through without."

Perhaps some of the pain was eased through sharing some early memories in his journal.

. . . The memory I wish to record here is perhaps the most exquisite: It was an incomparable night, the great bowl of the Notch brimming with the yellow moonlight which danced on the pale lake and the Great Stone Face looking down on it.

Everybody from the Profile House—guests, waiters, hostelers—was sitting about the shore; every boat from the boathouse was drifting noiselessly upon the

Charles F. Lummis, 1928. (*Courtesy Southwest Museum*)

lake; my little canoe and I were there. Suddenly from amid the ghostly birch trees that hemmed the western shore of the lake, there came a tenuous hint of sound. Hostlers and icemen grew dumb as the most cultured Bostonians, as that ghost of a voice rose across the water and filled the moonlight and set the tender leaves of the birches to an inaudible whisper that seemed to fill the very earth with a melody which I believe I have never heard rivaled. It was Carrero

the Master-Flautist who played Patti's obligatos. Not commercially but for friendliness and the very joy of the spot, he had consented to come out and play beside the magic lake.

I love that enchanted reed; and maybe the setting and the moonlight gave an unfair advantage. But I have never heard anything like it nor have I ever heard from an American audience so impressive a response . . . not the lubberly "applause." You heard people sigh: "Oh, God!" and "How heavenly!" and "Oh, please!" for an encore.

Arrange bottles & papers for Good Will . . . writing letters . . . infinite work with TR poem. . . . Head in best shape in a long time & I not quite so weak . . . 10 hrs. work on Poems.

Stenographers came filled with enthusiasm and departed after a few months apparently exhausted by the struggle. There was a notation in the diary on June 24:

Test of my weakness when I tried to clip my nails and it took the last ounce of my strength . . . too weak even to get enraged at the gyves on me when I want to run my last race good and clean . . . 1 anodyn in 54 days.

Jul. 4 . . . didn't venture to read anything but headlines. But greatly delighted by the photo of Will Rogers as he alighted from the plane after running the two National conventions. Best picture I ever saw of him—just the right angle to show how Will is enlarging his cranium. Nothing will ever give him the Swelled Head; but the incessant workings inside bulge the skull to a new square-roundedness—just as Porfirio Diaz & T. R. absolutely remade their skulls in my own acquaintance with them from hatchet heads to square heads. And Will is well on his way. 6th . . . Crab in very bad and dangerous shape. I say "It's got away from us, hasn't it?" Dr. Meland said, "Yes and I can't quite understand it. . . ." To Jerusalem and get lovely roses for Helen [secretary] Give Elena new skillet and pan. . . .

July 21st . . . MH [Marco H. Newmark] deadly despondent & sad about [fate of El Alisal]. We talk hard & warmly . . . in an hour & a half I have him comforted & believing with me this thing can be fixed on the lines I suggest [that the museum rent the house back to the family].

Jul. 10 . . . Finish Bronco Pegasus

11th . . . Start to take up work on Sp. Pioneers. Helen pleased . . . work self blind. 6 hrs. poems. 2 anodyne. 14 in 15 days.

14th. No Drink . . . Just nach'ly don't touch a drop of Juisque all day. 1st time in many months or a year. I haven't drunk a glass of milk in 68 years . . . & don't expect to in 68 more. It is only after a cow has been safely imprisoned in a tin that I can venture near enough to her to take her fluid in any guise.

Aug. 1. Another of my Red Chips on the Table—and I hope to play it for a good Jack Pot . . . Bertha's goldenrod almost ready to burst into bloom—so I shall still have the pleasure of sending her a bunch of her most beloved flower. Find exostosis under left eye . . . they can't treat it because X-Ray is still actively working.

3rd . . . To Hollywood Bowl to hear Frederick Converse's Tone Poem "California." . . . Roy Jones comes down with huge chair in his arms for me—says "Man who inspired fine piece of music, as Converse says you did, deserves this & more" . . . program gives me credit . . . same language he used on program of Boston . . . interesting to see what he did with my 2, "Chata Cara de Bule" & "Capotín"—wh between them ran through large part of the last of his composition . . . though I don't think he got out of Capotin the force & snap wh belongs to it.

13th. Grand & Glorious Day! Houghton Mifflin accepts Bronco Pegasus! . . . Greenslet's wire [head of Houghton Mifflin]: "Delighted to publish A Bronco Pegasus!" After this I am going to call them "poems." "Verse" is about my size and I have modestly used it; but this little wire has raised the denomination.

Aug. 16. Finish Spanish Pioneers . . . New edition all ready to be done up to express to McClurg. Another Triumph. . . . Next week I want to jump in on the new book, Flowers of Our Lost Romance.

Lummis took time to help one of his Indian boys, Juan "Biscocho" Jojola, "Johnny Biscuit," who years before had helped him in the building of the castle. Juan was a victim of the railroad strike when strikers had literally forced him with a gun at his head to join them.

Aug. 3 . . . Have written a letter to Jimmy Duffy, Gen. Pass Agt. of the Santa Fe, that would scorch the hair off an iron dog . . . while it is none of Duffy's funeral, he will send it along the line, I know. . . . The name I gave Juan, "Biscocho," still sticks to him since I took a picture of him as a little boy crawling out of an Isleta outdoor oven.

From time to time the old roar was heard.

Aug. 18. . . . Felt like I had stepped on a stingaree

when I observed that Mesa, Canon and Pueblo has a new jacket—idiot new line on the back title, "The Classic Southwest History" . . . not only idiotic but a fake and I'll make them eat it . . . more than a year ago they promised me that they would change the imbecile text they have carried for three years and substitute text I gave them . . . worse yet by God! they have put the same M C & P slop on the jacket.

Aug. 19. . . . Little Pat[9] three years old today and a lovely creature. She was rioting in the kitchen this noon as I ate my breklunch, then came demurely to the door and said, "Dr. Lummis, does the noise disturb you?" She has a great flair to call me Dr. Lummis now; and while I prefer "Grandpa" the other sounds so demure and cunning that we will let it go at that. . . .

Aug. 26 . . . Spoke to Quimu tonight about a little niche in the porch wall for the ashes of my oldest boy Amado and another niche for me. Q fine and thinks he can get an electric drill that would bite into flinty concrete wall. . . .

Aug. 29th. This is the Day I long have lived for! I have a childish or savage joy for magic numbers: had long hoped to get up to 5555. But that of course won't be as the last three 5's will take a year and a half or more. But this morning I slather out joyfully my 5000th blind shave! It is really no trifle—it is a bit of self-control and handiness that is good to keep.

. . . She [Bertha] & M. H. considerably flabbergasted that I am going to make a contract with the able Mr. Bresee (undertaker) for putting me into ashes at precisely so much. They both thought this most extraordinary—but admitted that if they had to change their room or move their store they would arrange for it.

3rd. Knibbs Foreword . . . "In spite of Dr. Lummis' modest disclaimer, he is always a poet—in his living, his friendship, his environment. Had he lived in the days of Bertran de Born he would have been a fighting troubadour, serving impartially with song or blade, and a keen edge of each . . . fearlessness and sincerity burning high and clear throughout these songs of his adventuring."

From David Starr Jordan . . . "It is not very reasonable that you should be growing old, and yet I, who

have been among the liveliest of my kind, am struck by 'my eldest partner, Father Time,' as Phillip of Spain is said to have remarked. But he is sure to whack us all once in a while.

Except that I cannot walk any distance, and cannot see worth anything, and am getting hard of hearing, I am getting on pretty well although nearly all of my pioneer friends have passed on."[10]

From Ruth B. Moran came this letter:

. . . I like [the verses on her father, Thomas Moran] oh so much, and I feel that father would thank you and feel honored to be included in your last book. You will, if you are able to, dedicate a volume to me, won't you—if you can write in only your name—to stay with me till I too reach the "Top of the Hill"—but it will never be so bravely and splendidly mounted. The last few feet of your ascent are perhaps—though so quietly made, your most splendid effort. . . . I shall never forget you—and the times we had together—you and Father and I . . . all beautiful memories, and all helpful in climbing the Hill to the Top. . . . My dear friend goodbye.

From Edith Ellis, author of *White Collars*, came this.

Wait for me, dear friend, I caught from you the real idea of living. I haven't learned to practice it thoroughly yet but I'm sure another sight of you and your manner of making a glow rest on mere existence will set me finally right. I'm selfish you see and offer no exchange except my admiration and some understanding of the monumental thing you make of life . . . you and your work and the lesson it is to see and love and praise the beautiful and significant things we all blend with by nature and history—raises itself above the unthinking herd like one of your beloved mountain peaks. . . . It must be glorious fun to be you—and to distil sorrow and pain and loneliness into such fellowship with nature and mankind & God. . . .

Lummis' final entries in his journal were brief.

[Nov.] 3rd. Knibbs and I tackle Pioneer Transportation. . . . He admires it greatly. Then Virginal Mule

9 Patricia Lummis, the oldest daughter of Jordan Lummis, later Mrs. Patricia de los Reyes.

10 Lummis, "Journal."

Tamer . . . enormously pleased . . . 8 hrs. Romance [Flowers of Our Lost Romance].

4th. M. H. unspeakably shocked at news of Helen's going. Tells me to spare no effort to find competent successor. Lovely visit. 8 hrs. Romance. O anodyne. 2 in 65 da. O swear, 6 cigars, 55 min. guitar. . . . Helen back 8:20, ill. I dict. Journal. Some letters. She read 27 pp. "Where did He Come From?" Arrange ad for new sec. She goes 11. I work infinitely. She will stay till 15th.

5th. Up at 12:15. Blind shower, shave. Fine letter from Amado Chaves.

This was the last day Lummis dictated for his journal. His diary continued.

Nov. 10. Big hemorrhage . . . gathering things for Good Will, clearing things up, throwing away . . . Helen types property directions. Rank (substitute secretary) forgot all about it and can't come. . . . Helen tries in vain for another. Goes 4:30. No secretary. I work on mail & records. Not a drink all day. No time for guitar.
11th. M. H. Newmark (½ sick) comes 2:30. Fine visit.

Lummis made a memorandum to himself: "Instructions and requests to Museum; Make full list of ownership of articles for children; Assemble all Journals on desk; Order tables and desk; List whereabouts of important things; Plates on dining room table."

On November 12, Charles Lummis wrote his last notes in his diary. His handwriting was quite strong and clear.

. . . Advance copy of Bronco Pegasus, 13 days late, *air mail $2.40. . . . Cannot find any secretary to take Helen's place. Nobody left. . . . Marco Newmark visit. Admires Bk. Show Q & B the Bk. [Bronco Pegasus]. Phone Knibbs on B. Will come Fri. Phone MH.*

So forty years of diary ended with the names of two well-loved companions. About nine o'clock that night Lummis had another hemorrhage. Yet Helen read to him from his book, and he sat up listening to his poems until midnight.

The next day the absent ones were sent for. Lummis was unconscious when Turbesé came, yet he seemed in some way aware of her presence. Late at night, when no one was near, she took up the guitar and began to sing one of the songs he had so loved. Suddenly his voice rang out as it used to: "Adios, adios amores, adios porque me ausento . . ." ("Farewell, farewell my loves, farewell for I must leave").

"That was good," he said as Turbesé finished the song; together they sang another.

As he had after the shooting forty years before, Lummis one day demanded his trousers, his watch, and other familiar belongings. He insisted on getting out of bed and walking around the room. It was as though he was determined to have one final journey of exploration and to fling a last contemptuous gesture in the face of the enemy.

From time to time he would come up out of the deep coma to say something concise and characteristic. To Turbesé he murmured, "You are more precious than fine jewels."

One night Keith heard him call out, "Make way! A Lummis in the field, meeting all comers."

On November 25, 1928—it was hard to tell at which moment—he met the Last Comer.

37

A Niche in the Wall

CHARLES LUMMIS, who had loved welcoming his friends at El Alisal, met them one last time under the old sycamore. He lay on the redwood board he had chosen himself, wrapped in his finest chief's blanket and covered with his favorite deep-red roses. Once again the clear voice of Alma Real was heard, accompanied by José Arias and the Spanish musicians. Old friend Joseph Scott spoke. And then it was El Cabezudo's turn with the consuming flame. In the niche he had selected in the wall he had built rest his ashes with those of his first son.

Much has been said of him. Edgar Hewett summarized him: "Editor - Explorer - Founder - Barbarian - artist - archaeologist - antiquarian - ethnologist - librarian - linguist - humanitarian - philanthropist - teacher - preacher - entertainer; many - lived, myriad - minded, golden - hearted. He lives in California, New Mexico and in the heart of a million friends."

John Collier remembered the days and nights when they had sat together in the Indian councils:

Ah, much is told, much shall be told of you:
  You who wrought great the immeasurable tale
Of Spain amid the hemispheres, who blew
  With trumpet-words life into ages pale.
Only the old sweet men, who long have known
  A friend great in the changed and conquering time,
The old sweet men welcome their own, their own;
  Lummis has gone, has gone into the prime.
Lummis has gone into the longed-for cloud,
  Has gone into the grass which answers prayer,
Has gone where Indians round the great drum crowd.
  The world soul takes its own. Lummis is there!

Gene Rhodes wrote in final tribute to his friend and patron: ". . . In twenty ways Lummis was the most remarkable man I ever knew—his scholarly thoroughness, his appalling industry, his rapier-like wit, and the militant heart that never feared to make a foe in a good cause. He finished what he started and he paid for what he broke."

THE WORKS OF CHARLES F. LUMMIS

PUBLISHED WRITINGS

Birch Bark Poems. Cambridge, 1879.

A New Mexico David and Other Stories of the Southwest. New York, 1891.

A Tramp Across the Continent. New York, 1892.

Some Strange Corners of Our Country. New York, 1892.

The Land of Poco Tiempo. New York, 1893.

The Man Who Married the Moon and Other Pueblo Indian Folk-Stories. New York, 1894. Reprinted in 1910 as *Pueblo Indian Folk-Stories.*

The Gold Fish of Gran Chimú. Chicago, 1897.

The Enchanted Burro. Chicago, 1897.

The King of the Broncos and Other Stories of New Mexico. New York, 1897.

The Awakening of a Nation. New York, 1898.

The Landmarks Club Cook Book. Los Angeles, 1903.

My Friend Will. Chicago, 1911.

In Memory of Juan Rodriguez Cabrillo, Who Gave the World California. Chula Vista, California, 1913.

Spanish Songs of Old California. Los Angeles, 1923.

Mesa, Canon, and Pueblo: Our Wonderland of the Southwest. New York, 1925.

A Bronco Pegasus. Boston, 1929.

Flowers of Our Lost Romance. Boston, 1929.

General Crook and the Apache Wars. Ed. by Turbesé Lummis Fiske. Flagstaff, Arizona, 1966.

Land of Sunshine. June, 1894–December, 1901. *Out West.* January, 1902–November, 1909. Virtually every issue of these two magazines contains articles written by Charles F. Lummis under his own name or a pseudonym.

UNPUBLISHED MANUSCRIPTS

"As I Remember." Handwritten manuscripts. Portions in the possession of Keith Lummis, the University of Arizona, Tucson, and the Southwest Museum, Los Angeles.

Diary. 1888–1928. Over forty handwritten volumes. In the possession of the Southwest Museum, Los Angeles.

Journal and letters of Charles F. Lummis to Maurice Newmark. 1911–1927. A typewritten WPA project on file at the Los Angeles Public Library.

OTHER SOURCES
BOOKS

Austin, Mary. *Earth Horizons: Autobiography.* Boston, 1927.

Bandelier, Adolph. *The Delight Makers.* New York, 1916.

———. *A History of the Southwest.* Ed. by Ernest J. Burrus, S. J. Rome, Italy, 1969.

Bingham, Edwin R. *Charles F. Lummis, Editor of the Southwest.* San Marino, California, 1955.

Brother Cornelius, F.S.C. *Keith, Old Master of California.* New York, 1942.

Dillon, Richard. *Heroes and Humbugs.* New York, 1970.

Gordon, Dudley. *Crusader in Corduroy.* Los Angeles, 1972.

———. *The Birch Bark Poems of C. F. Lummis.* Los Angeles, 1969.

Gugliotta, Bobette. *Katzimo, Mysterious Mesa.* New York, 1974.

Hunt, Rockwell D. *California's Stately Hall of Fame.* Stockton, California, 1915.

Jordan, David Starr. *The Days of a Man.* New York, 1922.

Judd, Neil M. *Men Met Along the Trail.* Norman, Oklahoma, 1968.

Keleher, Julia and Elsie Ruth Chant. *The Padre of Isleta.* Santa Fe, New Mexico, 1940.

Newmark, Harris. *Sixty Years in Southern California.* New York, 1926.

Newmark, Marco. *Jottings in Southern California History*. Los Angeles, 1955.

Perrigo, Lynn I. *The American Southwest*. New York, 1971.

Powell, Lawrence Clark. *California Classics*. Los Angeles, 1971.

——. *Southwest Classics*. Los Angeles, 1974.

Rhodes, May D. *The Hired Man on Horseback*. Boston, 1938.

Robinson, W. W. *The Story of the Southwest Museum*. Los Angeles, 1960.

Simmons, Marc. *Charles Lummis and Amado Chaves*. Cerrilos, New Mexico, 1968.

——. *Little Lion of the Southwest*. Chicago, 1974.

Starr, Kevin. *Americans and the California Dream*. New York, 1973.

Storke, Thomas M. *California Editor*. Los Angeles, 1958.

ARTICLES

Gilbert, Hope. "He Discovered the Southwest for America," *Desert Magazine* (September, 1944) 13–16.

Gordon, Dudley. "Southwest Crusader," *New Mexico Magazine*, Vol. XIX (October, 1941), 10–11, 31–32.

——. "Lummis as a War Correspondent in Arizona," *The American West*, Vol. II, No. 3 (Summer, 1965), 4–12.

Powell, Lawrence Clark. "Charles Fletcher Lummis and the *Land of Sunshine*," *Westways*, Vol. LXII, No. 1 (January, 1970), 20–23, 35.

——. "Song of the Southwest," *Westways*, Vol. LXV, No. 5 (May, 1973), 45–47, 82–87.